Accountability and Opportunity in Higher Education

Accountability and Opportunity in Higher Education

The Civil Rights Dimension

GARY ORFIELD

NICHOLAS HILLMAN

Editors

HARVARD EDUCATION PRESS

CAMBRIDGE, MASSACHUSETTS

Paperback ISBN 978-1-68253-147-1
Library Edition ISBN 978-1-68253-148-8

Library of Congress Cataloging-in-Publication Data

Names: Orfield, Gary, editor. | Hillman, Nicholas W., editor.
Title: Accountability and opportunity in higher education : the civil rights
    dimension / Gary Orfield, Nicholas Hillman, editors.
Description: Cambridge, Massachusetts : Harvard Education Press, 2018. |
    Includes bibliographical references and index.
Identifiers: LCCN 2017051127| ISBN 9781682531471 (pbk.) | ISBN
    9781682531488 (library edition)
Subjects: LCSH: Educational accountability—United States. | Discrimination
    in higher education—United States. | Educational equalization—United
    States. | African Americans—Education (Higher)—United States. |
    Hispanic Americans—Education (Higher)—United States.
Classification: LCC LC212.42 .A34 2018 | DDC 379.2/6—dc23 LC record
    available at https://lccn.loc.gov/2017051127

Published by Harvard Education Press,
an imprint of the Harvard Education Publishing Group

Harvard Education Press
8 Story Street
Cambridge, MA 02138

Cover Design: Ciano Design
Cover Photo: David Schaffer/Caiaimage/Getty Images
The typefaces used in this book are Sabon for text and Myriad Pro
for display.

Contents

The Access Crisis and the Move Toward Accountability

GARY ORFIELD

American society is facing a growing crisis of sharply escalating demand for college opportunity met with an unwillingness of political leaders to adequately respond. Instead of addressing this demand by investing in higher education, political leaders have shifted greater financial responsibility for the costs of higher education onto students and their families. This shift disproportionately affects the nation's lowest-income students, students of color, and the colleges and universities serving them. At the same time, there has been a sharp decline in the percentage of Whites among the college-age population and a dramatic rise in the share of Latinos; Blacks have held their own. The small share of Asian immigrants are the most educated and successful among the racial groups in a society with record levels of economic inequality. As the rates of school-age poverty have grown, the public schools have become increasingly unequal by race and class, further raising the stakes.

So as the real cost of college has multiplied over the last four decades, and few families have savings that can cover the cost, financial aid and loans have become essential for most college-going students. The demands are intense, as families and institutions across the country seek out and compete for limited resources. And with the public unwilling to pay for these resources through higher taxes, policy makers, hearing the demand for action, have increasingly proposed accountability policies as a solution, asking: Why can't colleges increase their output by lowering the time required and increasing the graduation rates? Shouldn't they be punished if they start recruiting too many out-of-state students to increase their tuition income, thus harming local students? Why are they admitting so many students who do not pay off their loans? Is it inefficient to enroll students who have been ill-prepared in inferior public schools and have weaker chances of ever finishing? Why not just pass a law and make the system more efficient?

However, as the research studies in this volume reveal, one person's efficiency is another person's exclusion. If college controls destiny—access to employment, income, and middle-class status—and the paths to college are a well-lit superhighway for some and a rocky path over mountains and through briars for others, we need to ask ourselves: Who is a push for efficiency going to hurt? Whose life chances are going to be squeezed out? What groups will do fine and which will suffer? Will the policy that sounds good become a harsh barrier for the institutions that struggle to widen the path for those who are not prepared for what may be their only real chance? Politically, it is logical to turn toward accountability. But, like many large and seemingly simple ideas, it is full of unexpected complexities and unacknowledged costs.

AMERICAN DREAMS AND NIGHTMARES

Today, the American Dream focuses strongly on college. Families dream of putting their children through college and launching them into successful lives, and working adults believe that going back to school will help them retool for the new economy. In an era when postsecondary education is almost required for secure access to the middle class, success in college is a requisite for serious upward mobility, and failure to graduate from college is a gigantic barrier to all future endeavors. For much of the twentieth century, a high school education was similarly important, and there was a vast expansion of free public high schools offering pathways to middle-class jobs. Colleges grew as the GI Bill veterans of World War II enrolled, and next came the vast expansion of free or low-cost community colleges and regional public universities. These institutions offered affordable tuitions, and the federal government invested in a large federal scholarship program, complemented by the work-study program, offering college degrees at a modest price. These investments expanded college opportunities and made higher education accessible to millions in a society with rising family incomes.

But since the 1980s, policy and economic changes have greatly increased the barriers to higher education even as it has become even more important for success. The extreme complexity of the higher education system and the growing stratification of the society and polarization of its politics have made policy making both more critical and far more difficult. The earlier expansion was fueled by rising public resources, but policy making since 1980 has had to cope with the impact of a succession of massive state and federal tax cuts that have shrunk the public sector even as the costs of health care, an expanding criminal justice system, and a large increase in the elderly population have made larger demands on diminished public resources.

Higher education, which is dependent on state governments, has been especially vulnerable. In a society with a near-universal wish for college yet limited resources, political pressure requires responses, but fiscal realities mean that those responses will not be adequate. And in a society where most of the children are now non-White and very far behind in college completion, the racial dimensions of these challenges are critical. Policies targeted at helping minorities have been highly controversial, and the issues are often ignored. Too many families have to face failure when they tell their children that there is no way for them to go to the college where they could succeed, or that their only choice is a community college where few succeed, or that going into the military and facing war is their only chance to someday go to college.

With such inadequate resources, there need to be ways to allocate scarce opportunities. Much of that happens through adoption of rules and regulations controlling access to different kinds of colleges and allocating assistance that makes it possible to afford choices. From the perspective of state and federal policy makers, it is about getting more done for less and wasting less money (and limiting bad debts) on programs with poor success records. This tends to be expressed in regulations and aid criteria that try to foster what the officials see either as positive policies and results that should be rewarded or as failed policies that should be sanctioned or changed. When there is a serious scarcity of funds, the ways policy makers go about designing rules and regulations become even more powerful, because they are able to set priorities that allocate opportunity without explicitly acknowledging who loses. Such policies can be adopted at the federal, state, or institutional levels, and students and families are affected by a mixture of all three.

In the Obama administration, for example, there was a major effort to expand federal authority though rule making and regulation that promoted consumer protections, pressured institutions with low outcomes scores, and sharply cut funds to private for-profit universities with weak records. But its strategy was sharply limited by congressional Republicans. In the succeeding Trump administration, the focus has shifted to proposed budget and program cuts that would implicitly regulate access, to greater deference to state priorities, and to policies more favorable to the private for-profit sector. Yet, there were no serious debates about the racial impacts of these decisions. And in an intensely stratified society where higher education is one of the only ways to make intergenerational progress and where minorities have always been far behind, these issues have huge consequences.

When, with a Republican Congress, the Obama administration reached a dead end on major legislation, such as its ambitious plan for community college aid, it focused on accountability strategies to get more results from public resources. However, the strategy of the Trump administration appears to be to relax the consumer protections and institutional accountability efforts that Obama found to be severely damaging for disadvantaged students. Instead, it will seek to transfer functions of the gigantic federal student loan program from education officials to the Treasury Department and sharply reduce the scope of aid available to disadvantaged students through several programs that have been important for decades. There is a proposal to end the policy of deferring payment of interest on student loans while students are still working on their degrees, which could create an earlier fiscal stress on low-income students. And policies granting loan forgiveness for public service employees are also under attack, which could result in a disincentive for people to pursue public-sector careers and would break a promise to those who have entered public service. Within this context, states will play a more central role in regulating colleges according to their own performance metrics and students' education outcomes.

Unfortunately, neither of these two very different approaches to accountability has seriously taken into account the racial consequences of these decisions for students of color. Although the society is profoundly polarized, and policies are certain to have differential impacts, the policy developments continue to proceed as if this were not the case. The higher education policy dilemmas that led to the Obama administration initiatives and to those of a number of state governments were rooted in very real problems. Hard choices were strongly shaped by long-term trends in state and federal government resources, priorities, and politics; convictions regarding federal versus state responsibility; and beliefs about the conditions of racial and ethnic inequality in public schools, communities, and families. They reflected the frustration at both the state and federal levels generated by an inability to respond to all demands for help and a search for defensible strategies. Massive tax cuts by successive conservative federal and state administrations and growing mandatory costs of health care, incarceration, and the needs of public schools, as well as vast unfunded retirement payments and other nondiscretionary costs, had eaten up much of the available funds. Three great forces—lower revenues, declining economic mobility, and an intensified demand from all sectors of society for access and aid—produced a chaotic jumble of policy and portended out-of-control costs.

Eventually the pressures on a poorly designed patchwork of policies unable to meet the demands of large segments of the population led policy makers to do things that made little sense in terms of equity but gave at least the appearance of action. Since it was easier to win congressional action through tax subsidies than direct expenditures, one solution involved giving entitlements to the more privileged sectors of society most able to actually pay for college, families that understand tax loopholes; but tax-based subsidies do not work for families with little tax liability. At the same time, policy was falling seriously behind in making four-year college possible for those at the bottom. No one wanted to make a bad situation worse, but some of the only policies that could be pursued without money had the unintended consequence of doing that—policies like raising entrance requirements, awarding aid only to those with high grades and test scores, and eliminating remediation. Unfortunately, it often appears to be easier politically to implement policies and rules that turn out to disproportionately aid students from families of high socioeconomic status, particularly when such policies can be framed as raising standards or eliminating waste.

With no clear leadership from the world of higher education, since each sector tried to protect its part of the shrinking pie, it was nearly impossible to take any bold action in favor of equity for the groups in most urgent need of mobility and least able to pursue college opportunity without major support. No clear program developed, and without fundamental restructuring of policy and alterations in the operation of many institutions, the dominant pattern remained one of distributing something (or the appearance of something) to all sectors.

To understand how we arrived at this juncture where crude methods of accountability became a central policy and where policies were commonly developed with little or no serious consideration of their racial consequences, it is important to examine the history of this deepening crisis and the links between policy and cycles of political change.

INCREASING BARRIERS TO COLLEGE ACCESS

US higher education policy changes take place within a policy and social context that has undergone major change. From the mid-1960s to the early 1970s, college was affordable, students could earn their way through public universities, admission to the great majority of schools was not very competitive, and the states were supporting and rapidly expanding colleges. The United States was still the world center of industrial production, and there were millions of unionized jobs paying family wages, so higher education was not needed for many middle-class jobs. The US led the world in the share of its residents who received affordable higher education; it was the nation that invented the idea of mass higher education in high-quality public universities that were affordable for millions. The US was a society with a very large White majority with a small, largely European immigrant population and an expanding middle class experiencing substantial gains in real incomes. But all of this was about to change.

During the civil rights revolution, higher education policies and regulations focused on racial equity. Most selective colleges enrolled significant numbers of students of color for the first time in their history through implementation of affirmative action plans and policies to support students of color with weaker preparation. Under the 1964 Civil Rights Act, affirmative action was imposed on segregated, mostly southern universities in the nineteen states that had long operated separate Black and White public colleges that violated the Constitution. Voluntary affirmative action was adopted by the great majority of elite private and public campuses outside the South, almost none of which previously had significant non-White enrollments.[1] US colleges had record numbers of non-White and poor students by the mid-1970s, following the creation of federal grants for low-income students and the Johnson administration's War on Poverty programs, including Upward Bound, which was designed to recruit and support students from groups that had previously been largely excluded from college.

But since the late 1970s, when California's Proposition 13 drastically cut taxes and the US Supreme Court narrowed affirmative action in the 1978 *Bakke* decision, barriers to college access have sharply increased. Also, tax cuts, which became widespread in the late 1970s and 1980s, worked to lower the priority of higher education in state budgets hit by rising healthcare and prison costs. These cuts were expanded in the 1990s when states began adopting tax and expenditure limitations ("Taxpayer Bill of Rights" laws), which disallowed states from increasing their budgets beyond inflationary and population growth rates. Colleges responded to severe cuts by slowing or stopping expansion and continuously shifting the financial burden to the students and their families, which they saw as the only possible source of major funds. State officials unwilling to raise taxes put the colleges in a position where their only option was to heavily tax the students through tuition raises, which, in turn, focused the blame on the colleges rather than the legislatures.[2] Financial aid was cut, tuition rose sharply, and the Federal Pell Grant, which depends on annual appropriations, covered a much smaller portion of soaring college costs. And the same state governments that reduced their support of higher education tried to shift the blame for the resulting problems onto the colleges by demanding more accountability, implying that colleges were wasting money and, under pressure, could make more progress without additional money.

Declining civil rights efforts to include historically excluded groups through affirmative action presented another barrier. The *Bakke* decision upheld the idea of affirmative action but seriously limited it.[3] Major changes under President Reagan widened the gap between costs and aid and deemphasized civil rights. Affirmative action enforcement was cut back, and high schools became more segregated and unequal as the Supreme Court abandoned desegregation policies.[4] Since the mid-1990s, nine states have outlawed affirmative action, and in 2014 the Supreme Court accepted the legitimacy of referenda writing affirmative action prohibitions into state constitutions.[5]

The tide of immigration from Latin America peaking in the period from 1980 to the Great Recession transformed the college-age population. The Latino population soared, and the proportion of White young adults fell sharply. After the baby boom, the United States saw a substantial decline in White birth rates and a vast and unprecedented immigration of poorly educated Latinos. A number of the most important states for Latinos were those that limited access to four-year colleges, forcing many students from weak minority high schools to begin in weak community colleges.[6] Black and Latino students attended increasingly isolated and unequal K–12 schools as school segregation reached a fifty-year high, concentrating students of color in schools that seldom prepared them well for college. The access problem was especially serious in the two larges states, California and Texas. In many states, undocumented students had a right to free public schools, established by the Supreme Court in the 1982 *Plyler v. Doe* decision, but were ineligible for any federal aid in public colleges. Population changes bringing in millions of low-income non-White families accelerated just as the country was turning in a far more conservative direction, cutting college budgets and raising barriers to higher education. The door was closing as the need grew, and families of color did not have the options available to families a generation earlier. In some states the failure to serve the expanding communities of color threatened to lower average education levels, even as employers were seeking stronger credentials. The largest growth of potential college students was among groups that were most behind in college completion: Latinos, followed by African Americans. Colleges were operating in a very rapidly changing society.

A SHIFT TOWARD THE MIDDLE CLASS AND ACCOUNTABILITY

In the political world, successive presidential victories by strong conservative presidents who won large majorities of the White vote led the Democratic Party to moderate its goals and shift its focus from poor and non-White students to less progressive policies providing more aid to middle-class families. Most American middle-class families were deeply worried about college affordability, which made it an important political issue. The "New Democrats" who created the Democratic Leadership Council (DLC) in 1985 deemphasized race and class issues and focused on working families and the middle class, not the poor, who vote less and have little representation by lobbies. The DLC provided the framework for the Clinton presidency and deeply influenced Obama-era policies.[7]

Higher education policy changed as both parties competed to help middle-class students and their families. In 1978, President Jimmy Carter, a southern moderate, signed the Middle Student Assistance Act, which began the process of moving a large share of federal subsidies from the poor to the middle class. Under Ronald Reagan and George W. Bush, Congress tried to do something for everyone in spite of huge tax cuts, but the result was a confusing and inefficient mix of programs and large poorly targeted subsidies through the tax system. And both Presidents Clinton and Barack Obama signed costly tax-subsidy programs that disproportionately helped middle-income and high-income borrowers. Political pressures pushed toward policies that sustained rather than challenged social stratification.

So while there was widespread demand for more aid and lower costs, there was no willingness to give colleges significant increases in public funds from the states, which historically supported much of their operating costs. A growing share of college budgets began relying on high tuitions paid with the proceeds of student loans, since families lacked savings to pay the rising costs. And a number of states shifted more of their aid away from poor students to middle-class students with high grades, even if those students had no financial need.[8] These "merit scholarships" were highly popular with the families whose children received them, but they took money from need-based programs that allowed low-income students to attend college. Many private colleges directed much of their aid to giving "tuition discounts" to attract students. For low-income minority students, often the only path was from inferior high schools segregated by race and poverty to weak community colleges with low graduation and transfer rates. This was usually a dead end, however, with students often exiting with no credential and significant debt.

After 2000, as tuition and loans continued to climb, federal policy makers grew increasingly concerned about the reliance on loans as a growing number of students were failing to repay their debts, especially low-income students from the least selective colleges. This introduction of serious risk into the federal loan system has created great pressure to do something to control it. But too often the result of all this pressure has been a difficult-to-understand set of compromises that seem to offer something for everyone but, in reality, actually reinforce persisting inequalities. The government offers tuition aid for needy families but often not enough to create actual access to four-year schools. So while opportunity is seemingly created, the gaps in aid packages often remain impossible to cross. For a family without resources, credit, or an understanding of complex policies, there often is no option but the nearest community college, which substantially reduces the chances of the student ever obtaining a bachelor's degree independent of a student's ability and widens the gaps in college completion based on family income.[9]

DEEPENING ECONOMIC AND RACIAL INEQUALITY

Today, the family income and wealth necessary to afford good precollege preparation and college costs are more unequally distributed than they have been for many years.[10] Millions of families have little or no savings or net wealth and are seeing their real incomes declining, so there is no way that they can contribute significantly to the college costs that are several times higher (in constant-value dollars) than they were a generation ago.[11] When more than half the families in major regions of the United States, including the entire South, the largest region, lack the income to pay for school lunches, how likely is it that they can make any real contribution to college? Many parents actually need help from their children, even as they are struggling to stay in college.

The Federal Pell Grant is the only broadly available, need-based source of grants, but it pays far less than a fifth of the average cost of attending a public four-year college, and it is programmed to decline as a share of costs. In 2015 House Republicans repeated a call to freeze the Pell Grant for a decade, as costs continued to rise.[12] Early in the Trump administration the grants have not been cut, and there is a plan to restore summer school aid, but key support programs have been proposed for elimination or severe cuts.

Controlling for inflation, the average cost of four-year colleges is now four times what it was in the early 1970s.[13] As costs have soared, institutional scholarship resources for the students most in need have fallen far behind the rising costs, and campuses faced with a severe fiscal squeeze are spending money on "enrollment management" strategies to bring in more students able to pay rather than focusing on attracting high-need students. These strategies often involve offering modest scholarships to high-scoring students who can pay most of the costs rather than adequately funding the much more expensive students who can pay very little and need extensive aid and remediation.[14]

Getting more high-scoring students also improves a college's prestige and helps draw more high-achieving students who don't need aid. Many public universities are actively recruiting and admitting out-of-state and international students who pay much higher tuitions. Giving tuition discounts to students without financial need helps colleges gather 80 percent of a high out-of-state tuition, while a poor in-state student needing remediation raises costs. Most colleges simply do not have the resources to fund the very substantial need and remediation of poor students.[15] This is seen not as a matter of preference but as a necessity for colleges whose finances are threatened by not meeting their enrollment goals. An accountability system focused on equal opportunity should reward rather than punish schools that admit low-income students even though they have problems that contribute to lower and slower average graduation outcomes. (And that is, of course, far more expensive than simply blaming them for low completion rates.) However, there is no national accountability policy for helping low-income and minority families increase their access to college or for developing new major assistance programs.

Struggles over affirmative action and race-conscious support policies, essential to integrating student bodies and faculties, continue to stir controversy, reaching the Supreme Court for the fourth time since 2000 in yet another challenge to the University of Texas.[16] In June 2016 the Court decided a key case, *Fisher v. University of Texas II*, and its decision surprised many observers by supporting affirmative action. However, President Trump began to move the Court in a conservative direction with his appointment of Neil Gorsuch and with active opposition to affirmative action, at risk again in pending cases against Harvard University and the University of North Carolina.[17] Student support services were slated for serious cuts in Trump's budget, and the popular work-study program, created more than a half-century ago, faces presidential proposals for drastic reductions.[18] There are working models of strategies to increase college-going and success for disadvantaged students, but most require significant resources and a serious long-term institutional commitment.[19] There is no willingness at either the national or state level to dedicate resources toward substantially expanding these efforts during a period when colleges often lack essential funding for basic campus functions. In other words, the social and polical context in which the accountability policy issues are being developed is one of self-perpetuating inequality and fiscal straightjacketing in which four-year colleges become only a dream for many.

THE CIVIL RIGHTS DIMENSION OF ACCOUNTABILITY

In the United States today, higher education is more important than ever in determining life chances, and economic and social mobility are significantly lower than in many peer nations.[20] Deep gaps in income and wealth perpetuate education inequality for racial and ethnic minorities. College access and success are basic civil rights issues in our changing society. Yet, although half of America's public school students are now from racial and ethnic minorities, and education success has always been profoundly unequal, there is little serious focus on policies that could remedy the segregated and unequal preparation for college.

Studies using federal data repeatedly show that US students of color are increasingly segregated in low-achieving, concentrated-poverty high schools.[21] School segregation intensified as the courts adopted colorblind policies which assumed that race could be ignored. As a result, many of the schools serving students of color were punished, or even dissolved, for their "failure" to achieve certain outcomes, provoking many qualified administrators and teachers to avoid working in such schools where they would likely be blamed for inequalities that were there long before they or the students had entered the schools.[22] And if Black or Latino students are only a seventh as likely as White or Asian students to be in strong high schools, as recent California research shows, the colleges those students attend are challenged to educate students with systematically unequal preparation.[23] Ignoring unequal preparation is a fatal flaw in designing policies for equity. President Johnson noted the dilemma in his 1965 Howard University speech: "You do not take a person who, for years, has been hobbled by chains and liberate him, bring him up to the starting line of a race and then say you are free to compete with all the others, and still just believe that you have been completely fair."[24] This consideration needs to be made in designing college accountability policies.

In a deeply polarized society, failure to think systemically about issues of race and poverty when formulating policy compounds inequality in many arenas. If, for example, we build subsidized family housing in a community with very bad schools segregated by race and poverty and dangerous streets, we may solve immediate housing needs for families but doom their children's future. It would be much more effective to also think about how putting subsidized housing in healthy, diverse communities gives students from poor families of color access to positive exposure to peer groups and stronger school opportunities. Ignoring the context of race and other institutions can waste scarce funds and unintentionally harm the children. Historically, we built many expensive high-rise public housing projects that turned out to be social catastrophes, totally isolating tenants in a syndrome of disadvantage—projects that did nothing to prepare the next generation for the social and economic mainstream and that we had to blow up because they ignored the realities of communities and lives.[25]

The same thing happens with education policies. Racial inequality is multidimensional and persistent. It is such a fundamental dimension of society that it must be carefully considered in designing policies; otherwise, well-intentioned policies can undermine institutions that are actually having strongly positive impacts. That happened often in No Child Left Behind. Many schools in non-White neighborhoods were closed and their teachers fired because their incoming students were so far behind before even beginning school. The accountability standards did not measure what difference schools actually made but instead falsely assumed that all schools deal with similar challenges.[26] Whites and more affluent residents tend to deny the persistence of unfair racial disparities and assume that there is little need to consider the fundamentally different contexts in which students receive an education.[27]

These differences in perspective often produce well-intentioned policies that only deepen already-severe inequalities and blame the institutions that try to serve those starting at the bottom. This book aims to show how failure to consider the basic system of stratification often can intensify rather than resolve the inequalities even when there is no intention of doing that. It shows how good intentions, and seemingly plausible regulations, can have perverse effects and attempts to point policy development in directions that would help equalize higher education opportunities.

HIGH-STAKES ACCOUNTABILITY RESEARCH

High-stakes accountability strategies based on a limited number of imperfect measures are often described as important breakthroughs by their advocates because they appear to be precise numbers and express a commitment to accountability. But they can be highly misleading. Since the public school accountability initiatives of the Reagan administration and many states in the 1980s, the idea that institutions need strict evaluation and tough sanctions has become a basic element of education policy discussions. After more than three decades of this approach, reaching its peak in the No Child Left Behind and Reach for the Top federal programs, vast numbers of American schools were branded as failures. There was virtually no resistance in Congress when those programs were abandoned and when the federal role in education was greatly limited and vast authority and discretion were turned over to state governments in the Every Student Succeeds Act of 2015. And many state education agencies contend with the same disputes. The development of sound and fair assessments seems, at first glance, to be relatively simple. But it actually requires accurate data, some of which do not exist, and appropriate interpretation so that institutions are evaluated for what difference they make, not for conditions that are beyond their control.

The authors of the new studies in this book find that the approach of using existing data is poorly targeted and could create severe problems for minority-serving institutions (MSIs) and the many minority and low-income students who have experienced much weaker precollege education. This raises a very serious civil rights question: Even without financial sanctions, do accountability reforms disproportionately harm schools or mislead consumers they are intended to help by discouraging enrollment and cutting support from state and private donors, thereby leading to regrettable unintended consequences?

The research in this volume operates at the intersection of accountability and civil rights, where authors carefully diagnose the source of education inequalities and offer alternative ways state and federal policy makers might hold colleges accountable without reinforcing inequality. They explore what factors are related to graduation rates and find evidence of very large impacts from experience before college and the financial situation of students' families. They find that MSIs do have a substantially lower graduation rate than other institutions but that they are disproportionately important for the education of minority groups that have always had unequal access to college and unequal success in higher education. Some of these institutions have graduation rates far lower than the national average—How should they be judged? Will accountability and sanctions be an effective solution to this inequality, or would the consequence be to make higher education still more unequal?

The authors explain why policy makers need, at a minimum, the appropriate data infrastructure to design better accountability systems. But more importantly, each chapter presents innovative analytical techniques that can help expand the way policy makers go about evaluating institutional performance data. Using input-adjusted performance metrics, variance decomposition, frontier analysis, and geospatial analysis, policy makers may find new tools to help design regimes that are able to account for many of the inequalities presented here. This book includes the work of a number of leading researchers who explore the predictable—and avoidable—consequences high-stakes accountability regimes have on reinforcing racial and economic inequality.

Minority-Serving Institutions Are Especially Vulnerable

There are three kinds of schools that are minority-serving institutions, as described in chapter 3 by Marybeth Gasman, Thai-Huy Nguyen, Andrés Castro Samayoa, and Daniel Corral. The first two are institutions that, historically, were created to serve Black or Native American students with a central mission to educate young people from those backgrounds, and they are run largely by people from their racial or tribal group. The third kind of MSI has more than a specified threshold number of students from underrepresented minorities. These are mostly Hispanic-Serving Institutions (HSIs), but others serve substantial groups of Blacks or Native Americans. For these colleges, recognition as a minority-serving institution is purely statistical and usually has nothing to do with their history or original mission, although this mission has now been adopted by some. There are colleges actively seeking out students of color and creating special programs and support systems for them; others merely happen to have these students and apply for associated funding.

The oldest MSIs are those founded by churches, philanthropists, and state governments to educate former slaves after the Civil War. The second Morrill Act in 1892 provided for state universities and accepted the "separate but equal" policies in the nineteen states that established separate colleges and profoundly unequal schools for Black students. Gasman and colleagues find that MSIs enroll about a fifth of all US students and that most of their students receive Pell Grants, so they are very dependent on eligibility for federal funding. These colleges tend to cost much less than the national average, in part because almost half of them are community colleges that draw many students from nearby heavily non-White communities, and they account for a disproportionate share of male graduates of color.

Since MSIs are institutions serving a large share of the college students who graduated from weak high schools and from families with far fewer resources, their students tend to take longer to graduate and graduate at lower levels. Thus, these schools, which produce a very substantial share of graduates of color, face special challenges. They usually have little money and are highly tuition dependent, and their low-income students make them particularly vulnerable to state and federal accountability ratings that are blind to the obstacles facing students of color. They also usually have much smaller per-student budgets. A colorblind accountability policy using unadjusted statistics could easily end up hurting these institutions and may even encourage them to screen out the very students these institutions best know how to serve.

Accountability regimes that fail to account for the racial and economic inequalities students face before ever entering MSIs will do little to reverse them. Drawing on a very rich data set from Texas, Stella Flores, Toby Park, and Dominique Baker offer in chapter 5 a solution for how policy makers might adjust for these differences. Though the federal data infrastructure makes it nearly impossible to conduct such analyses, Flores and colleagues use a rich state-level data set from Texas to examine the extent to which noncollege factors contribute to college outcomes. Their research shows that unequal precollege preparation is powerfully linked with unequal college outcomes; in fact, college characteristics account for only about one-third of college outcomes. If most of the outcomes are accounted for by things outside the control of colleges, then it is impossible to evaluate the contribution of colleges without statistically controlling for such massively important factors. Failing to account for this in an accountability regime will only reinforce inequality and unfairly penalize colleges for serving students who are products of our nation's unequal K–12 education system. But to make such adjustments is beyond the reach of existing data sets at the federal level and in most states.

In a similar study, Anne-Marie Nuñez and Awilda Rodriguez explore in chapter 6 whether it would be possible to adjust the graduation rate metrics to take into account factors outside the control of colleges. Using the federal IPEDS (Integrated Postsecondary Education Data System) data on colleges and universities, they adjust graduation rates according to financial aid data, enrollment data, and budgets for bachelor's-degree-granting HSIs, analyzing data from ninety-eight institutions. The study concludes that once "differences in institutional and student characteristics are accounted for, HSIs perform on par with their non-HSI counterparts." In other words, all of the apparent relative failure of these institutions is due to things beyond their control. From this perspective, policy makers should consider the possibility that policies themselves, and not necessarily colleges, are part of the accountability problem. An accountability regime that fails to use statistical adjustments will unfairly penalize colleges by overlooking the positive outcomes they produce.

In addition to regression adjustment analysis, Sylvia Hurtado, Adriana Ruiz Alvarado, and Kevin Eagan offer in chapter 4 a new way to analyze and measure institutional performance. Using a frontier analysis, they demonstrate a new way to statistically adjust performance metrics that consider student background and institutional resources. By using this technique, there are a number of MSIs whose outcomes appear to be superior to those found for similar students at more affluent colleges. They show that these institutions play an especially critical role in producing graduates of color and conclude that these institutions should receive special rewards for their success in the face of very difficult challenges rather than be rated poorly by the federal government. Across these chapters, a key lesson is that federal and state policy makers will need to make better data available to conduct these types of studies while also designing policies that adjust for these deeply rooted inequalities.

However, no adequate data exists to validly make these adjustments at the college level. And with an administration far less likely to expand federal data requirements than Obama's, these flaws limit any Trump administration effort to do so.

Accountability Regimes and the Illusion of Choice

Many states with big metro areas also have large rural sectors where the population has been declining for a half-century or more, and these areas are having a hard time supporting colleges and other needed services. A fundamental component of modern accountability regimes rests on the market-based belief that information and sanctions will foster competition, which in turn will help students make more informed choices about where to enroll. There are big areas of the country, however, where colleges are scarce. This means not only that there isn't a competitive market, but, if report cards or sanctions force the local college to close, there may be no higher ed opportunity at all.

In chapter 7 Nicholas Hillman shows that in these "education deserts" there are no real choices, and a sanction shutting down the local community college could simply eliminate any affordable public option for the low-income, and often minority, students who live there and cannot afford the much higher costs of a residential college. Many students are place bound (most community college students live within thirty miles of their school), and the level of enrollment is clearly related to proximity; it is much cheaper to live at home. Eliminating options or aid for students attending these schools would mean sharp drops in enrollment and institutional income, which further perpetuate education inequality in areas that are already struggling.

Financial Aid System Flaws

Sara Goldrick-Rab and Jason Houle argue in chapter 9 that the financial problem the government is trying to address with accountability measures is actually not caused by colleges and cannot be fairly addressed with accountability measures. They argue that what such measures treat as a symptom of college mismanagement or inefficiency is actually a fundamental problem of an increasingly unworkable financial aid system. The grant aid is too small for many families, and the only alternative is government-insured loans. Because disadvantaged students have less chance of finishing and earning enough to repay their loans, the government faces increasing losses as more loans default. In response, the government is taking steps that pressure colleges to condition loans not only on the student's need but, implicitly, on an estimate of the student's ability to repay, much as a bank would do. This, of course, would change the nature of the commitment to aiding students with need that has been a central element of federal aid for fifty years. Moves in this direction, such as the Parent Loans for Undergraduate Students (PLUS loan) program policy changes, may have already made the long-term crisis of minority college completion even worse.

Willie Kirkland takes a closer look in chapter 8 at the PLUS loan and the fiscal situation of students and families at Dillard University in New Orleans. A 147-year-old African American college committed to helping disadvantaged Black students, Dillard is still struggling to recover from severe damage from Hurricane Katrina. The hurricane destroyed substantial parts of the campus and caused a dramatic drop in enrollment, which triggered major cutbacks, including sharp cuts in full-time faculty. Ninety percent of incoming students at the college need financial assistance, and only one-fourth of those students receive enough in grants and loans to cover their costs. The rest have unmet need that neither they nor their families can cover. After all sources have been tapped and student loan eligibility for aid exhausted, the Dillard officials recommend PLUS loans to the parents or guardians, an undesirable but inescapable challenge for many families who have no lending alternatives. The Obama administration substantially raised the credit standards for the loans because of the risk, but this meant that in 2012–13, 80 percent of the Dillard parent applicants for PLUS loans were denied because of the policy change. The next year 73 percent were denied. This resulted in a notable decline in enrollment at a school that was still struggling to recover from Katrina's devastation. In this case, accountability policies that appear to be helping students afford college may indeed be doing just the opposite and may create new problems, such as encouraging students to drop out or having disproportionate impacts on Historically Black Colleges and Universities and other MSIs.

State Accountability

We are a country with fifty different state systems of higher education, and within each there are many individual colleges and sometimes several state coordinating agencies for more- and less-competitive universities and community colleges. These systems have widely differing policies on the state contribution to college operations, about state aid to students, and many other issues. But there have also been very broad patterns of cuts in the state share of college costs. In 2015, after recovery from the Great Recession, the decline from the pre-recession level of state funding was still 15 percent.[28] State policy makers have often responded to concern about costs and complaints about the low graduation rates on many campuses by linking the state funding that still exists in one way or another to student outcomes. The governing idea, much like the Obama proposals, is that accountability will spur efficiency and increase graduation rates.

As Nicholas Hillman and Valerie Crespín-Trujillo report in chapter 2, almost two-thirds of the states have such policies, and, as one would expect, they vary widely. In some states, they are adjusted to try to more accurately assess what difference the colleges make, not how selective they are in admissions. Others are simple outcome measures giving the most credit to those who get the best students and the least to those who offer a chance to the students with the fewest opportunities. It is very important for those trying to figure out the future of higher education opportunity to understand, evaluate, and bring together information from across the country about these measures. They will create either obstacles or incentives and support colleges trying to do the right thing to expand opportunity and to increase the productivity of our education system. Many of the problems explored in studying the federal measures are directly applicable to debates in the states.

In chapter 2, Orfield explores and draws lessons from the experience of the Obama administration in trying, with limited resources, to create a college information system intended to inform students and families about some key aspects of college success, costs, and job placement. The goal was to inject some serious accountability into the higher education system, but it had to be done without congressional support and with only the data that the federal government was already collecting from the nation's colleges. The country's higher education leaders and scholars raised serious challenges to the effort, which faced some of the same kinds of problems in holding colleges accountable for outcomes that were often more rooted in the inequality and segregation of the society and the public schools than in anything colleges had control over. But the administration persisted and created the nationally publicized College Scorecard, which has been widely used in spite of its limitations. The chapter discusses how this issue evolved within a frustrated administration wanting to make much larger changes in higher education than were possible once it lost control of Congress in the 2010 midterm elections.

CONCLUSION

As college access became a more visible and urgent issue for American families, and as the federal role changed from helping low-income families gain access to trying to help everyone within constrained budgets, presidents, governors, Congress, and state legislatures tried to respond with a complex set of grants, loans, and tax credits amid growing and conflicting demands. Gaps grew in student funding that introduced huge obstacles for the many families without significant savings, income, or wealth. Once the door had been opened to federal college subsidies for the middle class in the 1970s, the efforts to provide some kind of subsidy for everybody facing soaring tuition created increasingly incoherent and arbitrary policies and vested interests in maintaining them. What was left over for the poor was seriously inadequate. There was not enough money to provide Pell grants that covered even a fifth of the actual cost of attending a median four-year public university. But the overall federal cost increased substantially, and the states were shifting the burden to students. The feds were expected to help the students pay, but federal funds covered only part of the need, and student loans mushroomed, some beyond the capacity of former students to repay.

In its early days, the Obama administration used bailout funds for a substantial increase in aid but, later, without money, turned toward accountability and sanctions. Many state governments slashed their funding for colleges in the Great Recession and did not restore it but demanded more of campuses, usually not taking into account the extreme variation in student background and college missions and resources. The failures of fourteen years of high-stakes accountability with No Child Left Behind for public K–12 schools did not prevent policy makers from devising decontextualized assessments for colleges based on similar theories. College and state governments continued raising tuition, President Obama's proposals for new programs died in Congress, and there were funding cuts dealt in a succession of budget deals with Congress. Frustrated, the administration doubled down on the accountability and competition approach in spite of strong opposition from the nonprofit and public higher education communities and an increasingly hostile Congress. With resistance, it was only able to institute its College Scorecard.

The 2016 presidential election brought a sharp turn to the Right, and the Trump administration shifted policy-making authority much more to the states and reduced regulations for the private for-profit colleges and weakened civil rights enforcement. In the meantime, the states confronted many accountability challenges on their own, since most were short of funds and looked to receive less from the federal government. They faced many of the same issues that muddled the Obama initiative.

Though the GOP took control of the presidency and both houses of Congress in the 2016 election, the Senate majority was too small and focused on other issues to make major legislation outside the limited reconciliation process. And serious divisons among Republicans added to the complexity. When President Trump proposed some significant immediate funding changes in early 2017, Congress ignored most of them and enacted a spending plan for the rest of the fiscal year that continued existing programs. Fortunately, the education committees in Congress have a tradition of significant collaboration across party lines.

The basic policy landscape continues to be dominated by the clash between families' needs and colleges' search for needed revenue in the face of severely constrained budgets. Policy making is rich in rhetoric but poor in both resources and coherent priorities. In this crossfire, the shift of blame to the universities and the families through accountability policies remains attractive to some in both political parties, with Republicans focusing on the state level. The systematic analyses of the racial equity consequences of accountability policies in the following chapters document unintended consequences of these high-stakes policies. As studies demonstrate, high-stakes accountability without consideration of the background and resources of students and campuses is likely to make our higher education system even more unequal. Equitable accountability requires facing the issues our colleagues explore in their pathbreaking work.

CHAPTER 1

Obama's Accountability Efforts

A Case Study in Frustration

GARY ORFIELD

Barack Obama made college opportunity a central goal of his presidency. His campaign motivated young voters, and he received their support. As a former college teacher at the University of Chicago, he thought a lot about higher education. When he became president in the midst of the greatest economic crisis in eighty years, he had stimulus money to spend to get the economy going again, and he sent billions of dollars in the direction of colleges and student aid. He was able to dramatically change management of students loans, marking the greatest burst of federal higher education policy changes in a long time, and made a good start at addressing a number of issues that had been kicked down the road for years. Unfortunately, those first two years were both the start and, in many ways, the end.

The administration identified college access as a priority from the outset. Obama's proposal during his first year in office called for a substantial increase in college spaces, mostly in community colleges, and a major increase in financial aid for students. This was part of a broad plan to mobilize institutions across the country around the urgent effort to revive an economy in grave trouble. Billions were to be devoted to supporting community colleges and helping students. This was very important during the Great Recession, which devastated both higher education institutions and the families of college-age students. But Obama's hope for major new, substantive higher education law and major new programs died with the Republican takeover of the House of Representatives in the 2010 election.

Substantial increases in the need-based Federal Pell Grant and increased tuition tax credits were part of the huge but temporary fiscal stimulus package in those first two years, which gave the administration flexible and wide discretion in using funds intended to stimulate economic activity. The basic goal was to pump up economic activity and transfer dollars to students, virtually guaranteeing that they would be quickly spent and boost the economy. That, however, proved to be a unique, short-lived opportunity. As soon as the major financial institutions and the auto industry were saved, the threat of an immediate depression passed, and the conservative Tea Party gained momentum in the 2010 election, concern over the deficit became intense and budget growth was sharply limited.

The largest breakthrough for college access under Obama came with the decision to replace bank loans for students with lower-cost direct federal loans. In one hard-won congressional vote that shaped much of Obama's domestic legislative legacy, the administration enacted both the Affordable Care Act (ACA) and legislation taking federally guaranteed student loans away from private banks and originating all new loans directly with the federal government, thereby substantially lowering the cost to students.[1]

While the administration had fought to help poor students during the recession, it also quickly doubled down on President Clinton's tax subsidy for middle-class students. Under Clinton, the Pell grant had been allowed to lag, and a new tax-based subsidy was enacted to cover much of the out-of-pocket costs at many community colleges for two years. Clinton successfully pushed a tax benefit for former students paying off student loans in spite of serious objections from administration experts that it was an inefficient, very costly, and unfocused expenditure that did not enable people without funds to go to college but instead subsidized a higher-income group that had already graduated and had debts to pay off. It polled very positively in the Clinton reelection polls, however, and was enacted in spite of its equity problems. Tax subsidies, once given, develop a constituency and are very hard to end.[2]

This tax credit was greatly expanded in Obama's 2009 American Recovery and Reinvestment Act, the fiscal stimulus legislation, and was made available to families with much higher incomes and covered more years of education, thereby ballooning the cost. The quickly assembled package offered something for everyone but failed to target aid to the students who needed it the most. The credit was fully available only for those taxpayers who owed substantial taxes and filed long-form returns; yet, a large majority of low-income families file the short form, which requires no professional help but, at the same time, does not tap the great majority of subsidies and loopholes built into the tax system. The maximum benefit for a low-income student not owing taxes was $1,000 a year—a very modest help. The credit was a popular but very poorly focused subsidy most beneficial to those with substantial incomes and good accountants.[3]

Later, in the budget deal struck in the closing days of 2015, this regressive subsidy was made permanent in a deal between the White House and the Republican Congress. Obama briefly proposed cutting these subsidies to high-income families but withdrew that proposal within days following a storm of congressional protest from both parties. The administration found that the extremely favorable and very costly exemption of college savings accounts from taxation, either before college or when the increased funds eventually come out, was a significant benefit only to the most affluent Americans. These families have substantial funds to sock away for many years and are subject to high tax rates that make exemptions very valuable.[4] And they vote in large numbers. The same exemption is worth three times as much to a family taxed at the 36 percent rate as to a much-lower-income family paying 12 percent.

Tax benefits are rarely repealed or seriously examined, and they are not subjected to the annual appropriation process that controls all cash expenditures. That means this benefit will continue unless it is reversed by Congress.[5] Research has also found these subsidies to have no effect on expanding education opportunity, which should not be surprising considering who benefits most from the subsidy.[6] Most conservatives do not see tax exemptions as expenditures and oppose any significant increases in taxes, though these "loopholes" have exactly the same economic effect on the budget as expenditures do. Tax subsidies normally continue indefinitely, while subsidies that work through appropriations, like the Pell grant, require positive budget decisions each year and are squeezed when deficits rise. Congressional conservatives fiercely oppose substantial increases in domestic expenditures but normally leave tax subsidies unchallenged, defining the end of an exemption as a tax increase. Obama's something-for-everyone approach embedded more tax subsidies whose cost would grow rapidly.

President Obama often strongly criticized excessive college costs and student debts, noting that Pell grants for poor students had doubled during his term and tax subsidies for middle-class students had tripled. Yet, the gaps between aid and cost were still much larger than they had been in the past.[7]

The newspapers were (and still are) full of stories on the dramatic increases in student indebtedness, criticisms of the value of college education, and reports on the ways debt limits the life prospects of a generation of students.[8] As colleges continued to raise costs, the president searched for levers.

After substantial progress in his first two years, when he had stimulus money and a congressional majority, Obama ran into a wall of resistance to new resources, as funding was also reduced in many states. Congressional conservatives, alarmed at the debts generated from the stimulus program, were strongly opposed to new spending. Deeply frustrated, Obama turned to regulation. Because regulation is inevitable in allocation of scarce resources, the story of this effort has lessons for future state and federal policies. Understanding the ways in which accountability policies can have major unintended impacts on racial equity is the goal of this case study and the chapter studies of the complexities of accountability.

Obama and his administration frequently addressed equity and cost issues when conservatives took control first of the House of Representatives in 2010 and then the Senate four years later. The president made a series of proposals in his second term, some of which echoed initiatives demanding accountability in a number of states, and he visited campuses to promote them in widely publicized addresses. This chapter assesses those proposals and shows the possibility that accountability policies may unintentionally further limit the chances of students of color and the colleges that serve them if they do not take racial issues into account.

After the stimulus package and health-care reforms passed, the Obama administration turned its attention to regulatory reforms and to designing a new system for evaluating colleges. However, after harsh criticism of the ideas by many university leaders and experts, and with strong resistance to expanding federal control by the Republicans, the administration retreated in some important respects. Federal regulators maintained tough policies about for-profit colleges and colleges of education and pressed forward with "scorecards" and the release of data on all colleges they believed to be relevant to the assessment of college choices by America's families. Similar ideas have been implemented or are still being debated in various states, some of which are making decisions on the basis of the College Scorecard data, making this research relevant in many settings. The Obama administration story illustrates the difficulty of measuring college impacts, the unintended outcomes of accountability measures, probable impacts on institutions serving the most vulnerable students, and the need for much better basic data for valid assessments of institutional impacts and considers parallel state efforts and the policy context in which these ideas emerged.

FOR-PROFIT COLLEGES: THE USE OF EXTREME SANCTIONS

The one area of accountability that the Obama administration managed to attach very strong consequences to was for-profit colleges that often enroll large numbers of students of color. Sometimes, as in the evaluation of the for-profit schools, accountability enforcement is triggered by fraud, scandals, and investigations or prosecutions, or simply by the financial risk to the government of open-ended commitments cleverly exploited by promoters. When the government in the 1970s promised Pell grants to low-income students and student loans to any college meeting the federal government's low accreditation standards, the path was open for the creation of for-profit schools that provided low-cost education lacking many of the features of most nonprofit public and private colleges, such as substantial permanent faculties, research faculty, libraries, etc. These institutions set fees at levels students could afford after combining Pell grants and student loans, and they invested heavily in recruiting students who had little preparation for college and little or no understanding of college choice and financing. The colleges made a great deal of money, and for years their stocks soared.

The administration faced the problem of what to do about very large-scale defaults on federally guaranteed student loans, often pushed to the maximum, by counselors at for-profit colleges. Often these colleges recruited students on the basis that they could go to college at no cost, and they then set tuition so that a Pell grant and a maximum federal student loan would cover it. Students who arrived with no money and signed a stack of papers often did not realize that they would have to repay large loans even if they never got a degree or the kind of jobs the colleges promised. Many of these colleges invested much of their funds in advertising and recruiting, often giving students inaccurate information on the placement rates and income of their graduates. They enrolled students with few or no qualifications and had very low completion rates. They tended to promise that their degrees would mean great success in the job markets, but many of the claims were bogus.

The sector was highly profitable, required limited resources to enter, expanded to hundreds of campuses, and rapidly took over a large share of all federal aid. Students were often left with large debt and no credential, or with a credential that had little credibility with employers.[9] Graduates and the many dropouts often could not repay their loans, creating a serious budget problem for the federal government, which had guaranteed the loans, as well as the students, who faced long-term financial crises. Congressional conservatives and the Bush-era officials, who tended to think that private meant better and trusted the market to solve problems, just let this huge expansion of for-profit schools happen. After scandals were exposed in a two-year US Senate investigation ending in 2012, the Obama administration moved to more vigorously monitor these colleges' financial situations, exposing widespread problems in this sector that had been free of much of the regulation and oversight mechanisms aimed at the public sector. In 2015, the administration took dramatic action, sometimes freezing federal payments; large numbers of students found their campuses suddenly closed, since the companies could not survive for even a brief period without a constant flow of federal dollars. They had few reserves. When these colleges fought back, the federal courts supported the administration and upheld the action.[10]

This shows the kind of power that federal ratings could have with high-stakes accountability. As federal standards were tightened, the giant University of Phoenix reported a dramatic drop in enrollment.[11] The Obama administration took action against the massive Corinthian Colleges (with 107 campuses), which conceded that it had lied to the government about job placement rates, and briefly stopped federal funds, making it apparent that the for-profit system was facing financial disaster because it was almost totally dependent on federal aid. It lacked the financial standing to get even short-term bank loans, after burdening the government and many thousands of students with debt they could not repay.[12]

The Department of Education took action again in August 2016, forbidding ITT Educational Services from enrolling any more students receiving federal funds. It faced increasing sanctions and recently reported having only $78 million in cash, likely a death sentence for the business ordered to set aside $153 million to reimburse students who would lose their programs. Federal aid dollars had covered 70 percent of the company's budget in 2015, so when ITT collapsed, the government faced the huge cost of reimbursing students for debt they accrued at these defunct colleges.[13] A disturbing part of the story is that many of these campuses had admitted large numbers of Latino and African American students who were hurt by both the low-quality education and the large debts they carried, even though, too often, they never received a degree or credential. Closing the schools, however, closed institutions that had been far more enthusiastic about enrolling them than many other colleges had been.

This experience with abusive institutions and huge financial costs for the government was among the factors leading to pressure for more consumer protection and financial accountability. However, nonprofit institutions, especially those serving very disadvantaged students, strongly insisted that their situation was fundamentally different from that of the bad for-profits, since they were not after profit and cared about their students. Although the closed for-profit colleges enrolled many African American and Latino students, there has been limited study of the impact of the abuses or the closings on those groups. Faced with abusive practices and what were large and open-ended risks to the federal government, the temptation was to shut down institutions or to force them to judge risks and basically do underwriting for the federal loans. This would make them more sound on a banking basis but was in basic tension with the ideal of giving all students access to the money they needed to go to college.

The crackdown on for-profit colleges also revealed other risks associated with high-stakes accountability, including cheating or manipulation of the data for which the college is being held accountable. The Chicago City Colleges, a vast system of community colleges in the city, was put under severe pressure to raise very low graduation rates under the city's Reinvention plan. Between 2010 and 2015 the graduation rate for full-time students soared from an extremely low 7 percent to 17 percent. One contribution to the reported progress in growth of degrees awarded was merely the impact of changes in the process of awarding degrees. For example, the colleges decided to retroactively award associate degrees to students who did not finish the college's requirements but got a bachelor of art's degree after transferring to a four-year campus without an associate degree. A similar trend has occurred in community colleges that are subjected to state performance-based funding policies. The meaning of seemingly similar data over years can be changed in many ways, responding to accountability by creating a paper success. A basic message from this story, as well as the others, is that it matters very much what kind of data is used and how the impacts of the accountability are monitored.

Ironically, the great success of the Obama administration in cleaning up some of the abuses of the for-profit sector became one of the first targets for reversal by the Trump administration. Obama had been able to act very strongly because of scandals, huge risks for the student loan system from poor repayment, a major congressional investigation exposing scams, and the lasting damage done to many students. The Trump administration, in contrast, came in with a general hostility toward federal regulation and a strong belief in the private sector as a provider of education, and the new secretary of education, Betsy DeVos, appointed a leader from the for-profit sector to run student financial aid programs.[14]

Outside of the for-profit school scandal, however, the Obama administration had little latitude in trying to move toward evaluations with consequences for federal decisions. It had to rely on a hope that people and institutions would respond to its College Scorecard and the metrics it included (see table 1.1).

After a major reversal in the 2010 election, conservative Republican opponents heavily influenced by the far-right Tea Party movement, took over the House of Representatives, and the budget was drastically tightened as congressional opponents pointed to the huge deficits caused by borrowing for the bailout, the unfunded wars in Iraq and Afghan, and the George W. Bush administration's large tax cuts. Though many economists believed that more stimulus was needed for a full recovery, the budget cutters now had veto power over any significant new expenditures.

Without significant dollars or congressional support, the Obama administration had to continue trying to respond to deep concerns about college costs and indebtedness.[15] The states were experiencing similar problems, and many of them had cut taxes during the boom and had to savagely cut budgets in the Great Recession, since they were required to balance their budgets each year. The federal government also faced a growing threat posed by the inability of many recipients to repay their student loans, which were guaranteed, and had to pick up the cost of nonrepayment and the administrative expenses of collecting past-due loans. Congress had made student loan debt something that could not be expunged even in personal bankruptcy (except in extremely rare cases), something that could hang over one-time students' heads for life, damaging credit and limiting futures.

During his reelection campaign in 2012, President Obama faced a hostile Congress unwilling to provide new funds and the sequester agreement requiring ongoing budget cuts. He still promised progress on college access. He had no more money, and Congress was not willing to attempt cutting college subsidies to the middle class. He wanted to show leadership and called on colleges to lower their costs, although state funding was still far below its historic share of college costs. But he had no leverage, and there

Table 1.1   College Scorecard elements

Average annual cost of attendance	Graduation rate
Salary 10 years after beginning college	Percent receiving federal student loans
Percent receiving Pell grants	Median student loan debt
Average monthly student loan payment	Percent paying down the principle on debt
Students who return for their second year	Percent earning more than high school graduates
Race/Ethnicity of student body	College entrance exam scores

Source: US Department of Education, College Scorecard, 2016, http://www.collegescorecard.ed.gov.

was no significant response to this call. This is unsurprising, since, for example, faculty salaries had already been virtually frozen (in constant-value dollars) for decades, and regular faculty were being replaced by temporary adjuncts as campuses struggled with many kinds of deferred expenditures during and after the Great Recession.

SECOND-TERM PROPOSALS

The Obama administration needed an agenda of reforms that could be implemented without new money. It responded with a plan to better inform the public about college cost and quality, paralleling a 2006 recommendation of the Bush administration's Spellings Commission on higher education. The idea was that exposing and comparing the costs would put market pressure on colleges while also encouraging students to "shop around" to make better choices. The president also proposed a "student bill of rights," which aimed to provide better information about managing debt for former students, many of whom were shocked and confused by the complex public and private debts they found themselves facing after graduation. The plan, however, did nothing to reduce debts.[16]

In his 2013 State of the Union Address, setting out his goals for his second term, the president promised to increase college accountability, asking Congress to "change the Higher Education Act so that affordability and value are included in determining which colleges receive certain types of federal aid." Since most colleges are extremely dependent on students receiving various kinds of federal grants and loans to pay tuition, this could have been an extremely powerful and threatening move if enacted and implemented. With no likelihood of new federal program legislation, early in 2014 Obama decided to extend to higher education the basic approach his administration, like the Bush administration before it, had used in elementary and secondary education—accountability and sanctions. Because of the extreme political polarization in Congress, however, the administration lacked the votes to enact legislation for accountability policies. The Republicans were strongly opposed to the expansion of federal authority over colleges, and so were higher education leaders.

Obama pledged in 2013 to "release a new 'College Scorecard' that parents and students can use to compare schools based on a simple criteria— where [they] can get the most bang for [their] educational buck."[17] The next year, in the 2014 State of the Union Address, he said, "We're shaking up our system of higher education to give parents more information, and colleges more incentives to offer better value, so that no middle-class kid is priced out of a college education." (Donald Trump would make similar complaints about the high cost of college in his 2016 campaign.) Obama said, "We're offering millions the opportunity to cap their monthly student loan payments to ten percent of their income, and I want to work with Congress to see how we can help even more Americans who feel trapped by student loan debt."[18] This was the plan widely supported by economists, but it is difficult to implement without the Internal Revenue Service playing a central role in monitoring and collecting both earnings and loan debt. Instead, borrowers must opt into one of five different income-driven plans and reapply each year, but federal loan servicers (e.g., Navient, formerly Sallie Mae) have little incentive to encourage borrowers to enroll in these alternative plans. Enrollments were growing at the end of Obama's presidency. (Trump featured a similar plan as a solution for student debt in his campaign.)

President Obama held two college summits at the White House, in January and again in December 2014, announcing some modest federal and philanthropic commitments to college opportunity.[19] The midterm election in 2014 was a bitter disappointment, however, with the GOP takeover of the Senate and the Republicans winning a very large majority in the House as well as capturing a number of state governments. This left the administration severely weakened for its last two years and policy making across the country largely in the hands of conservatives, except for what could be accomplished by executive initiatives.

With little prospect of new programs or major legislation, accountability became the dominant goal. The White House launched the promised College Scorecards "to help empower students and families with more transparent information about college costs and outcomes, so that they can choose a school that is affordable, best-suited to meet their needs, and consistent with their education and career goals." The plan promised "clear, concise information on cost, graduation rate, loan default rate, amount borrowed, and employment for every degree-granting institution in the country" to equip "students and families to compare colleges and make the best decision for their future."[20] It was an attempt to use market forces to keep down costs and raise the graduation rate while protecting the government from loans that would default.

The central measures for the initial report cards were to be a mixture of things important to students and families and to the government's control of costs. Graduation rates, the cost, and whether the schooling led to a well-paying job and not deep debt—these metrics were important to families. The government wanted to know whether students in a school were repaying their loans at a high rate. Though these metrics may seem helpful, none of them is easy to quantify. For example, earnings are likely to differ across majors and by student's race/ethnicity or gender, yet none of this is reported in the Scorecard. Similarly, student loan repayment rates fail to account for the type of repayment plan a student is enrolled in, and most of the Scorecard data are only accounting for students receiving federal financial aid. And the outcomes of previous cohorts of students are not necessarily good predictors of future cohorts. This leaves fundamental questions about the legitimacy of comparisons along these seemingly neutral dimensions. Yet, these are not unobtrusive measures of quality; they are intentionally obtrusive measures. And the measured colleges are not passive; there are many things they can do to try to change the outcomes, or at least the apparent outcomes.

Obama's goal was to address problems of constantly rising cost and disappointing completion rates. This strategy, if the numbers were to be accurate comparisons of the colleges, rests on several assumptions. The first is that all colleges have the resources to produce a high graduation rate, but some use them more effectively than others. If this were true, there would be no need to equalize resources to fairly judge outcomes. In reality, however, there was no money to equalize key resources. A second assumption is that all colleges have relatively similar student bodies with students who would graduate at high rates if only the college were efficient. A third assumption is that the students and their families have sufficient resources to permit students to achieve and remain in school, if only the school's management became more efficient. A fourth assumption is that a college's resources can be activated by a credible threat of a devastating sanction affecting its income. And a fifth assumption is that colleges have direct and unambiguous control over any of these outcomes. As the following chapters suggest, these central assumptions are incorrect in many cases, which means that the comparisons are often misleading.

A rating system depends, of course, on the validity of the data the government is collecting for other purposes and a determination that they can now be validly used to create the ratings. Data designed and collected for other purposes often do not work well for validly assessing different goals. And an accountability system without valid input and outcome data cannot be fair. If it is not fair, some institutions will be undervalued and face losses based on faulty comparisons that might imply, for example, that a college which intentionally took on students from inferior high schools was less effective than one whose students were exceptionally well prepared.

EVALUATING THE COLLEGE SCORECARD

Higher education leaders and associations were strongly critical of President Obama's idea, arguing that the higher education system and American society are much too complex to equitably use one-dimensional outcome measures.[21] Many objected to the administration's proposed plans and regulations, claiming that such a system would "create perverse institutional incentives and limit access to higher education for certain student populations."[22] The basic claims were that the proposed ratings were both misleading and would likely hurt the very institutions most dedicated to helping vulnerable groups of students. It is true, of course, that no institution likes to be ranked and judged by powerful external forces. Yet, while some of the criticism was self-serving, the colleges also raised valid issues.

A fundamental problem was that there were no input measures about student backgrounds in the proposed rating system. If a college's mission is to educate poorly prepared students from weak schools and families with few resources, is it fair to rank its outcomes against a college that serves few such students and enrolls well-prepared students from families with substantial resources and highly educated parents? Few educators could support the validity of such ratings. Because of strong resistance from colleges and the obvious limits of such ratings based on existing data, the administration promised to consider adjustments that take into account the different circumstances colleges face and not to issue comparative rankings based on problematic measures. Deputy Undersecretary Jamienne Studley, who led the effort for the Department of Education, made this commitment in September 2014, but the College Scorecard was published the next year with no adjustments.[23]

Though the government did not publish comprehensive comparative ratings of colleges, Undersecretary Studley wished to see a rating system similar to that of *Consumer Reports*, indicating that rating a college should be as easy as rating a blender.[24] The Department of Education later praised specific institutions that had high scores on a measure, without qualifications or adjustments that would have been needed to judge what should be credited to the college rather than other factors. The fundamental goal of the Scorecard was to enable families to compare colleges to better inform their choices. This was, of course, an implicit rating system of comparative data based on the credibility of the US Department of Education, which presented the Scorecard as impartial data. If the measures were invalid, however, so were the comparisons. Though emphasizing different aspects, the early indications are that the Trump administration shares the basic assumption that crude unadjusted outcomes are valid measures of success.

Differences in Resources and Student Population

When the US government issues official statistics on institutions and advocates their use in evaluating the colleges, it raises the stakes. The Scorecard operates on the theory that publication of data can and should be used by consumers and the government to make decisions about institutions and that this will pressure those institutions to improve their prices and outcomes. Implicit in this logic is a belief that institutions are responsible for the results, so putting a strong spotlight on the information will force them to improve. If they fail to improve, they should be shut down (the "creative destruction" of free markets) as students stop enrolling. The measures assume, for example, that a college can be reasonably held responsible because a number of its students do not repay their student loans. They assume that colleges should be held accountable for their graduates' employment, which is a fundamental goal of students and families investing in college. But that may, of course, be affected by factors, including changes in the regional job market, racial discrimination in the labor market, and many other factors outside the control of a college.

It also assumes that all colleges are, or should be, vocational. This is, of course, directly contrary to the mission of many liberal arts colleges, which believe a broad general education is the best preparation for graduate and professional work and for creativity. It further assumes that a single college is responsible for the student's eventual outcome, ignoring the fact that students attend multiple institutions—so which college should be credited or blamed for a transfer student's eventual outcome? Also, there is an implicit belief that colleges and universities will use this data to learn about their own practices, but the Department of Education provides colleges with no resources to build their capacity (professional development, technical assistance, etc.) to use this data for institutional improvement.

By simply providing public information and threatening to penalize underperformers, policy makers believed a report card system would improve education outcomes. The assumptions about the impact of Scorecards are, of course, empirical hypotheses—they may or may not be true. Since they assume the great power of colleges to transform outcomes and ignore other important influences, such as previous education, family resources, and connections, it is very likely that they represent, at best, serious oversimplifications. Since a college has little or no power after a student graduates, the only way that a college can reasonably lower its risk of a bad rating is to give better information to students and, most importantly, to screen out students who are predictably at risk. Although most federal student aid is given on the basis of financial need and is designed to help the disadvantaged, administrators who look at probabilities and statistics know that better-prepared students who do not face labor-market discrimination are more likely to graduate, to finish on time, and to get a better job. So these seemingly neutral standards can unintentionally create an incentive for colleges to look more skeptically at admitting students of color from inferior and segregated high schools and from families with fewer resources, since they will probably make the institution's statistics look worse.

The validity of report cards and ratings depends on the quality of data used. A fundamental difficulty is that the federal government collects only very limited relevant data, none of which was designed for this purpose. The available federal data says very little about the cost or effectiveness of higher education institutions; they are mostly data on enrollment, reported cost to students, financial aid, graduation rates, loan default rates, and a few other items. There are a handful of longitudinal survey data sets, a major one in each generation, that follow a cohort of students through higher education, but they draw on samples of large areas and cannot support any reliable conclusions about individual institutions. So, in the absence of a student unit record data system (which is currently outlawed to protect confidentiality), very little can be said with any certainty about the impact of any college. Collection of new data—especially data following individual students by institution over time at the institutional level and assessing where they were on entering the college—would be very expensive, would be resisted by institutions, and would involve years of delays. Trying to reach conclusions with existing data involves using crude data with very few controls for the differences in student background, thus creating very serious risks of incorrect and oversimplified conclusions about institutions.

The demand for new data necessary for evaluating the quality of colleges was explicitly rejected by Undersecretary Studley at our 2014 Capitol Hill presentations, who was managing this project. She insisted that the administration would not expand data demands on colleges. (This has also been a clear theme by GOP policy makers in the Trump administration.) Mandating new data collection involves working with the Office for Management and Budget, college associations, state governments, and congressional committees that were under the control of GOP conservatives, so they were not in a position to do it and were thus limited to the inadequate data already collected.

So, the practical question facing policy makers, if no new data is produced, is whether it is better to distribute and highlight statistics that are severely flawed and use often misleading data or to have none at all. To researchers insisting that conclusions be based on accurate information that is on point, this is an unacceptable choice. But to policy makers, it is a strong temptation, especially when political constraints make it impossible to substantially expand required data from all colleges.

The Scorecard data, according to the Obama administration, provided consumers and policy makers with an accessible, understandable way to measure the relative effectiveness of different colleges and universities. Interestingly, the Spellings Commission, which also called for assessing colleges, called for adjusting information about colleges based on student background, focusing on the difference colleges make rather than simple comparisons of outcomes that may or may not reflect anything the colleges does. The idea in this Bush-era report was that ratings should take into account "students' academic baseline when assessing their results" rather than simply providing comparative information on outcomes.[25] In other words, the ratings should explicitly recognize that colleges are starting with very different groups of students and are not responsible for those initial differences, something that would be difficult to do. The Obama-era Scorecard did not do that. So while, to nonexperts, the results appear to be statistical evaluations of the differential impacts of the colleges, in reality they have profound flaws.

For this reason, the College Scorecard creates serious risks of underestimating the value of colleges serving disadvantaged students and giving excessive credit to schools with more privileged students, as do many similar rating and ranking systems by states and private organizations. The US higher education system includes campuses that serve a vast number of students, ranging from some of the most selective colleges in the world, where most of the new students already have at least a year of college credits before enrolling, to some that have very few students prepared to do any kind of authentic college work before remediation. The latter are almost totally driven by tuition, much of which is financed by student loans—loans taken out by students and families with few assets. The former enroll students almost certain to learn and already connected to powerful opportunity networks and ample family resources, but the latter enroll students who have struggled in weak high schools, who are very much on their own, who often face the necessity to work many hours while in college. Many have no safety net.

To compare colleges serving these different groups on the same outcomes, as if were dealing with the same kind of students, guarantees mistaken conclusions. The result is to downgrade colleges serving Black and Latino students whose families have, on average, less than a tenth the wealth of White and Asian families, and most of whom have had inferior education in segregated schools and attend colleges with far more limited resources. Comparisons of outcomes would mean losses for many colleges with large Latino and African American enrollments unless the ratings are adjusted to control for those differences.

It has been clear in research for at least a half-century that academic outcomes are strongly related to family resources and previous education.[26] Data show that a great many students of color attend colleges with lower graduation rates, come from families with far fewer resources, have much worse preparation for college, tend to spend more time finishing college, receive lower grades, and, even after they succeed in graduating, have more problems in the labor market. Some of these problems are related to college experiences, but others arise from discrimination in public schools before college and in job markets after college. Campuses cannot reasonably be held accountable for problems that are rooted in conditions of unequal income and wealth, poor parental education, a different first language, weaker schools, negative peer groups, dangerous neighborhoods, continuing labor-market discrimination, and many other conditions that tend to perpetuate inequality.

The United States has a public school system increasingly segregated by race and class that systematically provides the weakest schools serving disadvantaged students with the most limited precollegiate curriculum and inexperienced teachers, thereby widening the differences.[27] For example, one-fifth of American students are growing up in homes where English isn't the home language, and they often never acquire equal facility in academic English. This means that their knowledge outside of English is often underestimated in English language tests. Can we ignore basic facts about the powerful impact of precollege inequalities?

Yet, policy makers and families deciding about college choices do want some way to evaluate the colleges. Rating plans face the question of whether there is a single race-blind, class-blind standard of excellence that can be fairly applied without taking those differences into account and still produce accurate comparative ratings. If this standard does not exist, what is most fair? How can we fairly evaluate the success of colleges whose basic mission is to serve low-income students of color? How do report cards and rating systems change the incentives and the behavior of colleges created for that important purpose? Could they punish the very institutions we should be trying to strengthen in order to break the vicious cycle of intergenerational inequality?

Without massive initiatives to equalize opportunities in high schools, supportive colleges are often the only alternative for students from weak backgrounds. Critics say these gaps should have been fixed before college. But since there have always been serious gaps, and all policies that promised to end them have failed, it makes the most sense to recognize the reality of huge gaps among students attending different colleges. The alternative virtually guarantees unfair and counterproductive ratings and sanctions directed against minority-serving institutions. This is exactly what happened in the ratings of public schools used to impose sanctions in the No Child Left Behind Act.

The Employment Metric

Finding out whether students are employed after graduation is a reasonable accountability measure, particularly for students whose college program is aimed at a particular job. Many students and families pursue higher education to increase job and income prospects and to secure a position in the middle class, which is often why families invest heavily in college. From the perspectives of both the students and the government, it is very important that students taking on substantial debt for higher education be able to repay them. And there are clearly very weak programs that exploit and make false promises to students who do not leave with marketable credentials, cannot find employment in their field, and default on their loans, putting a shadow over their lives. Not all of those programs are in the for-profit sector.

The fact is, however, that young recent college graduates have notably different experiences in the labor markets by race, region, and field, which may have nothing to do with the college they attend. A 2014 report notes:

> The unemployment rate of young college graduates who are racial and ethnic minorities tends to be higher than that of young white non-Hispanic college graduates, in good times and bad. The unemployment rate of young black college graduates was 8.1 percent in 2007, rose to 20.0 percent by 2010, and has since improved to 13.1 percent. The unemployment rate of young Hispanic college graduates was 6.7 percent in 2007, rose to 13.8 percent by 2010, and has improved to 7.8 percent.[28]

To the extent that there is discrimination in the labor market, students' employment and earnings penalty should not be blamed on the college, something that would create an obvious incentive for colleges to avoid enrolling minority students and thus deepening economic inequality.

A number of recent studies examining the effects of race on the success of phone or written inquiries to potential employers show continuing bias in job markets.[29] A job applicant with an African American–sounding name or accent is much less likely to get an interview or a job. These biases have real-world impacts. A report from the Center for Economic and Policy Research noted that "white high school dropouts were more likely to have a job than blacks with some college education."[30] The study also found that more than half of recent Black college graduates were working in jobs that did not actually require a degree. The racial dimension of these economic factors would tend to create lower accountability report card scores, particularly for institutions serving African American students, which would be blamed on the colleges rather than external discrimination.

Possibilities of jobs and income vary greatly by major and by local job markets, but they are lumped together in single numbers for employment and income. A college that specializes in liberal arts education is going to look less successful in income after graduation than one with lots of business and medical training programs directly linked to jobs. If an accountability system rewards colleges with mediocre programs in an area with a great job market and very well-prepared and supported students and punishes those producing significant numbers of successful graduates in an area where students face multiple obstacles and the job market is limited but the field is important, the system is clearly counterproductive. If it devalues a college that imparts the classics of Western philosophy or is preparing students for divinity school yet gives great credit to a college training people for the gambling industry, a single number gives the wrong impression of a college's contribution and could lead to academically and socially indefensible choices. These problems do not mean that labor market success is not very important, only that it is hard to fairly measure the impact of colleges without far more data and without considering the varying missions and contributions of various institutions.

The Costs Metric

A recurring theme from the Obama administration, and a basic feature of the Scorecard, was the desire to control college prices. It believed that publishing college costs would be a good service to students and families and also create positive incentives for college efficiency. The actual cost of college as reported in the Scorecard, however, is not the published tuition and living costs but, rather, that number minus the grant aid a student receives. So the colleges strongly prefer to publish the net cost, the calculated average real out-of-pocket dollars a student must pay after receiving an aid package. The Department of Education agreed to use the colleges' own estimates of average net costs reached by subtracting the average aid package from the total cost. This is an economist's view of average costs, but, of course, there is no assurance that any given student will get what the colleges say is the average aid package. Receiving adequate financial aid depends on understanding the system, making the right applications at the right time, packaging them well, and being ruled eligible for that amount of money through a complex process with many variables.

What families need to know is the *actual cost to them*, since they have to make the decisions, and the aid package is usually not known until later. Research shows that it is the published "sticker price" (before subtracting average aid) that has a very powerful impact on decisions made by low-income students and their families. Particularly when parents are not college graduates, the complexity of the aid and student loan systems often creates a decisive barrier. Net price is a more comfortable number for college officials, since it is much lower than sticker price; however, students and families often assume that it is the real total price, an inaccurate conclusion that reflects a misunderstanding of college costs.

More than nine-tenths of college admissions officers surveyed in 2015 said that the cost of the college is important to families. Yet they reported deep concerns about using net price data, which was sometimes outdated, stating that "individual family circumstances are often such that the [net price data] failed to capture the subtleties of a situation, and thus is incapable of providing an accurate calculation" and that it "provides an estimate, not a guarantee of financial aid." These admissions officers noted that some families do not realize that aid in the form of a loan is not a grant and creates a long-term debt. They also said that the federal cost template was not accurate.[31]

A 2014 Brookings Institution study found widespread confusion among students about the cost of their education. Using data from the federal government's National Postsecondary Student Aid Study and a selective university, the report found that fewer than a third of first-year students had a reasonable estimate of the debt they were taking on and that many students receiving loans did not even realize that they had debts as a result.[32] Obviously, these results demonstrate that both parents and students need far better information, but the report expressed little confidence that net price data would solve the problem. In fact, net price data, presented as total cost, could easily obscure the depth of future debt that students would bear after graduating or leaving school.

The Loan Default Rate Metric

The cohort default rate metric is the only loan repayment metric used by the federal government. If a college's default rate exceeds 30 percent for three years, or 40 percent in a single year, it faces a potentially devastating sanction of losing access to Title IV financial aid. Whether or not this rate provides any meaningful information for potential students and their families making college choices—as part of the Scorecard data—is an open question.

The Obama administration used very high default and low employment rates at some colleges as primary tools in attacking and shutting down some large for-profit multicampus institutions via gainful employment regulations to protect students from predatory and fraudulent colleges. Those sanctions were so severe that many colleges simply shut down when their eligibility for federal funds was terminated or greatly postponed. Whether through the cohort default rate policy or gainful employment regulations, the threat of sanctions has introduced new risks for colleges. However, in turn, some colleges are responding in perverse ways. For example, one in five community colleges have already opted out of the federal student loan system largely because of these potential sanctions. For colleges serving very disadvantaged groups of students who face more future financial risks, this move can create a basic conflict with their mission, when they choose safety from federal sanctions over admitting students who badly need the aid.

CONCLUSION

Federal and state accountability policies that ignore differences in the students various colleges serve and the resources they possess can easily reach false conclusions. The Obama initiative (and many parallel state initiatives) to evaluate colleges and create incentives and sanctions to trigger better choices by parents and place more pressure on colleges to ensure debt repayment was a significant response to the frustration of the nation's families and leaders with rising costs, poor graduation rates, and the risk of student defaults. However, the initiative never reached the point of defining clear goals or making a commitment to gather better data and adjust them to reflect the difference various colleges make in dealing with very different local situations and student bodies. One of the things that was curiously lacking on an issue so fraught with implications for racial equity and stratification in the society was any clear focus on the civil rights dimensions of these proposals. Those issues were only seriously raised by researchers, by the leaders of the minority-serving colleges that were likely to suffer under these plans, and by some educators and advocates who took a broad view of the responsibilities of higher education.

The studies in this volume show very clearly that if the country is to move in this direction, and it is likely that there will be more accountability in the future, much deeper thought about implications and much better data are urgently needed. Data and research are needed to explore what effects are attributable to individual colleges as opposed to external factors, including discrimination, that clearly impact college and labor-market success. Ultimately, serious thought about these issues may force higher education policy makers to clarify where they stand on the role and responsibility of higher education in our society, because serious accountability measures will impact the behavior of colleges, and that will impact society as a whole. Moving in this direction without much better information and research designs is likely to make the outcomes even more unequal. These are not decisions to be made by default. The stakes are far too high.

CHAPTER 2

State Accountability Policies
Can Performance Funding Be Equitable?

NICHOLAS HILLMAN AND VALERIE CRESPÍN-TRUJILLO

Over the last two decades, state governments have been steadily reducing their financial support for public universities and colleges and increasingly responding to public demands for college opportunity by insisting, and often threatening with sanctions, that the institutions become more efficient in graduating their students. The goal of graduating more students is widely shared, but it is very important that the accountability standards do not injure institutions serving the most disadvantaged students or reward those that only admit the best-prepared students who are most likely to graduate on time. While standards can produce incentives to increase equity in college opportunity, they can also, in the name of efficiency, creative incentives for colleges to exclude students who are less likely to graduate, thereby improving their institutional score. How accountability is designed and measured matters greatly and could have serious racial and ethnic consequences for academic institutions and communities.

The year 2012 was a turning point for state higher education finance. That year the average public college received more revenue from student tuition dollars than from state appropriations, a trend that has continued.[1] This cost shift has both symbolic and material consequences for the future of public higher education. It represents a significant step toward the steady privatization of public higher education, but it also makes college less affordable and thus increases student loan debt, which has increased inequalities in college access and done nothing to close the gap between the haves and have-nots.[2] This shift has also ushered in a new era of accountability policies, such as *performance funding*, that fundamentally change the way states allocate resources to colleges.

This chapter uses data from the Delta Cost Project database, which is generated from the National Center for Education Statistics' Integrated Postsecondary Education Data System, to examine recent trends in state performance funding and assess the impact performance has on colleges. We implement an ordinary least squares regression through a difference-in-difference framework to examine five outcome variables focused on representational diversity (racial/ethnic and socioeconomic) in public four-year colleges operating under this funding mechanism. By exploring performance funding through this lens, we offer evidence about the policy's implications for equal education opportunity and whether this form of accountability can help states reverse inequalities in their public higher education systems or further exacerbate existing disparities.

Today, thirty-two states operate some version of performance funding that allocates state appropriations according to such outcomes as graduation and retention rates, affordability, or the number of degrees conferred. Proponents argue that existing state funding models do not provide sufficient incentives for colleges to help students succeed.[3] By allocating scarce state appropriations according to performance, rather than by campus needs, colleges will now have an incentive to enroll and graduate more students. Moving to this new model will not only improve education outcomes, but it will increase transparency and more closely align colleges with state education goals.[4]

While this accountability logic has popular appeal among politicians and advocacy organizations, it stands on weak empirical and theoretical footing. The research evidence both inside and outside of higher education suggests pay-for-performance regimes often do not produce their intended results and in some cases may actually foster inequality and lead to other negative outcomes. To date, most of the research on state performance has focused on how it affects student retention and degree completion, the two primary policy goals of most performance funding states.

This chapter extends the literature by focusing on the unintended consequences of performance funding, namely how it affects colleges serving low-income and racial/ethnic minority students. The chapter begins with a summary of trends in state higher education finance and the various ways states incorporate equity into their performance funding models. This is followed by a review of the research literature on how performance funding affects student outcomes and then an analysis of whether performance funding states have reduced access for low-income and racial/ethnic minority students. The chapter concludes with a discussion of why these trends are important and how performance funding regimes are likely to do little to reverse or improve education inequalities.

TRENDS IN STATE HIGHER EDUCATION FINANCE

The financing of public higher education is a shared responsibility between government, students (or their families), and philanthropy, and this relationship is vital for understanding the causes and consequences of recent finance accountability trends.[5] Historically, during economic downturns states often divested from public higher education because some policy makers viewed it as a discretionary budget item and saw colleges as having other ways of raising revenue, thus shifting responsibility away from the state and on to students in the form of higher tuition.[6] When economic times were good, or improved, states tended to invest in public higher education and keep tuition rates relatively lower. But since the Great Recession, state funding has become increasingly unstable.[7] As states recover from the recession, financial support for colleges and universities has slowly increased, but the concern over scarce resources has made a lasting impression on state governments and led them to adopt new models to allocate funding to their public institutions.

Performance Funding

The emergence of performance funding stems directly from these trends, where state funding is either volatile, scarce, or difficult to increase. At least thirty-two states now use performance funding models, and more states are developing them.[8] With students now carrying a greater financial burden, states are putting pressure on colleges to be more accountable with respect to their performance outcomes.

Traditional funding models do not emphasize performance outcomes; rather, they finance institutions via enrollment formulas, fixed-cost funding, inflation-adjusted increases, and changes in operating and maintenance expenses. These input-oriented financial models have come under increased scrutiny in recent years from state governors and legislators as well as from advocacy groups and philanthropic organizations for doing little to encourage colleges to graduate more students.[9] Instead, these critics maintain, performance funding models create the right incentives for colleges to focus on increasing degree completions while also being more accountable to students.

In designing their performance funding models, states use common accountability metrics and apply different performance weights to different sectors of institutions. The most frequently used performance indicators include measures of credit completion, student progression, and credential or degree completion.[10] Funding models differ according to how much money is tied to performance versus how much is allocated by traditional mechanisms (e.g., Illinois commits as little as 1 percent to performance funding while Tennessee commits its entire budget to performance funding).[11] It is important for policy makers to consider how dedicating even a small percentage of a state's budget to performance funding can translate into a substantial amount of funding for any single college (e.g., Illinois appropriated over $3.8 billion to public higher education in 2014, meaning that 1 percent represents close to $200 million available to campuses).[12] While certain supporters of performance funding advocate for a large enough incentive to motivate institutions to make significant changes, even a relatively small level of funding has the potential to make a significant impact on institutions' budgets and could be extremely meaningful for any given campus.[13] Table 2.1 summarizes the key design features of funding models for public four-year colleges and universities, including stated performance goals, the share of the higher education budget dedicated to measure of performance, and whether or not states use indicators of equity included in their models.

States often include in their funding formulas a variety of performance measures, among them research productivity, faculty-to-student ratios, and job placement rates. One such performance goal that is particularly important for education equality is the enrollment of traditionally underserved students.

FINANCIAL INCENTIVES FOR EDUCATION EQUITY

Due to performance funding's focus on student outcomes, institutions may be encouraged to enroll students who are viewed as better prepared to succeed in college or to recruit students who bring in increased tuition revenue (e.g., out-of-state students and foreign students). However, certain performance funding models include rewards for meeting statewide equity goals, which can be used as an incentive for enrolling students of color and low-income students who have traditionally been underserved in higher education. The practice of designing formulas to include these metrics is in line with recommendations by proponents of performance funding who suggest offering colleges and universities incentives for completion gains among hard-to-reach groups, especially low-income and underrepresented populations.[14]

As shown in table 2.1, states include a number of alternative measures of "equity" in their funding models. Some states focus only on socioeconomic diversity, while others embed racial/ethnic diversity in their models by prioritizing enrollment and completion for minority students. Still others reward colleges for enrolling more at-risk, nontraditional students, veterans, transfer students, and first-generation students.[15] The way states define and measure these groups varies widely across models, and there is little consistency across states in terms of the targeted populations, strategies for improving their success, or why one population is prioritized over another. Additionally, no states currently use input-adjusted performance metrics. As a result, performance funding models embed vague notions of equity into models without truly identifying or addressing structural inequalities that shape education outcomes.

Potential Negative Consequences

Offering bonus points for target populations is a first step in addressing inequalities, though it is far from sufficient. If policy makers truly want to leverage accountability for promoting civil rights, they would not embed (and certainly not as an afterthought) these metrics within complicated formulas. Trying to influence diversity through performance formulas will only distort the incentive system by increasing the likelihood that negative consequences will emerge over time. Using financial incentives to motivate institutional changes may actually encourage colleges to be less willing to admit, retain, and support *all* students. In a public sector where horizontal equity between institutions does not exist, it is plausible that performance funding will widen existing inequalities resulting in certain institutions receiving disproportionately larger subsidies from the state. For example, colleges serving the least diverse student body and those with the greatest resources are often highly correlated with each other; therefore, it is likely that the least diverse and most well-resourced institutions could be better off with performance funding regimes. Colleges serving the most diverse mix of students and those that already have the least resources may be disproportionately

Table 2.1 States with performance-based funding (PBF) models for four-year institutions

	Year adopted	Equity measures (y/n)	Equity metrics
Arizona	2012	No	
Arkansas	2011	Yes	Number of Pell recipients enrolled; graduation rate for Pell recipients; graduation rate for minority, first-generation, at-risk, nontraditional, or transfer students
Colorado	2014	No	
Florida	2014	No	Number of Pell recipients enrolled
Illinois	2011	Yes	Degrees for Pell recipients; degrees for low-income students; degrees for minority, first-generation, at-risk, adult, nontraditional, or transfer students
Indiana	2009	Yes	Degrees for minority, first-generation, at-risk, adult, nontraditional, or transfer students
Kansas	2005	No	
Louisiana	2009	No	
Maine	2013	Yes	Degrees for Pell recipients; degrees for minority, first-generation, at-risk, nontraditional, or transfer students
Massachusetts	2013	No	
Michigan	2013	No	
Minnesota	2013	No	

Mississippi	2011	Yes	Degrees for Pell recipients; degrees for minority, first-generation, at-risk, nontraditional, or transfer students
Missouri	2013	No	
Montana	2014	No	
Nevada	2011	*No	
New Mexico	2007	Yes	Degrees for low-income students
North Carolina	2012	No	
Ohio	2009	Yes	Number of minority students enrolled; number of Pell recipients enrolled
Oklahoma	2002	No	
Oregon	2007	No	
Pennsylvania (PASSHE)	2000	**Yes	Number of minority students enrolled; number of Pell recipients enrolled
Tennessee	1979, 2010	Yes	Degrees for low-income students; degrees for minority, first-generation, at-risk, adult, nontraditional, or transfer students
Utah	2013	No	
Virginia	2007	No	

Notes: *Nevada's model includes equity measures for two-year institutions. **Pennsylvania's model has an accountability measure for faculty diversity.

Sources: US Department of Education, *Using Federal Data to Measure and Improve the Performance of U.S. Institutions of Higher Education,* https://collegescorecard.ed.gov/assets/UsingFederalDataToMeasureAndImprovePerformance.pdf; HCM Strategists, "Driving Better Outcomes," http://hcmstrategists.com/drivingoutcomes/; National Council of State Legislatures, "Performance-Based Funding for Higher Education," http://www.ncsl.org/research/education/performance-funding.aspx.

harmed by performance regimes, even if equity is symbolically present in the funding model.

Figures 2.1 and 2.2 show that Tennessee colleges serving the largest number of Black and low-income students have fared the poorest under the state's model. Conversely, institutions serving the fewest Black or low-income students have benefited the most under the state's performance model.

Performance funding proponents point to Tennessee as a state that rewards colleges for serving at-risk students. However, if this were really the case, the relationship shown in figures 2.1 and 2.2 would be just the opposite, with colleges serving the most diverse student body benefiting the most from the funding model. Instead of creating an incentive to enroll and graduate more students, Tennessee's model may induce colleges to become more risk averse by increasing selectivity or reducing access, which has the effect of pushing out underrepresented students. This has been the case in other states, where performance incentives have encouraged colleges to turn away students requiring enhanced supports.[16]

LITERATURE REVIEW

To assess the impacts of performance funding, researchers have increasingly turned to quantitative research designs that compare outcomes of states using performance funding with states that do not. This literature examines both national trends and state-specific case studies. In the national studies, researchers often use states as the unit of analysis and assess whether those that adopted performance funding produce more graduates than states that did not. Proponents of performance funding believe states that use traditional budget models will perform at poorer levels and that college completions will rise at a faster rate after adoption of performance funding. To test this assumption, researchers have examined statewide trends in both associate and baccalaureate degree production, finding that performance funding states do not outperform other states.[17] Interestingly, these studies found mixed results across the states, with some producing significantly fewer graduates after adopting the policy while others experienced small growth after several years of implementation. Other national studies use colleges as the unit of analysis and reach similar conclusions, even after differentiating between "old" and "new" performance funding models.[18] These studies reveal broad national trends that could mask positive results occurring within specific states.

Figure 2.1   Tennessee colleges' budget changes (x-axis) relative to the share of black students (y-axis)

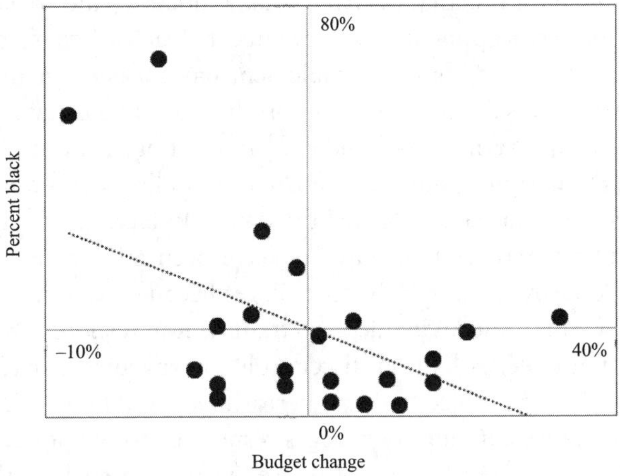

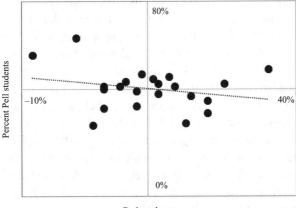

Sources: Tennessee Higher Education Commission, Tennessee's Outcomes-Based Funding Formula, https:// www.tn.gov/thec/article/2015-20-funding-formula; US Department of Education, "Integrated Postsecondary Education Data System," https://nces.ed.gov/ipeds/.

Figure 2.2   Tennessee colleges' budget changes (x-axis) relative to the share of Pell grant students (y-axis)

Sources: Tennessee Higher Education Commission, Tennessee's Outcomes-Based Funding Formula; US Department of Education, "Integrated Postsecondary Education Data System."

Accordingly, researchers have conducted several state-specific case studies that look much more closely at patterns within each state. State case studies have focused on Indiana, Pennsylvania, Tennessee, and Washington. Performance funding proponents have pointed to each of these states as examples of how best to design and implement pay-for-performance models, implying these states are most likely to produce positive results and contradict findings from the national studies.[19] Interestingly, the findings are consistent with the national studies: performance funding states do not outperform those states that never adopted the policy. In fact, these states have produced negative outcomes that may not have been anticipated or desirable under the policy regime. In Indiana, colleges became more selective and reduced access without improving degree attainment in response to the policy.[20] Pennsylvania colleges had no discernable improvements over similar colleges that were never subject to state performance funding regimes.[21] In Washington, the state's community colleges responded to the policy by producing more short-term certificates as opposed to more associate degrees.[22] And in Tennessee, retention and graduation rates did not improve in the years after the state increased its financial incentive.[23]

This literature finds that states with traditional budget models perform just as well and sometimes better than performance funding states. While this may surprise performance funding proponents, it is consistent with findings in the fields of economics, public policy, education, and public health. Across this literature, there is little evidence that financial incentives induce positive outcomes when applied to complex public organizations like schools, hospitals/clinics, and job-training programs.[24] In fact, there are many cases where incentive systems reduced organizational performance. After adopting versions of performance funding, doctors avoided sicker patients, cancelled riskier operations, and had higher rates of misdiagnosis.[25] Elementary school teachers became more likely to teach to the test.[26] Local job placement centers increased short-term but not long-term labor outcomes.[27] This is not to say that performance funding regimes cannot improve performance; in fact, there are some examples where performance actually improved. However, these improvements tend to be short-lived and occur among organizations that are already performing at high levels or that have the capacity to respond to financial incentives.[28]

Literature suggests pay-for-performance regimes work best when the task is predictable and routine, there is only one principal and one agent, goals are unambiguous and measurable, and the process of achieving the goal is clear and controllable.[29] The classic example of a pay-for-performance success is a windshield installation company that experienced large performance gains in response to the financial incentives it provided to its employees, who had a routine task they could perfect over time, a job that was under their direct control, and a clear performance goal.[30] But the process of producing a new college graduate does not conform to these criteria: no single university employee has direct control over "producing" a new graduate, the process is unpredictable and occurs over the course of several years, and there are several additional learning goals along the way to a diploma that matter for colleges and universities. Indeed, the literature shows that introducing high-stakes funding incentives into complex organizations like a college or university can encourage, not deter, negative behaviors, including gaming, cream skimming, and crowding out of intrinsic motivation.[31] To avoid losing funds, colleges may become more selective in order to improve performance outcomes, or they may be less inclined to enroll low-income students or students of color if the college has a poor track record of helping these students succeed.[32] Consequently, using performance funding to improve education outcomes is likely to fall short and could even exacerbate education inequalities. Yet states continue to adopt and expand performance funding policies with the belief financial incentives create conditions to improve education outcomes. The evidence inside and outside of higher education gives good reasons to anticipate that negative and unintended consequences could work against stated performance goals.

DATA AND ANALYSIS

Because some campuses report financial data from other campuses within their larger system (e.g., Penn State University–Main Campus includes all twenty-four Penn State University campuses) in the Delta Cost Project database, nested observations like these are omitted from the analytical sample.[33] The analytical sample includes non-nested public four-year colleges and universities (n=411) for the years 2005 through 2013 (t=9), resulting in a panel data set containing 3,699 total observations. All finance data are adjusted to 2013 dollars.

Outcome Variables

Five outcomes variables are of interest to this study. The first three focus on representational diversity: the percentage of students who are Black, Hispanic, or White. The fourth examines the socioeconomic status of each campus measured by the percentage of students receiving federal grant aid (e.g., Pell grant recipients). The fifth is a measure of college selectivity based on the percentage of applicants who were accepted during the fall of each academic year. These five outcomes offer a comprehensive overview of college access, namely representational diversity (racial/ethnic and socioeconomic) and selectivity.

Analytical Techniques

To assess the impact performance has on colleges, we implement an ordinary least squares regression through a difference-in-difference framework. In adopting performance funding policies, states introduce a plausible source of exogenous variation that may induce colleges and universities to change their accessibility or selectivity, and this framework allows us to observe the performance differences between states subjected to the policy and those not subjected to the policy, both before and after adoption years.

To improve our internal validity, we add a robust set of control variables, including the number of years performance funding has been continually in place, in-state tuition and fees, the share of operational revenues funded by net tuition revenue, expenditures per full-time equivalent student, and the percentage of students enrolled part time. We also include institutional fixed effects to account for unobserved characteristics of each college that are relatively stable over time and year fixed effects that account for unobserved factors similarly affecting all states in each year. Also, linear state-specific trends allow outcomes to take different trajectories across the states during the period before the study.[34] To account for autocorrelation and panel heteroscedasticity that would downwardly bias standard errors, we cluster standard errors at the institution.[35]

KEY FINDINGS

In states providing financial incentives to diversify the student body, colleges should have increased access for Black and Hispanic students. Also, colleges should have expanded the share of students receiving Pell grants, and these outcomes should not come at the expense of becoming more selective.

But our results do not bear this out. We found that even when states set aside bonuses or premiums for serving low-income, adult, or otherwise at-risk students, enrollment did not increase for Black students and declined for Hispanic students (table 2.2).

Table 2.2   Regression estimates of performance funding's impact on various outcomes

	White (I)	Black (II)	Hispanic (III)	Pell grant recipients (IV)	Selectivity (V)
All PBF states	0.498	0.108	−0.348***	0.235	−1.144
"Equity" PBF states	0.570	0.527	−0.422*	1.977*	3.843
Observations	3,699	3,699	3,699	3,699	3,699
Institutions	411	411	411	411	411
R^2	0.31	0.052	0.555	0.48	0.03

Notes: These models control for time-variant controls, including policy duration, enrollment profile, and institutional finances. The models also include linear trend and fixed effects. Robust standard errors are in parentheses, *<0.10, **0.05, ***0.01.

These results make us less sanguine about the ability of bonuses and premiums to advance civil rights. We found that that which embed equity measures in their funding models are experiencing nearly identical results as those states without such measures. There is one exception, where the share of Pell students increased by approximately two percentage points in those states that embed bonuses. While this is a helpful measure, it is important to note that percentages can be driven by either the numerator or denominator; a college could increase this figure not by enrolling more Pell students but by reducing the number of non-Pell students. The results also show that performance funding states enroll fewer Hispanic students after the policy, and this difference is larger in those states claiming to promote equity (rising from 0.348 to 0.422 percentage points).

IMPLICATIONS FOR EQUITY

Performance-based funding is rapidly spreading across the country during a time of rapid demographic change. These two trends have the potential to work against one another if performance funding models are not designed to improve access, persistence, and completion for underrepresented students. Our analysis reveals broad trends occurring among performance funding states and concludes that current models do little to improve campus racial/ethnic diversity. In some cases, the funding model may result in less access for Hispanic students, even when states embed equity measures within their regimes, and current efforts do not appear to promote access for Black students.

This chapter cannot explain *why* these patterns occur, but it can show *that* they occur. To the extent public colleges are reducing representational diversity in response to performance funding, states may want to find ways to prevent these responses. But how?

Embedding equity metrics within performance funding models may be too weak an instrument for inducing desired change. Instead, states could prioritize equity into their funding system by identifying colleges that serve the most diverse student bodies and then ensuring these schools have the capacity to serve these students well. In other words, focus on equity and capacity building *prior to* having colleges compete for scarce financial resources tied to performance metrics.

Another strategy could be to state in the performance model more precisely and explicitly what the state's diversity goal is. One of the most consistent failures of pay-for-performance regimes is having ambiguous goals that work against stated diversity goals. Table 2.1 identifies states that include equity measures, but some of these measures may be too vague to help colleges know how to respond. For example, the funding model rewards colleges for improving enrollment and completion for at-risk students. Colleges may interpret this deficit language in any number of ways. Perhaps they see Pell students as the most at risk, which is why their share of enrollments grew in equity model states. Also, in an era of legal uncertainty around race and affirmative action, colleges may emphasize socioeconomic diversity over racial/ethnic diversity, which could result in enrolling more Pell students and not changing the share of Black students and even reducing the share of Hispanic students on campus.

State policies that do not prioritize, clarify, or create clear pathways for improving inequities will do little to reverse them. Performance funding appears to suffer from this fate, as our results show that embedding equity into the model does not actually improve racial/ethnic diversity on college campuses. Instead of embedding equity as one of many design features, states may need to take bolder strides to reverse inequities. The growth in Pell grant enrollments is a promising finding, and this is likely because some states use it as an equity goal. Yet, states shy away from specifying racial/ethnic diversity goals, and doing so likely weakens their ability to improve diversity on campuses. It is also possible that campuses have little incentive to diversify their student bodies if they believe doing so will make it more difficult to improve on other performance outcomes. After all, serving students who universities have traditionally served well is a surefire way to increase retention and graduation rates. Public colleges are already highly segregated, and, as figures 2.1 and 2.2 illustrate, it is possible that those already serving the least diverse student body are most likely to win the performance funding race. States may want to reverse these priorities by focusing first on equity and ensuring that all colleges have a fair baseline from which to serve students, and then, after reaching this baseline, they can compete for performance funds.

As states continue to divest from public higher education, and as incoming students are increasingly more diverse, performance funding models will need to adapt. Using the funding formula to prioritize equity is a step in the right direction, but we should not expect this approach to make much of an impact. For a larger impact, states likely need to focus on ways to build the capacity of colleges where underserved students enroll, which will likely yield far greater outcomes.

CHAPTER 3

Accountability and the Key Role of Minority-Serving Institutions

MARYBETH GASMAN, THAI-HUY NGUYEN,
ANDRÉS CASTRO SAMAYOA, AND DANIEL CORRAL

Minority-serving institutions (MSIs) account for about one in every ten postsecondary institutions in the nation.[1] There are more than 500 MSIs, of which 38 are Tribal Colleges and Universities (TCUs), 105 are Historically Black Colleges and Universities (HBCUs), and 279 are Hispanic-Serving Institutions (HSIs).[2] Over 50 percent of students across these institutions receive Federal Pell Grants, and tuition is, on average, about half as much as that of comparable majority institutions. This makes MSIs more affordable for many students of color from underresourced backgrounds than most Predominantly White Institutions (PWIs). MSIs are vital to achieving civil rights for all in the United States, and, in many ways, they hold other institutions accountable by setting an example and showing what can be done for and with students of color even with limited resources.

Our data and research approach are grounded in a commitment to fostering greater civil rights for students, especially students of color, and we think that an exploration of the contributions of MSIs can provide new approaches and perspectives that are beneficial across higher education. Often, policy is made without adequately considering the unique features and challenges of the MSIs. Because MSIs serve many students who have had inadequate preparation in unequal schools, as well as fewer family resources, accountability policies that ignore these distinctive features in assessing performance can seriously damage institutions that are helping students beat the odds.

Some MSIs were intentionally created to serve students of color, while others have entered this category due to demographic change in their recruitment areas. Although we cluster MSIs together in this chapter, it should be noted that HBCUs were created due to historic discrimination in higher education in the United States (in almost all states that segregated education by law) and that TCUs were created during an era of self-determination for communities that were isolated and also in response to the historic miseducation of Native Americans. At their core, both have a mission to empower and uplift their students, and, by and large, their curricula and co-curricular programs are aimed at providing culturally relevant learning experiences.[3] HSIs, however, are determined by demographic concentrations and federal definitions of institutions that serve large numbers of Hispanic students. Many were created as general-purpose institutions without a special founding mission to serve Hispanics. There is also great diversity within HSIs, with some boasting student populations that are 98 percent Latino and others hovering near the federal requirement of 25 percent.[4] In fact, 48 percent (n=135) of all HSIs have 50 percent or greater Hispanic enrollment, well exceeding the 25 percent or greater requirement.

Like MSIs, two-year institutions represent greater access to postsecondary education for racial minorities and low-income students. And of the 1,132 two-year colleges in the United States, 16 percent are designated MSIs.[5] These two-year MSIs make up 43 percent of all MSIs.[6] Two-year MSIs also enroll and award degrees to a disproportionate number of students of color. MSIs are playing a significant role at every stage of postsecondary education.

MSIs can play crucial roles for the nation's economy, especially with respect to elevating the workforce prospects of disadvantaged populations and reducing the underrepresentation of minorities and disadvantaged people in graduate and professional schools and the careers that require postbaccalaureate education and training.[7] However, more than other US colleges and universities, MSIs must contend with the recent focus on outcomes-based funding at the state level due to their vulnerable financial situations and history of underfunding.[8] Many do not have the reserves or resources to withstand cuts in federal aid. Unless policy takes MSIs' unique situation into account, the federal government's focus on rating colleges and universities and publishing a performance-based scorecard has the potential to disproportionately hurt these institutions.[9]

MSIs serve many important and unique roles in fostering college access for students. To illustrate those very special roles and challenges, in this chapter we briefly describe MSIs' special importance for bringing men of color into and through college, preparing students of color for jobs in the STEM fields, and preparing teachers of color for our diverse schools.

UPLIFTING MEN OF COLOR

MSIs are especially central for minority males, the group experiencing the greatest gaps in college access. Improving the education attainment of men of color requires the inclusion of MSIs. Based on fall 2013 data, over 25 percent of men of color with full-time college enrollment are found at MSIs. Interestingly, this number increases to nearly 34 percent of men of color with part-time college enrollment, which includes a large share of community college students. MSIs also confer a large portion of their degrees to men of color. Of the 193,702 bachelor of arts degrees conferred to men of color in 2012–13, 19 percent (n=37,187) were awarded by MSIs.

The role that MSIs play in educating men of color must be considered when both the state and federal governments are evaluating the contributions of these institutions. According to the US Department of Education, data indicate that boys and men of color are disproportionately at risk.[10] There are large disparities in preparation for boys and young men of color at all levels. For example, "Black and Latino males are conspicuously overrepresented on most indicators associated with risk and academic failure."[11] These factors contribute to the undermining of families and local communities.[12] As a result of these circumstances, men of color are also more likely to be the victims of violent crimes.[13] MSIs can and do play a large role in countering these statistics and changing the lives of men of color, and the role they play is disproportionately larger than their majority institution counterparts.

Disaggregating enrollment data allows us to compare MSIs' disproportionate enrollment of certain racial and ethnic groups. For instance, table 3.1 shows that MSIs enroll 38 percent of all full-time Hispanic men in the nation, and almost a quarter (24 percent) of all Black men. Although within-state demographics are responsible for some of these percentages, MSIs continue to do the lion's share of the work with men of color even in states that are not as diverse as California and Texas. MSIs reach out to

Table 3.1   Men's college enrollment, fall 2013

		All institutions	Non-MSIs	MSIs	% in MSIs
American Indian/ Alaskan Native:	full time	33,995	27,276	6,719	20%
	part time	22,749	17,964	4,785	21%
Asian American:	full time	345,528	304,076	41,452	12%
	part time	171,681	132,703	38,978	23%
Black/African American:	full time	525,887	398,540	127,347	24%
	part time	340,006	265,171	74,835	22%
Hispanic:	full time	688,697	427,757	260,940	38%
	part time	540,173	279,042	261,131	48%
Native Hawaiian/ Pacific Islander:	full time	14,770	13,060	1,710	12%
	part time	11,102	9,184	1,918	17%
White:	full time	2,986,579	2,875,732	110,847	4%
	part time	1,586,270	1,439,399	146,871	9%
Two or more races:	full time	143,922	132,468	11,454	8%
	part time	66,074	55,412	10,662	16%
Total	full time	4,739,378	4,178,909	560,469	12%
	part time	2,738,055	2,198,875	539,180	20%

these students through their admissions offices and tap urban areas including Detroit, South Chicago, Los Angeles, the San Francisco Bay Area, and Washington DC, offering opportunity to men of color.[14] Part-time enrollments for men of color at MSIs are even higher. These institutions enroll 48 percent of all part-time Hispanic men and 22 percent of all Black men. Additionally, 50 percent of MSI students are Pell grant recipients, as compared to 36 percent at colleges and universities overall. MSIs' commitment to low-income students should be considered as both states and the federal governments employ outcomes-based funding formulas.

Much like their enrollment data, the percentages of degrees conferred to men of color by MSIs demonstrate their commendable labor in educating this population. As mentioned earlier, of the 193,702 bachelor's degrees conferred to men of color in 2011–12, 19.2 percent (n=37,187) were awarded by MSIs. Contextually, it is important to note that MSIs conferred only 7.8

percent of all bachelor's degrees in 2013. Despite accounting for a modest number of degrees conferred, MSIs award a substantial number of degrees to underserved populations compared to majority institutions.

SUCCESS IN STEM

Another sign of the importance of MSIs is their role in meeting the national priority for STEM education. Many majority institutions are particularly weak in graduating students of color in the fields of science, technology, engineering, and math, although many students initially enroll with expressed interests in those careers. MSIs are committed to advancing the achievement of racial minority students in STEM, as shown by their disproportionate contributions to STEM success. Despite making up less than 3 percent of all US postsecondary institutions, HBCUs award nearly 17 percent of all baccalaureate degrees in the sciences to Black students, and almost 37 percent of Hispanics earning a baccalaureate degree in the sciences and engineering graduated from a HSI.

The continued security and health of our nation depend on new, emerging, and innovative discoveries in STEM. These discoveries, in turn, determine new possibilities in technology, manufacturing, and health care. However, colleges and universities are not producing sufficient STEM graduates to satisfy the demand of our economy.[15] Reports from prominent national and academic institutions insist that improving the education attainment of individuals from the most disadvantaged backgrounds—racial minority students—is a solution in mitigating the challenges of meeting this workforce demand.[16] Most certainly, MSIs, with their successful record of enrolling and graduating minority students, should receive consideration and attention for their efforts in improving the representation of students of color in STEM.

The underrepresentation of racial minorities in the STEM fields and workforce can be linked to challenges, or leaks, early on in and throughout the P–20 pipeline. Minorities are less exposed to the developmental opportunities that provide, strengthen, and shape their skills, dispositions, and experiences toward subsequent achievement in STEM—opportunities offered by well-resourced homes and schools rich with financial, social, and cultural capital.[17] For instance, enrollment in accelerated math and science courses in secondary school is found to heavily influence students' achievement in college-level STEM courses as well as maintain their persistence through degree completion.[18] Unfortunately, recent data from the US

Department of Education demonstrate that underrepresented minorities are less likely to be enrolled in college preparatory and AP/honors-level courses, further discouraging the likelihood of their success in STEM fields.[19] Despite an increase of minority enrollment in postsecondary education in the past thirty years, these gains have not manifested into improved and equitable representations in the STEM workforce.

According to recent data from the National Science Foundation, across all occupations in science and engineering, Hispanics or Latinos are underrepresented by 9 percent, Blacks by 7 percent, and American Indians or Alaska Natives, Native Hawaiians, and Pacific Islanders by less than 1 percent.[20] Asians are overrepresented by almost 8 percent, but disaggregated data by ethnicity may illuminate the struggles experienced by some communities within the Asian diaspora (see table 3.2).[21] The disparities in occupational achievement in STEM along racial lines become even graver at the baccalaureate level.

The unequal representation of minorities in the STEM workforce can be attributed to the type of institution students attend and the quality of their collegial experience. When it comes to performance in postsecondary STEM classes and earning a baccalaureate degree in STEM, minorities do not perform as well as their White counterparts.[22] And although a lack of preparation at the secondary level can certainly hinder minority performance in STEM, several studies have suggested that the dynamics of the college environment may be the primary culprit.[23] Minority students—especially Hispanics and Blacks—underperform in STEM because of a competitive climate commonly found at majority institutions that undermines their confidence and sense of belonging.[24] In contrast, minority students achieve more in STEM under more collaborative conditions that include the increased presence of minority peers and faculty mentors.[25] Accordingly, these conditions have been observed at several MSIs.[26]

MSIs, by virtue of their historical and legal missions, are charged with the responsibility of supporting the education achievement of racial minority students. This is evident in their disproportionate contributions to STEM education. Table 3.3 presents the number of baccalaureate degrees across STEM fields awarded to Blacks, Hispanics, American Indians, and Alaska Natives and the percentage contributions by each respective MSI.[27] As noted, HBCUs award nearly 17 percent of all baccalaureate degrees in the sciences to Black students. In the physical sciences and engineering, respectively, 33 and 19 percent of all Blacks in these fields graduated from a

Table 3.2 Distribution of employed scientists and engineers by occupation, ethnicity, and race, 2010

	All degrees	Hispanic or Latino	American Indian or Alaska Native	Asian	Black or African American	Native Hawaiian and Pacific Islander	White	More than one race
Total	21,903,000	7%	0.3%	12%	6%	0.3%	74%	1%
S&E occupations	5,398,000	5%	0.2%	18%	5%	0.2%	70%	1%
Science occupations	3,829,000	5%	0.2%	19%	5%	0.2%	69%	2%
Biological/Life scientist	597,000	5%	*	19%	3%	*	71%	2%
Computer and information scientist	2,204,000	5%	*	23%	6%	*	65%	2%
Mathematical scientist	190,000	2%	*	19%	4%	*	71%	*
Physical scientist	321,000	5%	*	14%	4%	*	76%	2%
Psychologist	210,000	6%	*	3%	5%		83%	2%
Social scientist	309,000	5%	*	8%	5%	*	80%	2%
Engineering occupation	1,569,000	5%	*	17%	4%	*	72%	1%
S&E-related occupations	6,957,000	6%	0.3%	11%	6%	0.4%	75%	1%
Non-S&E occupations	9,549,000	8%	0.3%	8%	7%	0.3%	75%	1%

Notes: * suppressed for data confidentiality and reliability reasons; S&E = science and engineering. Detail may not add to total because of rounding and suppression. Scientists and engineers are individuals with a bachelor's or higher degree living in the US with an S&E-related degree or occupation. Persons of Hispanic or Latino origin may be of any race.

Sources: National Science Foundation, National Center for Science and Engineering Statistics, Scientists and Engineers Statistical Data System, 2010.

HBCU. Almost 37 percent of Hispanics with a baccalaureate degree in the sciences and engineering graduated from a HSI, even though HSIs make up less than 6 percent of US colleges and universities.[28] HSIs also graduated 37 percent of all Hispanic students in the physical sciences and mathematics. TCUs award 2 percent of American Indian and Alaska Native baccalaureate degree holders in the sciences and engineering, almost 10 percent in the agricultural sciences, and nearly 3 percent in computer science, despite representing less than 0.5 percent of all postsecondary US institutions. Put simply, based on absolute production of STEM graduates, MSIs, although small in numbers, are an influential force in shaping the opportunities and achievement of minorities in STEM.

MSIs possess the resources that cultivate STEM achievement and talent in their student populations. At the institutional level, the importance of racial concordance between students, faculty, and staff is important to minority students' sense of belonging and to their engagement in campus and academic life.[29] It can be comforting to some students that they share, to some degree, a common life narrative with those teaching and guiding them. The large presence of minority faculty also means that professors may be more sensitive to the achievements and struggles their students are experiencing.[30] And similar to the influence of faculty and staff, the large presence of peers from similar backgrounds can minimize feelings of isolation and tokenism, both of which are commonly experienced by minority students at majority institutions.[31] In short, MSIs seem to be developing a "culture of science" in which students are able to develop a science identity by seizing opportunities for research and engagement without neglecting their racial identity.[32] Given the nation's need for additional STEM workers and the dearth of diversity in the STEM workforce, MSIs should be credited in outcomes-based funding measures for the substantial role they play in the STEM arena.

PROMOTING TEACHER EDUCATION

Institutions of higher education play a vital role in K–12 education by inspiring, instructing, and certifying the future teachers and administrators of the nation's schools. As the demographic composition of K–12 public school students continues to reflect the nation's racially diverse population, examining and strengthening the role that MSIs play in producing the future minority teachers of our nation becomes a national imperative. Given the

Table 3.3 Bachelor's degrees awarded by all institutions to Black, Hispanics, and American Indian and Alaska Native US citizens and permanent residents by field and the contributions to target groups by HBCUs, HSIs, and TCUs (percent), 2012

	Race/Ethnicity			Institution type		
	Black	Hispanic	American Indian and Alaska Native	HBCU (%)	HSI (%)	TCU (%)
All fields	172,868	176,699	10,743	16.7	37.0	2.4
S&E	49,683	58,146	3,411	17.8	33.8	2.2
Science	46,465	50,973	3,102	17.7	33.3	2.4
Agricultural sciences	704	1,407	213	32.1	26.8	10.8
Biological sciences	7,073	8,891	576	28.1	37.9	0.0
Computer Sciences	4,847	4,210	231	14.3	29.0	2.6
Earth, atmospheric, and ocean sciences	119	323	47	7.6	28.5	0.0
Mathematical sciences	964	1,277	58	29.5	37.3	0.0
Physical sciences	1,305	1,428	87	33.4	37.5	0.0
Psychology	12,709	13,353	711	17.8	39.2	0.1
Social sciences	18,744	20,084	1,179	12.5	28.2	3.8
Engineering	3,218	7,173	309	19.0	37.5	0.0
Non-S&E	123,185	118,553	7,332	16.3	38.5	2.4

Note: Data are based on degree-granting institutions eligible to participate in Title IV federal financial aid programs and do not match previously published data that were based on accredited higher education institutions.

Sources: National Science Foundation, National Center for Science and Engineering Statistics, special tabulations of US Department of Education; National Center for Education Statistics, Integrated Postsecondary Education Data System, Completions Surveys, 2002–12.

high need for teachers of color, there is some urgency in shining a light on the role of MSIs.[33]

Between July 1, 2012, and June 30, 2013, there were 102,481 bachelor's degrees in education (BEd) conferred in the United States. Within various racial and ethnic groups, MSIs can play a significant role. For example, though MSIs conferred 7,235 (7.1 percent) of these degrees overall, they were responsible for 40.5 percent of all BEds conferred to Hispanics and almost 30 percent to Blacks and African Americans.

Of the 159 MSIs (38 percent of all MSIs) that conferred BEds in 2012–13, 74 were HBCUs, 75 HSIs, and 10 TCUs. Almost three-quarters (72.55 percent) of all HBCUs confer BEds, whereas this percentage drops to a quarter for the other MSIs. These degrees are greatly needed; in 2011 only 1.5 percent of teachers in public schools were Black men. MSIs, and HBCUs more specifically, can change this statistic by continuing to play a significant role in educating Black men.

It is important to note that HSIs confer the bulk of BEds among MSIs. In 2011–12, HSIs conferred 6,230 of the 11,588 degrees awarded (51 percent), whereas HBCUs conferred 2,263 (18 percent); TCUs 64 BEds, accounting for less than 1 percent of all education degrees.

We know that there is a consistent shortage of teachers of color in the K–12 sector.[34] MSIs' role in preparing students to serve as future teachers is an opportunity for policy makers to reconsider the metrics in emerging outcome-based rubrics. We would suggest that, much like the advancement of underrepresented minorities in STEM, the diversification of the teaching profession should be considered a marker of institutional success.

ACCOUNTABILITY POLICY MUST NOT DAMAGE MSIS

Minority-serving institutions are beginning to gain attention for their work with low-income students and students of color, but progress is slow. Because these institutions are diverse in nature and have fewer resources than their majority counterparts, they struggle to bring attention to their strengths and challenges. To ensure that high-stakes accountability regimes are fair and effective, it is necessary for MSIs to garner attention for the unique role they play in US higher education.

Disregard for MSIs at the state or federal level will impede the overall effort of improving the education attainment of the nation. MSIs possess significant influence in advancing the nation's agenda on minority male achievement, teacher education, and STEM education—much of this through their presence in the two-year system. But instead of considering the most elite colleges and universities in our nation (many of which have low racial minority presence) as leaders and exemplars of achievement, it may be helpful to look to MSIs as potential partners in addressing our nation's most pressing issues in education. In order to do this, those at the federal policy level must also examine MSIs within their historical and social context. MSIs represent a collective of underresourced institutions and serve students from impoverished communities. When assessing their potential to aid in elevating our nation's education and workforce, we encourage leaders and policy makers to be critical in their comparisons of institutions and to recognize that such comparisons may unfairly distribute federal resources. With this in mind, we make the following recommendations to policy makers, researchers, and practitioners:

Policy makers

- MSIs are the best place for investment in increasing college attainment by underserved communities. MSIs are serving students who need much more support because of the inequality of their preparation, and that must be taken into account in assessments of their performance.
- When evaluating the performance of MSIs, consider and reward the significant contributions they make in high-need areas such as teacher education, education attainment among men of color, and STEM.
- Don't leave MSIs out of policy conversations. Leaving them out continues to privilege majority institutions that typically have more resources and fewer low-income students of color. Moreover, leaving MSIs out leads to the full-scale stratification and racial polarization of our already deeply stratified society.
- Look to MSIs for solutions to shortages of teachers of color; they have a track record of preparing students of color in education-related fields, especially those that work in minority communities.
- The United States needs a million additional STEM workers. Look to MSIs for success in the STEM arena and for ways to diversify the current STEM workforce.
- Consider the richness of MSI student bodies—including part-time, transfer, and swirling (going in and out of college) students—when evaluating their graduation rates and overall performance. These institutions have the student bodies of the future, not the past.

Researchers

- Look at successful programs in teacher education, teacher placement, and teacher longevity and use these programs to inform practices throughout the nation.
- Study the way STEM learning is structured, as well as MSI student support mechanisms.
- Examine MSIs' contributions to the health of their local communities through their teaching partnerships and their commitment to serve as resources for their communities. Appropriate metrics must be developed to fairly assess their contributions.

Practitioners

- Urge MSIs to build coalitions rather than leaving them to operate in silos. Coalitions are stronger and provide these institutions with a common voice through which they can have a collective impact.
- Cultivate pride in the MSI designation. The data demonstrate that MSIs continue to make strides in educating those who have the most to gain, even in the face of inhospitable financial times. To be called an MSI should be a marker of pride; these institutions model effective institutional resilience and capacity to transform the lives of a racially diverse student body.

CHAPTER 4

Using Institutional Accountability Measures That Serve Diverse Populations

SYLVIA HURTADO, ADRIANA RUIZ ALVARADO,
AND KEVIN EAGAN

Current reports, rankings, and accountability systems claim to make institutional performance transparent to students and parents but often fail to take institutional differences into account, rewarding elite institutions and reproducing resource inequalities among institutions serving high percentages of underrepresented students. Consistent reports show that six-year graduation rates are highest at the most selective institutions and are lowest at those institutions that are least selective.[1] However, selective institutions use more stringent admissions criteria and tend to have substantially more resources than the least selective four-year institutions. The most selective institutions also serve substantially fewer low-income, first-generation, and underrepresented minority (URM) groups. If institutions only admit the best-trained, most highly qualified students, and those campuses have highly resourced support services for students, the results are likely to be very positive when compared to students from less-well-funded colleges with many low-income students from schools and families with fewer resources.

In this chapter we use two methods of metrics, input-adjusted performance indices and efficiency scores, to identify some key campuses as engines of social mobility that are doing better than expected for the population of students they serve and among institutions with comparable resources. Identifying institutions that serve as engines of social mobility and using more appropriate metrics is an equitable and fair way to judge institutional efforts and advance the populations that remain underrepresented and underserved and that attend institutions which are largely accessible and affordable.

After President Obama's introduction of the American Graduation Initiative in 2013, college completion programs and initiatives quickly rose to the forefront of the national education agenda. The Lumina Foundation, the Bill & Melinda Gates Foundation, and the College Board, among others, which had previously articulated various goals, strategies, and performance benchmarks, found alignment with the initiative's promise. Many of these efforts commonly recognize that the country's overall college completion rates will be affected by disparate outcomes for first-generation, low-income, and URM students, specifically African American, Latina/o, and American Indian/Alaska Native students.[2] Given their growing share of the college-age population and their significantly lower completion rates, advancing college completion for these vulnerable populations is critical to meeting national education goals to sustain the US economy.[3]

Largely due to these concerns and a desire to increase transparency for "consumers" purchasing a college education, initial plans for tying federal student financial aid to institutional performance based on a national ratings system have created some controversy.[4] In particular, critics have expressed concern regarding the treatment of broad-access institutions under such a system. These institutions offer access and affordability but may score poorly on raw metrics in a national or state ratings system because they serve a large number of first-generation, low-income, and URM students whose success requires different forms of support. Therefore, it is imperative that any future discussion of college ratings or other high-stakes accountability systems are based on research that takes into account these challenges.

In this chapter we provide insights into ongoing research that predicts college completion rates in order to identify nonprofit, four-year institutions that are closing the gaps for first-generation, low-income, and underrepresented minority students. There is a lack of current research on campuses that serve large numbers of students from these three groups. We also demonstrate the utility of different metrics that can better account for completion in areas vital to advancing the nations' STEM-related goals.[5]

Both metric projects are part of ongoing studies conducted at the Higher Education Research Institute (HERI) at the University of California, Los

Angeles. Focusing research on these institutions will provide a more nuanced approach to serving an increasingly diverse student body. In turn, an awareness of specific groups will allow institutions to construct more targeted interventions to advance the success of the students who are currently least represented in US higher education.[6]

INSTITUTIONAL DIFFERENCES AND GRADUATION METRICS

While the Obama-era college rating proposed in 2013 has been sharply cut back by congressional opposition, the US Department of Education and White House have released new data via the College Scorecard in 2015 and 2017. Unfortunately, the data includes some measures of college access, affordability, and postcollege employment outcomes that have yet to be adjusted appropriately. *TIME* magazine illustrated the problem with these measures when it gathered data from the Integrated Postsecondary Educational Data System (IPEDS) on 2,500 higher education institutions and created individual rankings based on each of the College Scorecard's proposed measures (access, affordability, and outcome), as well as a holistic ranking based on the three weighted equally.[7] We compared exemplars of our results to those graduation rates in the *TIME* calculator to show the relationship between student input-adjusted measures and unadjusted measures. The US Department of Education has proposed releasing College Scorecard data for underrepresented groups but had not done so as of this writing.

Even with multiple criteria, as proposed by *TIME*, using raw (unadjusted) graduation rates as reported on IPEDS for judging institutional performance is problematic. Raw graduation rates implicitly reflect the types of students who attend the institution (described as student input), institutional resources, and institutional practices/policies (e.g., admissions policies, differing graduation requirements, and contextually based decisions). Alexander Astin argued that these "outcomes only" assessment metrics fail to take into account the characteristics of students who attend specific colleges.[8] He advocated for student input-adjusted metrics to more accurately assess the impact of college. Subsequent reports on degree attainment published by HERI created graduation equations and graduation rate calculators to help institutions evaluate graduation rates in a way that considers the composition of the student body.[9] Building on this previous work, we constructed student input-adjusted performance indices for campuses based on the six-year completion of a cohort of students who began college in 2004.

We used these indices to identify four-year campuses that are doing better than expected for first-generation, low-income, and URM students. At HERI, additional work is under way that uses the indices to identify practices that may be unique to high-performing institutions for these groups.[10]

One of the questions raised about input-adjusted measures is whether we should expect lower graduation rates for different campuses. This is a simplistic question, as almost every institution doing better than expected is also working on policies and programs to further enhance their rates to aspirational levels and/or to match the success of peer institutions or system sister campuses. For institutions doing better with students who have a higher probability of dropping out, it is important to understand the policies and practices that are in place in these contexts. The major point of our work is to give more credit to institutions doing better than expected for the most vulnerable students and serving as major engines of social mobility in the country. Just as a one-size-fits-all solution does not often work for different students, the same is true for institutions with lower resources and institutional capacities that serve local communities, as most minority-serving institutions are regionally focused.

The student input-adjusted graduation metrics, however, depend on following a single first-time, full-time cohort of students. Much like the raw completion rates reported in IPEDS, there is no accounting for the education and graduation of students who transfer in and/or institutional resources. One approach that does account for this is stochastic frontier analysis, which produces efficiency scores that account primarily for institutional resources in rates of degree productivity over time (as is typical in econometric models).[11]

These econometric models compare institutions with similar resources—full-time equivalent (FTE) faculty, undergraduate enrollments, and financial expenditures—to determine how close a campus's *actual* degree output is coming to its *expected* output, or its efficiency score. These models provide more accurate comparisons of institutions' productivity over time by crediting campuses that educate and graduate higher numbers of part-time and transfer students, who are likely to attain degrees at a different rate. Likewise, the calculation of these efficiency scores takes into account institutional resources, as campuses' rates of degree productivity are compared against those of institutions with similar levels of human capital (student enrollments), financial capital (expenditures per full-time-equivalent student), and labor (FTE faculty).

Input-adjustment results in regression to the mean, and a regression-type approach, will be more sensitive to outliers (very well-resourced or very poorly resourced institutions, or campuses that have an incredibly high level of degrees produced). The frontier approach uses a statistical model that results in estimates which consider differences across institutions in terms of their resources and overall degree production. With regression-based input-adjusted measures, you simply know whether a campus is doing better than expected. With the frontier approach, you can identify the top producer for a given set of characteristics, as many campuses can be on the "frontier." Campuses on the frontier could be considered as the top or as best producers within a group of similarly resourced institutions. If analyses suggest that an institution could produce the same number of degrees with fewer faculty or students, that institution may be considered inefficient.

This is reflected in the ongoing work in STEM at HERI, and we have conducted models focused on STEM degree productivity in the aggregate as well as for minority populations, the results of which are summarized here. Both performance indices and efficiency scores provide alternative ways of assessing institutional performance when it comes to populations that will gain the most from college access and completion.

DATA AND RESEARCH DESIGN

The data we use here come from three sources: the 2004 Cooperative Institutional Research Program (CIRP) Freshman Survey, the National Student Clearinghouse (NSC), and IPEDS.[12] The CIRP survey includes information about student background characteristics, precollege experiences, and anticipated college experiences and behaviors. The NSC data include student records on enrollment and degree completion from 2004 through 2010. The IPEDS data provide institutional characteristics. The merging of these three data sources allows for the examination of six-year degree attainment for a first-time full-time undergraduate matched sample of 25,304 URM, 36,586 first-generation, and 34,264 low-income students at 356 four-year nonprofit higher education institutions. The institutions included are those where nearly full cohorts of entering freshmen took the survey, making these students a representative sample of the URM, first-generation, and low-income students at each campus. The URM sample is 33.3 percent first generation, 60.8 percent female, and 35.8 percent low income (those with annual parental income below $30,000). The first-generation sample is 22.8

percent URM, 60.5 percent female, and 32.8 percent low income. The low-income sample is 31.3 percent URM, 64.6 percent female, and 41.5 percent first generation.

The STEM degree production efficiency score results reported here are found in several papers, and efficiency scores are based on existing federal data on all four-year institutions.[13] Instead of a single cohort, the efficiency analyses draw from several years (2004, 2006, 2008, 2010, and 2012) of student cohort data from IPEDS. The models include measures of total STEM degrees produced each year (overall totals and totals for specific racial/ethnic groups). They also account for campuses' undergraduate enrollment, graduate enrollment, FTE faculty, and expenditures per student.[14]

A comparison of raw graduation rates, even when separated by underrepresented subgroups, masks differences in the characteristics of the students who enroll at different types of institutions, favoring those institutions that are most selective. To identify four-year institutions that may be less selective but are still successfully graduating first-generation, low-income, and URM students at higher-than-expected rates, we employed the frontier approach.

HERI researchers also developed a calculator for institutions to use to determine their expected degree completion based on their students' input characteristics.[15] The calculator is based on a prediction equation developed using logistic regression. The model for the degree completion prediction equation accounts for many important factors cited in the literature, including student background, academic preparation, parents' background, student finances, activities in high school, college choice factors, students' self-rating, goals and values, anticipated college experiences, and institutional-level measures. Using the prediction equation and the same data set, we produced an expected graduation rate for URM, first-generation, and low-income students at each college and university in the sample. The expected rates were then subtracted from the actual six-year graduation rates to produce a performance index for each population, allowing for the identification of institutions where particular communities are most successful.

This analysis generated a list of 108 four-year institutions with positive performance indices for all three groups, which we used to create a dichotomous dependent variable indicating whether an institution was part of these 108 or whether it actually performed worse than expected for one or more groups. Nine institutional-level measures representing control, selectivity, and various financial indicators were logistically regressed on this outcome to identify characteristics of institutions that are serving as engines of social mobility by exceeding expectations.

TOP PERFORMERS FOR TARGETED GROUPS

Among 356 institutions, 108 institutions were coded as positive performers (doing better than expected); 43 of these had a performance index of 10 or higher for *two or more* of the groups, and only 16 institutions had a performance index of 10 or higher for *all three* groups. That is, these institutions were doing much better than expected given the characteristics of the low-income, first-generation, and racial/ethnic minority groups they enrolled. Descriptive analyses demonstrate that these institutions fell into three categories: (1) expected and actual graduation rates below 50 percent; (2) expected graduation rates below 50 percent but actual graduation rates above 50 percent; and (3) expected and actual graduation rates above 50 percent. Figure 4.1 shows the expected and actual URM completion rates for sample institutions in each of these three categories. In each example, the rates are at least 10 percent higher than expected. These differences are promising indicators that institutions are actively improving the rate of degree attainment for target groups even if their overall performance appears low when looking at the raw completion rate.

Additional descriptive analyses compare the URM performance index for the sixteen institutions with performance indices of 10 or higher for all three groups to their holistic ranking in *TIME* (based on the three rating criteria being considered by the Department of Education). Figure 4.2 shows that there is no relationship between how well an institution is performing for URM and this holistic rating. However, there does appear to be a relationship between the percent of the undergraduate student body that is URM and the graduation rank assigned by *TIME* (see figure 4.3). Specifically, the higher the percent of URM at an institution, the lower its graduation rank. This simple example shows how detrimental a simplistic rating system can be for institutions serving underrepresented populations. For instance, the two minority-serving institutions in the best-performing group of sixteen have the highest percentage of URM students and the lowest graduation ranks, even though they are clearly highly accessible in terms of admission and their students are graduating at considerably better-than-expected rates.

Figure 4.1 Examples of performance index category groups for institutions with PIs of 10 or higher for URM, low-income, and first-generation students

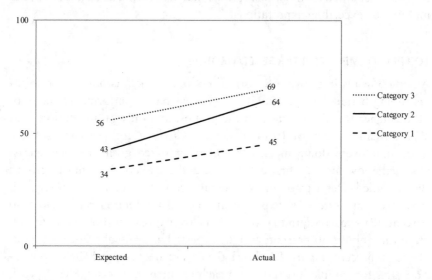

Figure 4.2 *TIME* holistic rank vs. URM performance index

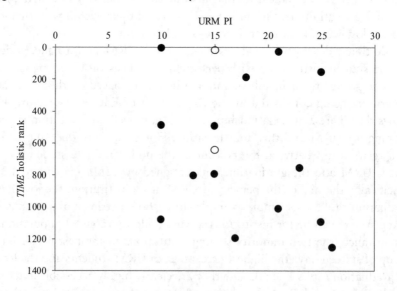

Note: White dots indicate minority-serving institutions.

Figure 4.3   *TIME* graduation rank vs. percentage of URM students

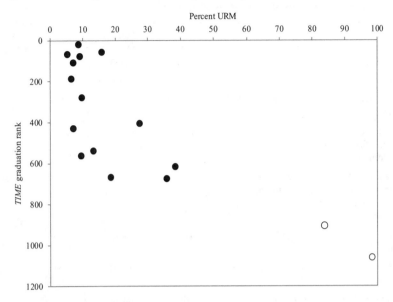

Note: White dots indicate minority-serving institutions

Table 4.1 shows the results of the logistic regression predicting positive performance indices for URM, first-generation, and low-income students. The findings show that more selective institutions have a lower likelihood of having a positive performance index for all three groups (b=-.004, p<.05). This means that despite having greater resources, they are more likely to perform worse than expected for one or more of these vulnerable populations. Yet, all ten of the top-ranked institutions in *TIME*'s graduation rankings are in Barron's "most competitive" category. The less selective institutions that perform better than expected for underserved and underrepresented populations are not the ones topping the charts and receiving the credit. Two additional variables were significant in the regression model: the average amount in federal grants received by first-time full-time undergraduates and expenditures on instruction per full-time-equivalent student. Institutions where students tended to receive more federal grant aid had a greater likelihood of outperforming for first-generation, low-income, and URM students (b=1.224, p<.05), as did institutions that devoted more funds to instruction (b=.891, p<.05).

Table 4.1   Logistic regression model predicting positive PI for low-income, first-generation, and URM students (n=356 institutions)

	B	Exp(B)	S.E.	Sig.
Control: private	–.159	0.853	.691	
Selectivity	–.004	.996	.002	*
Percent full-time undergraduate URM students	0.151	1.163	0.921	
Average amount of federal grants received by full-time, first-time undergraduates (natural log)	1.224	3.401	0.596	*
Revenue from affiliated entitites, private gifts, grants, and contracts, investment returns, and endowment earnings, per FTE (natural log)	–.156	.855	.184	
Expenditures for instruction, per FTE (natural log)	0.891	2.439	.408	*
Expenditures for student services, per FTE (natural log)	.438	1.550	.345	
Total number of full-time instructional faculty, per FTE	–8.485	0.000	7.013	
Share of operating revenues from net tuition (includes basic revenue streams, investment returns, sales and services of educational activities, and auxiliary enterprises)	–0.712	.491	0.928	
Constant	–15.815	0.000	5.017	

TOP PERFORMERS IN STEM

Table 4.2 lists means and standard deviations for each efficiency component by race/ethnicity and gender. Institutions are most efficient in their production of STEM degrees for White students, with an average efficiency score of 59 percent. Institutions also award STEM degrees to Asian students relatively efficiently, with an average efficiency score of 55 percent. Campuses' STEM degree production efficiency for Black (40 percent), Latino (42 percent), and American Indian (46 percent) students fell more than ten percentage points below the levels for White and Asian students.

Table 4.3 presents the results of models that regressed efficiency scores against a set of institutional structural characteristics. Across all models,

Table 4.2   STEM efficiency descriptive statistics

Efficiency scores	Mean	SD
Men	0.48	0.20
Women	0.63	0.08
American Indian	0.46	0.19
Asian	0.55	0.11
Black	0.40	0.18
Latino	0.42	0.18
White	0.59	0.13

except for STEM degree production for Asian students, we see statistically significant patterns where public institutions operate more efficiently than their private counterparts. We present the findings as unstandardized regression coefficients. Thus, the efficiency with which public institutions produce STEM degrees for White students exceeds that of private campuses by roughly 5 percent. This result is counter to what we have found in STEM completion models, which are cohort based and do not account for students transferring into institutions.[16] In the cohort-based STEM completion models, private institutions typically outperformed their public counterparts, but our analysis shows the opposite when resources are taken into account.

With minority-serving status, we find that Historically Black Colleges and Universities (HBCUs) produce STEM degrees for Black students significantly more efficiently than Predominantly White Institutions (PWIs), and the gap is wide. The efficiency with which HBCUs produce bachelor's degrees in STEM for Black undergraduates is 25 percent higher than the average for PWIs. Similarly, Hispanic-Serving Institutions (HSIs) produce STEM bachelor's degrees for Latino students significantly more efficiently than do PWIs, and the gap between these two institutional types is roughly 22 percent. STEM degree production efficiency is also higher at HSIs relative to PWIs for Asian students by 6 percent.

CONCLUSIONS AND IMPLICATIONS

An institution's degree attainment rate is tied to the characteristics of students it enrolls as well as the availability and use of resources. Findings using two different analytic approaches demonstrate that improving degree

Table 4.3   Institutional characteristics predicting STEM efficiency

	Men			Women			American Indian		
	Coef.	S.E.	Sig.	Coef.	S.E.	Sig.	Coef.	S.E.	Sig.
Hispanic-Serving Institution (versus predominantly White)	−0.04	0.02		−0.01	0.01		−0.05	0.03	
Control: Public (versus private)	0.09	0.01	***	0.02	0.00	***	0.03	0.01	***
Institution has a hospital	0.01	0.02		0.00	0.01		0.01	0.02	
Historically Black College or University (versus predominantly White)	−0.02	0.02		0.02	0.01	**	−0.04	0.02	*
Research University (versus liberal arts)	0.01	0.01		0.00	0.01		0.04	0.01	*
Masters Comprehensive University (versus liberal arts)	−0.04	0.01	***	0.00	0.00		0.00	0.01	
Professional School (versus liberal arts)	0.16	0.08		0.02	0.04		0.11	0.09	
Urbanicity: City (versus suburban)	0.00	0.01		0.00	0.00		0.02	0.01	
Urbanicity: Rural (versus suburban)	0.06	0.01	***	−0.02	0.00	***	0.03	0.01	***
Selectivity (average SAT composite score)	0.05	0.00	***	0.01	0.00	***	0.00	0.01	
Proportion of Part-Time Faculty Employed	−0.01	0.02		−0.02	0.01		−0.01	0.02	
Average Faculty Salary	0.02	0.00	***	0.01	0.00	***	−0.03	0.01	***
Proportion of Undergraduates Enolled in STEM Majors	0.09	0.01	***	0.04	0.00	***	0.04	0.01	***
Explained variance	27%			17%			6%		

Note: Reference categories are in parentheses.

	Asian			Black			Latino			White	
Coef.	S.E.	Sig.	Coef.	S.E.	Sig.	Coef.	S.E.	Sig.	Coef.	S.E.	Sig.
0.06	0.01	***	−0.12	0.02	***	0.22	0.02	***	−0.06	0.02	***
−0.03	0.01	***	0.02	0.01		0.00	0.01		0.05	0.01	***
−0.02	0.01	**	−0.01	0.02		−0.01	0.02		0.02	0.01	
−0.12	0.01	***	0.25	0.02	***	−0.16	0.02	***	−0.04	0.02	**
0.02	0.01	**	0.08	0.01	***	0.03	0.01	**	0.06	0.01	***
0.00	0.01		0.04	0.01	***	0.00	0.01		0.05	0.01	***
−0.07	0.05		−0.11	0.08		−0.14	0.08		0.08	0.06	
0.01	0.01		−0.01	0.01		0.00	0.01		0.00	0.01	
−0.02	0.01	**	−0.03	0.01	***	−0.02	0.01		0.02	0.01	**
0.01	0.00	***	−0.01	0.00	**	0.00	0.01		0.02	0.00	***
0.02	0.01		0.02	0.02		−0.03	0.02		−0.02	0.02	
0.02	0.00	***	0.00	0.00		0.04	0.01	***	0.00	0.00	
0.02	0.00	***	0.06	0.00	***	0.01	0.01	***	0.02	0.00	***
25%			25%			19%			12%		

attainment will involve more than an examination of graduation rates as reported in IPEDS. Student input-adjusted metrics are useful because they take into account accessibility, and results show that many less-selective institutions are doing better than expected for vulnerable students. More importantly, those doing better than expected have students with higher federal grant aid and also spend more on instruction per student. This is as it should be; campuses should provide not only enough aid to help students focus their efforts and energy on college but also sufficient instructional support with adequate faculty resources to develop students' talents.

Using a metric that does not account for student characteristics fails to acknowledge the challenges institutions encounter with students who have high needs for financial, academic, and social support. Many broad-access institutions could not significantly improve student graduation rates without altering their admissions policies (changing the characteristics of their student body), which would limit postsecondary opportunities for low-income, first-generation, and URM students. Moreover, broad-access and minority-serving institutions would likely experience significant enrollment declines as a result of restricting enrollment, and the for-profit sector could increase its share of students with high needs. Therefore, crediting institutions for their raw completion rate above all else could induce discriminatory changes to admissions policies.

To create student input-adjusted models nationally or on the state level, we need to ask institutions to provide more data on their student populations currently missing from IPEDS, such as average test scores, parental education levels, and income, as well as many other factors that influence retention (e.g., intention to transfer). One of the advantages of this analysis is that many students took the CIRP Freshman Survey, which allowed us to statistically control for a wide range of personal factors and expectations to produce performance indices and graduation rate calculators for institutions. Currently, not all institutions administer this survey, even though HERI has administered it to a representative sample for fifty years.

In contrast, we produced the STEM efficiency scores using currently available data on IPEDS. Unfortunately, the data are missing many indicators of student input characteristics, which further illustrates the need for richer data to inform policy making. Taking into account institutional resources using efficiency scores, we find that HBCUs and HSIs are more efficient at degree production for Blacks and Hispanics, respectively, in

STEM fields. The metric included transfer and part-time students, faculty labor, and institutional financial resources in its calculations. This metric is fair to institutions because it compares productivity and use of resources among similarly situated institutions. Higher efficiency in the production of STEM degrees among minority-serving institutions has a direct impact on diversification of the scientific workforce. Institutions with high efficiency scores in STEM also hold the promise of high-paying jobs for individuals with STEM degrees. Continued support should be provided to these institutions to help their efforts in developing URM student talent and meeting national goals in science training.

It is important that high-stakes accountability systems help support institutions that do the lion's share of educating students who stand to gain the most from a college education. By educating these students, they decrease racial and income gaps and create economic vitality in diverse communities across the United States. Broad-access institutions play an important role in this revitalization effort by remaining accessible and affordable. Identifying the institutions that are engines of social mobility may be an ideal way to nurture investment in low-income, first-generation, and URM education, thereby rewarding institutions with strategic policies and practices that ensure student success. Without acknowledging student and institutional resources, some campuses may feel pressured to take shortcuts to raise attainment rates. There is no question that all institutions must raise their graduation rates, but not at the expense of limiting access, which will surely cause further decline in overall US college degree attainment rates. We should continue to strive for policies and metrics of institutional accountability that are fair to vulnerable students and to the institutions doing their best to educate them.

The next steps in research are to understand the context, practices, and institutional policies at highly productive institutions. The institutions identified in this paper are performing far better than expected with regards to retention and graduation rates. However, if we use traditional standards to measure success, such as national rankings based on overall graduation rates, we may ignore similar institutions. These institutions are key engines of social mobility in part because they do more than others to develop the talents of students who would otherwise not attend college. Subsequent studies need to be conducted to specifically examine intentional institutional practices that improve graduation rates for vulnerable students. Ongoing work at HERI employs the use of case studies of institutions doing better than expected on first-generation, low-income, and URM student retention and, with comparable resources, doing much better in graduating URM students in STEM to identify the institutional practices and organizational strategies in these engines of social mobility.

CHAPTER 5

Accountability Across the Education Pipeline
The Contribution of Unequal High Schools on College Completion

STELLA M. FLORES, TOBY J. PARK, AND DOMINIQUE J. BAKER

One of the key issues defining the new public agenda in American higher education is the disconnect between rising college enrollment rates and stagnant college completion rates.[1] Adding to this educational dissonance is that some student populations are increasingly more likely than others to not complete college despite decades of interventions along the education pipeline.[2] In a society that has always been stratified by race and ethnicity, where there has been a major gap in high school achievement scores since the National Assessment of Educational Progress was created more than a third of a century ago, we continue to see gaps in college completion for certain racial and ethnic groups.[3] The College Board reports that the graduation rates of first-time full-time students seeking bachelor's degrees at four-year colleges in 2010 were 68.9 percent for Asian students, 62 percent for White students, 50.6 percent for Hispanic students, and 40.3 percent for African American students.[4] At the same time, two critical trends have surrounded the college completion story in the United States: the changing demography of US college students and the increasing costs of failing to complete college. In 2010 Hispanics comprised the largest minority in the nation and on both two-year and four-year college campuses.[5] In the same year Texas was home to the nation's largest Black and Hispanic four-year undergraduate populations, providing an excellent location to examine these issues.[6]

The costs of not completing college are unfortunately increasingly pronounced, causing potentially damaging effects across generations.[7] Such costs are particularly visible in terms of wages. For example, college graduates can still expect to earn almost twice as much as their non-college-educated counterparts, earning on average $1.6 million more in their lifetime.[8] High school graduates can expect to earn 68 percent more than non–high school graduates, while those with associate degrees or some college are likely to earn 26 percent more than high school graduates. In a time when the majority of all births are now non-White and the majority of our K–12 public school students are also non-White, the costs of not educating underserved populations, particularly underrepresented minorities (URM) who we identify as Black, Hispanic, and Native American students, with postsecondary credentials are a matter of state and national economic welfare.[9] Given this emerging crisis in college completion for Black and Hispanic students, and the unprecedented demographic growth of the URM student population, we focus this analysis on the college completion gaps between URM students and White students.

However, demographic changes are not the only force shaping US K–20 education. At the same time that the demography of our nation is changing the composition of schools, colleges, and universities, we also see increased movements for accountability, often defined differently by the various sectors of education. This new stage of higher education accountability involves states and the federal government exploring ways to hold institutions accountable for the success (e.g., graduation rate, earnings) of their students. Increasingly, states and the federal government have discussed, and in some instances implemented, accountability policies that serve to reward certain institutions for helping students succeed and to penalize other institutions for hindering student success (often measured as retention rates and certificate or degree completion).[10] Some policies carry real penalties, such as loss of a portion of state appropriations, while others are more strategic goals for institutions.

While useful for evaluating institutions and their ability to prepare students for life after college, there are equity concerns with these types of accountability policies. For example, Nicholas Hillman and colleagues studied the state of Washington's performance-based accountability system, which rewarded institutions for persistence and certificate or degree completion.[11] They found that the introduction of this policy caused students to earn more certificates with no statistically significant effects on either persistence or associate degree completion. This would be an unintended consequence of the policy: institutions increasing the number of students with short-term degrees with fewer labor market returns. In an era when the value of the bachelor's degree is higher than ever, organizational movements that fail to address bachelor's completion rates may add increasing costs to a state economy even if unintentional.

These types of unintended consequences need to be investigated as states and the federal government plan for higher education accountability policies. For these reasons, this chapter expands the field and policy makers' understanding of the ways factors outside of institutions' control can influence collegiate success. As the United States enters a new critical stage of higher education accountability that is not necessarily independent from K–12 accountability movements, we hope this analysis will contribute to a better understanding of the racial and ethnic gap in college completion by offering a perspective that focuses on factors that include, but are not limited to, the postsecondary experience.

We examine the extent to which these potentially influential factors explain the college completion gap between URM students and White students and, more specifically, the White-Hispanic and White-Black gaps between students. Using a combination of state administrative data and national data sets, we seek to disentangle the differing influence institutional-level (high school and postsecondary) and individual-level characteristics have on college completion. We also consider the role played by the higher education institutions URM students are most likely to attend: Hispanic-Serving Institutions (HSIs), degree-granting institutions with a full-time-equivalent undergraduate enrollment that is at least 25 percent Hispanic; and Historically Black College and Universities (HBCUs), institutions founded before 1964 with the mission to serve Black students.[12] HSIs now serve approximately 60 percent of all Hispanic college students in the nation, and the percentage is likely to be higher in states with larger Hispanic populations, such as California, Texas, and Florida.[13] HBCUs serve nearly 11 percent of all Black college students in the United States.[14]

The minority-serving institutions (MSIs) in Texas we examined include 64 HSIs, with an undergraduate enrollment of 188,785 as of 2004, and nine

HBCUs, with an undergraduate enrollment of 19,781 as of 2004 (there are no Tribal Colleges and Universities in the state).[15] Finally, while both HSIs and HBCUs have a significant presence in Texas higher education, they differ from each other in a few key dimensions. First, the majority of HBCUs are four-year institutions, whereas a significant percentage of HSIs are two-year institutions.[16] MSIs in general are more likely to have open admissions policies and to serve a larger percentage of students who are Federal Pell Grant recipients than their non-MSI peer institutions.

We use Texas as a case study due to the availability of state administrative data that captures the K–20 school experience for all students in the state. In addition, Texas ranks second in the nation (after California) in terms of its Latino population and the number of institutions classified as HSIs. Texas is third in the nation in terms of its Black population (after New York and Florida) and the number of HBCUs (after North Carolina and Alabama). Nationwide, HSIs educate more Latino students as a proportion of the college-going population than any other postsecondary institution. HBCUs are the only institutions that have educated Black students continually for the past 150 years, and they are the institutions most likely to produce Black bachelor's degree recipients in science and engineering who are likely to pursue a doctorate.[17] In light of these facts, we ask the following research questions:

- What is the extent of the college completion gap by race and ethnicity among Texas's most numerous student groups?
- What factors contribute most to this completion gap, and how much of this gap is explained by individual versus institutional factors from high school to postsecondary attendance?

Our cohort of focus includes students in Texas who graduated from high school in 2002 and entered a four-year institution that fall. We use variance decomposition analysis to determine what percentage of the college completion gap is explained by the various factors of the student groups assessed, including a covariate for attending a MSI (a HSI or HBCU). Variance decomposition analyses have been applied in previous research to examine gender wage gaps and gaps in college completion by institutional sectors, such as two-year versus four-year colleges.[18] We apply this tool to gain a fuller understanding of the college completion gap between URMs and White students, with a particular focus on the influence of the MSI.

CONCEPTUAL FRAMEWORK

In assessing what factors contribute to the URM-White bachelor's degree college completion gap, we incorporate a conceptual framework that includes a high-school-to-college-completion pipeline perspective. It is based on available state administrative data, which include students' demographic characteristics, high school context, curriculum participation, and the quality of the postsecondary institution in which they enroll.[19] We have adapted the framework used by Stella Flores and Toby Park, which groups key factors in the high-school-to-college-completion process, including students' individual characteristics and academic preparation; high school and community context, including working while in school; and postsecondary characteristics.[20] To supplement this conceptual framework, we incorporate two bodies of literature relating to the theoretical traditions used to explain college access and completion that are grounded in human capital theory and empirical analyses that note influential factors in college enrollment and completion by race and socioeconomic status (student characteristics, high school context, and postsecondary characteristics).

A Human Capital Perspective: Is It the Individual, the Institution, or Both?

The theoretical model incorporated for this analysis is one of student decision making (as it relates to an individual's decision to enroll and complete college) as well as the institution's response to students' decisions, which are based in human capital theory.[21] This larger explanatory framework has been used to examine outcomes for URM students across various postsecondary institutions.[22] Gary Becker, for example, finds that a student's decision to attend college includes her assessment that investing in education carries not only a cost but also her expectation that the cost might increase her human capital in ways that translate into skills or benefits she can exchange for income in the labor market.[23] Weighing the costs and the benefits, both monetary and nonmonetary, thus becomes part of the student's decision whether or not to invest in a college education.

John Bound and colleagues complement this framework by accounting for recent surges in college enrollment, and institutional responses to this enrollment, based on institutional capacity to serve new enrollees.[24] The authors hypothesize that, as the returns to a college degree increase, more students may be enticed to enroll in college. However, as students who previously might not have attended college do enter the college market, they find themselves competing with students who would have entered college regardless of the return they get on a college degree. This leads to two likely outcomes. First, while the increasing returns on a college degree might be expected to lead to an increase in college completion, the preparation levels of new students entering the college system are likely quite varied and in some cases inadequate, which can lead to a decrease in the college completion rate. Second, from the supply-side perspective (that of institutions), an increase in the number of students who are entering colleges and universities with varied abilities may change the amount of resources available to students at these institutions, especially if state budgets do not keep up with the changing demand for higher education services. For example, institutions might need to put more resources toward remediation and other courses designed to help new students become more college ready.

Because public colleges and universities comprise the majority of higher education institutions in the United States and in Texas, institutions' capacity to respond to student demand is an essential part of the college completion question. We build on this work by also observing the roles of both the individual and the institution in the context of declining student resources over time.

Precollege Factors in College Completion

Our framework considers research that incorporates additional modifications to the human capital model, as has other research on college access and completion.[25] Clifford Adelman, for example, finds that taking a math class one level beyond algebra II, such as trigonometry, doubles a student's odds of completing a bachelor's degree.[26] Others have found that engaging in rigorous coursework, such as Advanced Placement (AP) and International Baccalaureate (IB) courses, and participating in dual high school/college enrollment programs may increase the odds of gaining access to college and, in some cases, completing college, although studies of the causal effects of taking AP/IB courses have yielded mixed results.[27]

Racial concentration (or racial segregation) in schools has an important and negative role in student achievement in high school grades. Eric Hanushek and colleagues find that racial segregation in Texas explains a "small but meaningful portion of the racial achievement gap" as measured by test score differences between Black and White students.[28] Specifically, the higher the percentage of Black peers in a school, the lower the achievement rates for Black students; no significant effect was found for White students. While the authors do not examine the role of Hispanic racial concentration on Hispanic student achievement, previous work on racial segregation suggests patterns similar to, if not more exacerbated than, those for Black students.[29] Attending school in an urban context also seems to lead to consistently negative effects on college enrollment, particularly for underrepresented minority students who attend urban high schools.[30] The relationship between working and high school completion—whether either factor complements or excludes the other—has also recently received increased attention.[31] James Bachmeier and Frank Bean find, for example, that Mexican-origin youths' school attendance is conditioned on their participation in the labor force, a behavior generally not found among other racial and ethnic groups.[32]

College-Level Factors Promoting Completion

Finally, several studies have examined college choice and completion in the United States by institution type.[33] A good deal of research has focused on the effect college selectivity has on college completion rates.[34] Other institutional characteristics, such as funding per student and the percentage of tenured faculty, also have been explored, particularly at the two-year and four-year college levels. Bound and colleagues find that factors affecting completion rates differ by postsecondary sector. For example, institutional characteristics are more likely to explain declining college completion rates at four-year institutions, whereas students' level of academic preparation is more likely to explain declines in college completion rates at two-year institutions. They focus, however, on income level rather than race and ethnicity, which leaves unanswered the question of how race and ethnicity factor into college completion outcomes over time.[35]

DATA AND RESEARCH DESIGN

Although precollege factors play a distinct role in college completion, it can be difficult to isolate these factors when explaining the URM-White college completion gap. But this is precisely what is needed in high-stakes accountability policies, because failing to do so will reward colleges serving the most privileged students while unfairly penalizing those serving the most disadvantaged. To account for these factors, researchers can implement the Blinder-Oaxaca variance decomposition method and its extensions, providing a more precise explanation of the factors behind education inequality.[36] Indeed, when researchers use these decomposition techniques, they consistently find that precollege factors (e.g., student characteristics and academic preparation) explain more of the variation in education outcomes than do college-level factors.[37]

In this analysis, we use decomposition techniques to more fully understand the extent to which precollege and college-level factors explain the variation (expressed in percentages) in college completion between URM students and White students. We conduct the analyses and present our findings for the White-Black and White-Hispanic gaps separately. To conduct our analysis, we use student-level, restricted-use longitudinal state administrative data from the Texas Education Agency and the Texas Higher Education Coordinating Board. We focus on a cohort of seniors who graduated from high school in Texas in 2002 and immediately enrolled in a four-year (public or private, depending on year of entry) institution within the state. We use college completion within six years as our outcome variable.

At the individual level, we include students' gender, economic status (as designated by qualifying for free and reduced-price lunch), limited English proficiency (LEP) status, successful completion of a trigonometry course, completion of either an AP or IB course, performance on the state math exam, dual enrollment (doing college coursework while enrolled in high school), and an indicator for working during the spring high school semester immediately preceding graduation. Our high school context variables include the pupil-teacher ratio, school enrollment, the percentage of URM students in the school (Black and Hispanic), per-pupil expenditures, and whether the high school is located in an urban setting, as defined by the US Department of Education. We also include controls for community context, including the unemployment rate in the county where a student attended high school and whether a student's high school is located within twenty-five miles of a postsecondary institution. Finally, we control for such postsecondary characteristics as the percentage of tenured faculty members, the faculty-student ratio, full-time equivalent enrollment, per-pupil instructional expenditures, and whether the institution is designated a HSI or HBCU.

Table 5.1   Mean values for Hispanic, Black, and White students

	Hispanic	Black	White
Six-year college completion	0.51	0.44	0.66
Individual and academic characteristics			
Sex	0.45	0.39	0.46
Economic status	0.48	0.31	0.03
LEP status	0.01	0.00	0.00
AP/IB course	0.62	0.41	0.67
Trigonometry course	0.61	0.47	0.70
Math exam score	52.48	49.48	54.05
Dual enrollee	0.29	0.13	0.38
Working	0.12	0.16	0.14
High school context			
Pupil-teacher ratio	14.98	15.33	14.87
Enrollment (100s)	17.85	19.20	17.87
Per-pupil expenditure (logged)	8.38	8.35	8.36
Urbanicity	0.56	0.61	0.31
Percentage minority	0.74	0.66	0.32
County unemployment rate	7.25	6.32	6.06
Proximity to postsecondary education	0.83	0.85	0.77
Postsecondary characteristics			
Minority-Serving Institution	0.58	0.37	0.08
Historically Black College or University		0.37	0.01
Percentage tenured faculty	0.48	0.47	0.47
Student-faculty ratio	0.07	0.07	0.07
Enrollment (1,000s)	18.82	15.16	25.61
Per-pupil expenditures (logged)	9.87	9.84	9.98
Observations	9,837	5,139	25,875

RESULTS

Descriptive statistics for students by race or ethnicity are provided in table 5.1.[38] We note that these samples include only students who graduated from high school and immediately enrolled in a public four-year institution in Texas in 2002. We begin to follow this population of students in their tenth-grade high school year to include the influence of course-taking patterns and academic preparation in our analysis. We then follow an analytic sample of 35,712 students for the White-Hispanic cohort and a sample of 31,014 for the White-Black cohort (25,875 White, 9,837 Hispanic, and 5,139 Black) for a period of six years to compute our college completion rates: 65.5 percent for White students, 51.4 percent for Hispanic students, and 43.6 percent for Black students.

Precollege Characteristics

Key differences emerge between the URM student groups and their White counterparts. We see a vast difference between the economic status of Black and Hispanic students and that of White students, as indicated by the percentage of students of each race that is economically disadvantaged and attends a four-year institution in Texas. While the gap as stated is large between the URM and the White students, the income difference between Hispanics and Whites is significantly larger than the income difference between Blacks and Whites. We find that 3.4 percent of White students in this data set are economically disadvantaged, as indicated by participation in the federal free and reduced-price lunch program; this compares to 48 percent of Hispanic students and 31 percent of Black students.

In terms of academic preparation, AP/IB participation rates are fairly close for Hispanic and White students (62 percent Hispanic, 67 percent White) but considerably lower for Black students (41 percent). Participation in other college-preparatory high school courses also varies by race, often by large margins. For instance, participation in a trigonometry course is 70 percent for White students, 61 percent for Hispanic students, and 47 percent for Black students. Similarly, dual enrollment rates are 38 percent for White students, 30 percent for Hispanic students, and 13 percent for Black students. Average performance on the statewide math exam has the least variation, with scores of 54 for White students, 52 for Hispanic students, and 49 for Black students.

Finally, Black students who enroll in a four-year college show the highest rate of being employed while in high school (16 percent), followed by White (14 percent) and Hispanic (12 percent) students. Previous research finds that Hispanic students are actually more likely to choose to enter the labor force after high school than to attend college.[39] This factor may shed light on why Hispanic students who enroll in four-year colleges have the lowest high school employment rate of the racial and ethnic groups examined. Hispanic students who know they are going to attend a four-year college may be investing more in academics than in labor force participation during high school (by either choice or circumstance) than their peers who are more likely to work after high school than attend college.

In terms of the high school context, the pupil-teacher ratio, enrollment, and per-pupil expenditures are fairly similar among the three samples. There are sizeable differences, however, in the percentage of students graduating from urban high schools (61 percent Black, 56 percent Hispanic, 31 percent White), the percentage of URM students enrolled in the high schools from which the students graduated (74 percent Hispanic, 66 percent Black, 32 percent White), the high schools' proximity to a postsecondary institution (85 percent Black, 83 percent Hispanic, 77 percent White), and the county unemployment rates (7.2 percent Hispanic, 6.3 percent Black, 6.1 percent White).

Finally, the postsecondary institutions in which the samples enroll are also varied. A full 57.8 percent of Hispanic students enroll at a HSI, whereas only 8 percent of White students do so. In comparison, 37 percent of Black students enroll in a HBCU, compared to 0.1 percent of White students. Black students and Hispanic students are also more likely to enroll at institutions with smaller populations (Blacks average 15,161, Hispanics 18,824) than White students (average 25,606). Interestingly, we did not find large differences across racial groups for such factors as the percentage of tenured faculty and the student-faculty ratio. However, per-pupil expenditures were slightly lower at the schools attended by Black and Hispanic students, and the size of the student body was smaller at institutions attended by Black and Hispanic students.

Given these differences in student characteristics, high school and community context, and the postsecondary context in which White, Hispanic, and Black students enroll, it is important to consider how these factors contribute to the college completion gap between White and URM students who attend four-year institutions in Texas.

Table 5.2   Variance decomposition estimates

	White-Hispanic gap (14.1 percentage points)			White-Black gap (21.9 percentage points)		
	Variance estimate (1a)	% of Total variance (2a)	% of Variance explained (3a)	Variance estimate (1b)	% of Total variance (2b)	% of Variance explained (3b)
Individual & Academic Characteristics						
Sex	0.00	–0.7%	–0.7%	–0.01	–2.3%	–2.4%
Economic status	0.02	17.1%	17.8%	0.03	11.9%	12.6%
LEP status	0.00	0.0%	0.0%	0.00	0.0%	0.0%
AP/IB course	0.01	3.6%	3.7%	0.02	8.2%	8.7%
Trigonometry course	0.01	7.1%	7.4%	0.03	11.9%	12.6%
Math exam score	0.01	5.0%	5.2%	0.01	3.2%	3.4%
Dual enrollee	0.01	5.0%	5.2%	0.01	5.5%	5.8%
Working	0.00	0.0%	0.0%	0.00	0.5%	0.5%
Total individual characteristics	0.05	37.1%	38.5%	0.09	38.8%	41.1%
High school context						
Pupil-teacher ratio	0.00	0.0%	0.0%	0.00	0.5%	0.5%
HS enrollment	0.00	0.0%	0.0%	0.00	–1.4%	–1.4%
Per-pupil expenditure	0.00	0.0%	0.0%	0.00	0.0%	0.0%
Urbanicity	0.00	–2.1%	–2.2%	0.00	–0.9%	–1.0%
Percentage minority	0.05	37.1%	38.5%	0.05	22.8%	24.2%
County unemployment rate	–0.02	–10.7%	–11.1%	0.00	0.5%	0.5%
Proximity to postsecondary institution	0.00	0.0%	0.0%	0.00	0.0%	0.0%
Total high school context	0.03	24.3%	25.2%	0.05	21.5%	22.7%
Total precollege	0.09	61.4%	63.7%	0.13	60.3%	63.8%
Postsecondary context						
Hispanic-Serving Institution	0.02	12.9%	13.3%	0.02	9.1%	9.7%
Percentage tenured faculty	0.00	–2.1%	–2.2%	0.00	–0.5%	–0.5%
Student-faculty Ratio	0.01	7.9%	8.1%	0.01	3.7%	3.9%
Enrollment	0.02	12.1%	12.6%	0.03	15.5%	16.4%
Per-pupil expenditures	0.01	4.3%	4.4%	0.01	6.4%	6.8%
Total postsecondary context	0.05	35.0%	36.3%	0.08	34.2%	36.2%
Total variance	0.14			0.22		
Total variance explained	0.14	96.4%			94.5%	
Total Variance unexplained	0.01	3.6%		0.01	5.5%	

Variance Decomposition Analysis

Results from the variance decomposition are provided in table 5.2. The mean difference in college completion rates between Hispanic and White students is 14.1 percent, while the difference between Black and White students is 21.9 percent. That is, of students who entered a four-year institution in Texas, 51.4 percent of Hispanic students graduated college within six years, as compared to 65.5 percent of White students and 43.6 percent of Black students. Part of this difference is likely related to the fact that HBCUs offer more accessible entry to four-year colleges for Black students and are open to students with weaker preparation records. In our variance decomposition model for the White-Hispanic comparison, we explain 96.4 percent of this difference (or roughly 13.5 percentage points of the total 14.1 percentage point difference in Hispanic and White college completion rates) and 94.5 percent of the difference in the completion gap between Black and White students (or roughly 20.7 percentage points of the 21.9 percentage point difference in Black and White college completion rates).

We also present both variance estimates for each covariate and collective variance estimates for individual characteristics, high school characteristics, and postsecondary characteristics. For ease of interpretation, we present these estimates as percentages of total variance, including a percentage for the portion of the variance unexplained—that is, the percentage of the completion gap not explained using our set of covariates. In columns 2a and 2b we provide the percentage of the breakdown of the total variance explained by the variables in our model. Columns 3a and 3b express these percentages as a share of the total variance explained (eliminating the portion of the variance we fail to explain using our modeling technique). As we explain such a large share of the variance, these percentages do not change to any great extent, although they do increase slightly. Given this, we discuss our findings as they appear in columns 2a and 2b as a percentage of the total variance in college completion rates between White and URM students.

Hispanic students. Individual characteristics and academic preparation collectively constitute 37.1 percent of the total variance in college completion rates for Hispanic students. More specifically, economic status alone contributes 17.1 percent of the total variance, or roughly 46 percent of the total variance explained by the combined contribution of the individual and academic factors measured. High school context explains 24.3 percent of the total variance. Nearly all the variance explained by high school and community context factors is accounted for by attendance at a high school with a high percentage of minority students. Together, precollege characteristics (a combination of individual and high school context factors) contribute 61.4 percent of the total variance, which means that more than half of the college completion gap is explained by precollege characteristics. Finally, postsecondary context explains 35 percent of the total variance, with 12.9 percent of the total variance explained by HSI status alone. Put differently, roughly 37 percent of the postsecondary context influence is explained by HSI status.

Black students. For Black students, individual characteristics and academic preparation constitute 38.8 percent of the total variance in college completion rates. Economic status alone contributes 11.9 percent of the total variance for these students, or approximately 31 percent of the total variance explained by the combined contribution of the individual and academic factors measured. However, academic coursework is the largest source of total variance in this category, particularly having taken trigonometry. We see that factors related to academic preparation contribute 30.5 percent of the total variance, or approximately 74 percent of the variance explained by individual and academic factors combined.

In terms of high school context, 21.5 percent of the total variance is explained. Almost all the variance of this contribution to the college completion gap is explained by attendance at a high school with a high percentage of minority students. Together, precollege characteristics contribute 60.3 percent of the total variance. Therefore, similarly to the White-Hispanic findings, more than half of the White-Black college completion gap is explained by precollege characteristics. Postsecondary context explains 34.2 percent of the total variance, with 9.1 percent of the total variance explained by HBCU status alone. Put differently, roughly 28 percent of the postsecondary influence is explained by HBCU status.

Visual Representation

To further aid in the interpretation of both sets of results, we provide three panels in figure 5.1. This figure breaks down the variance by individual, high school, and postsecondary characteristics (panel A); individual and high school characteristics in a combined precollege category to postsecondary characteristics (panel B); and the influence of attending a HSI or HBCU (White-Hispanic and White-Black model, respectively) in the postsecondary characteristics category to precollege characteristics (panel C).

In panel A we note the sizable portion of the White-Hispanic variance that is explained by individual characteristics; much of this contribution comes from economic status. In panel B, we note that more than half (61 percent) of the White-Hispanic achievement gap is explained by precollege characteristics, and just over one-third (35 percent) is explained by postsecondary characteristics; the remaining 4 percent is left unexplained. Finally, panel C highlights the percentage of the variance (roughly 13 percent) explained by HSI designation. For the White-Black completion gap (panel A), we note the sizable portion of the variance that is explained by individual characteristics; much of this influence comes from economic status and coursework. In panel B, we note that more than half (60 percent) of the achievement gap is explained by precollege characteristics, with just one-third explained by postsecondary characteristics. The remaining 5.5 percent is left unexplained. We note that panel B reflects that similar shares of the variance are explained by precollege factors rather than postsecondary factors for both the White-Hispanic and the White-Black college completion gaps. Finally, panel C highlights the percentage of the variance (roughly 10 percent) explained by the HBCU designation.

LIMITATIONS

Our sample includes those students who graduated from high school and immediately enrolled in a four-year public postsecondary institution in Texas and who had complete records at the time of our analysis. While this approach allows us to incorporate characteristics of these students starting in ninth grade and to track them through six full years following high school graduation, it also has some limitations. First, our sample consists of a high-achieving group—a sample of students who finished high school on time and successfully enrolled in a four-year institution in the fall immediately following high school graduation. As such, our results may not generalize to the overall population of White and URM students. Second, while our data represent some of the most robust in the nation for this kind of longitudinal analysis, we are not able to track students who left Texas higher education (approximately one-tenth of students).

One important thing the data do provide is a statewide snapshot of large-scale factors that may be contributing to the current gap in college completion. That is, despite these two limitations, our study presents a complete picture of our analytic sample (n=40,851) and provides insight into the vari-

Figure 5.1   Variance decomposition by factor

Panel A: Decomposition by factor

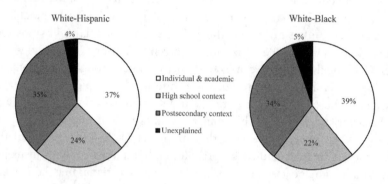

Panel B: Decomposition by factor (grouped)

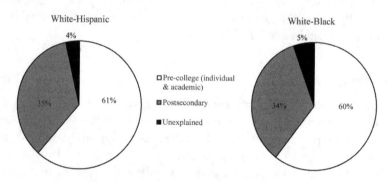

Panel C: Decomposition by factor (with MSI status)

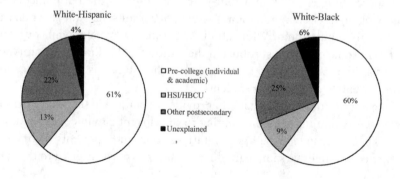

ous factors that may influence the White-Hispanic and White-Black college completion gaps between students.

DISCUSSION

One goal of this analysis is to offer a novel approach to examining the college completion gap by race and ethnicity in a state with a racially and ethnically diverse student population and a large number of minority-serving institutions—both HSIs and HBCUs. Our data show that the college completion gap in Texas is not unlike the figures at the national level, where, measured against their White counterparts, Hispanic students experience at least a fourteen percentage point gap in college completion, while Black students experience a twenty-two percentage point gap (we do not include Asian or American Indian students in this analysis for reasons of representation or sample size). Confirming the racial college completion gap, however, is only the first step in the analysis. Indeed, through these efforts to disaggregate what contributes to the racial college completion gap and determine how this evidence may relate to accountability policies based on metrics such as college completion, we find three key stories.

First, in our examination of the White-Hispanic and the White-Black completion gap, we find remarkable similarities across the racial group comparisons in terms of our categories: postsecondary characteristics explain just over one-third (35 percent and 34 percent, respectively) of the completion gap, while precollege characteristics explain well over half (60 percent and 61 percent, respectively). Of particular importance is the fact that these results corroborate previous work that examines contributions to the completion gap using different data sources.[40]

In sum, postsecondary characteristics explain a much smaller portion of the completion gap than individual factors and schooling outcomes initiated prior to enrolling in higher education. Indeed, of all the factors we examined to explain the college completion gap, attending a high-minority high school is the largest explanatory variable. Given these results, it would be unfair to rank or award funding to institutions based upon factors over which they have no control.

The second story of interest is that there are distinct differences by racial group in the individual factors that influence college completion. As previously noted, the two key factors driving the White-Hispanic achievement gap are attending a high-minority high school and poverty or economic disadvantage, as indicated in the data. Hispanic students who attend a four-year institution on average do not have gaps in academic preparation (defined by select math courses and access to AP/IB courses) compared to White students. However, Hispanic students are dramatically more likely to be lower income or more economically disadvantaged than their White counterparts. Interestingly, these Hispanic students are much more likely to be both observationally and non-observationally different from their Hispanic student peers who attend two-year colleges as a first-choice institution, which is the most likely outcome for Hispanic students in Texas and in the nation. As such, while these students are more "advantaged" than their peers who begin their postsecondary education at a community college, they are still deeply disadvantaged in terms of economic status relative to White students who begin their postsecondary education at a four-year college.

While attending a high-minority high school also explains a large portion of the college completion gap between Black and White students, the most critical group factors that explain this gap relate to academic preparation. While the data do indicate a significant difference in the percentage of students from each group who are economically disadvantaged, the gap is not nearly as large as that between Hispanic and White students. The factors of most relevance in the Black and White gap are those related to the rigorous coursework regarded as essential to college readiness and success, such as high-level math courses and AP/IB coursework, as well as early college enrollment opportunities, such as dual-enrollment courses.

Though the overall story of how precollege and postsecondary characteristics contribute to the racial college completion gap is similar between Blacks and Whites and Hispanics and Whites, the driving factors differ significantly across the racial comparison groups. These differences raise questions about how to invest in underrepresented communities based on the distinct needs seen in Texas and whether a larger, scalable programmatic intervention can attend to the differences that drive the college completion gap. Ultimately, the results suggest that college completion is both a financial story and one of academic preparation. Proposed policies that would rank and potentially award funding based on complex measures such as college completion without attending to what leads to these outcomes would be incomplete and unfair and would not account for both the academic preparedness of students and their financial capacity.

The third story involves how to interpret the role of the MSI across the racial comparison groups. For Hispanics, 37 percent of the postsecondary influence is explained by HSI status, while 28 percent of this context is explained by HBCU status for Black students. Previous work indicates that MSIs are more likely to be nonselective and to enroll a much higher percentage of Pell grant recipients and nontraditional URM students than non-MSIs. These factors may contribute to the influence each MSI has on the variance explained by postsecondary characteristics. While recent work finds that there is no significant difference in college completion rates between Black and Hispanic students who attend a MSI in Texas and between similar Black and Hispanic students who attend a non-MSI after conditioning on precollege factors, the current analysis compares Black and Hispanic students to White students.[41]

We therefore remain cautious of any high-stakes accountability system that includes punitive measures without accounting for the fact that MSIs are likely struggling to meet goals using the existing level of resources to serve much larger student populations. In other words, these institutions are likely to be at a disadvantage compared to their non-MSI peer institutions, as they provide an opportunity to attend college to groups of students who otherwise may not have had such an opportunity.

Nonetheless, additional analysis not included here indicates that the contributing influence of the MSI, particularly the HSI, to the college completion gap has actually decreased over time, which suggests that there may be programmatic or policy interventions that can address this gap—or, rather, that pointing to the influence of the MSI to explain the college completion gap is not a permanent finding. Thus, MSIs would be unfairly punished in any system that ranks or awards funding to colleges and universities based solely on such metrics as college completion, despite the fact that students who are similarly prepared graduate at equal rates at MSIs and non-MSIs. Without accounting for precollege factors, high-stakes accountability systems are most likely to harm MSIs—the very institutions in which many Black and Hispanic students are most likely to enroll.

RECOMMENDATIONS

Many have stressed the need for state higher education systems to have more accountability, similar to that in the K–12 sector, with a particular focus on college completion. Others point to the abandonment of a similar federal effort focused on accountability for achievement in public schools, the No Child Left Behind Act, which was harshly criticized for the unintended harm it inflicted on many high-poverty schools. The federal government replaced this strategy of accountability with a radically different one in the 2015 Every Student Succeeds Act (the reauthorization of NCLB), which now incorporates provisions for college and career readiness by state context, suggesting that a K–20 review of achievement may grow in importance. At the same time, there has been a persistent college completion gap between underrepresented minority students and White students, which is often absent from any discussion about college rankings or funding schemes that involve performance metrics. As such, we have conducted this analysis using unique longitudinal data to provide a more detailed and comprehensive picture of what might be contributing to the college completion gap. We do this in the hope that more targeted interventions may help reduce or close these pronounced racial gaps instead of focusing solely on ranking or funding colleges and universities based on college completion metrics. In this vein, we offer a series of recommendations.

Our first recommendation is to compare various state administrative databases with national databases to create a clear picture of the variation in college completion gaps for each state's URM student population. Various states have K–20 databases in place, although many also have a long way to go in improving their data systems.[42] These K–20 databases offer more nuanced analyses of what factors are most likely contributing to the completion gap, which can help to improve or at least complement the national databases currently in place. This is particularly important if any national ranking or funding policy were to be enacted that would use college completion as a main metric.

Second, we suggest that any such policy would also take into account student inputs. Ultimately, our data suggest that college completion is not just a postsecondary issue. Therefore, we offer additional recommendations for potential interventions based on the findings of our different racial group comparisons. The mechanism most effective in increasing the enrollment of Hispanic students may indeed be financial aid, and our findings support the notion that, of the metrics assessed, poverty is a key driver of the White-Hispanic college completion gap.[43] A greater emphasis on the financial aid needs of this student population, both before and after college enrollment, may be the most direct approach to increasing Hispanic college completion rates and Hispanics enrollment in four-year institutions. Given our finding that academic preparation is a significant factor in increasing Black students' college completion rates, it appears that investing in greater college readiness at the high school level and providing effective remedial course-work in postsecondary education are essential to the college success and completion of this population.

CONCLUSION

Assessing the White-Hispanic and White-Black achievement gaps is not a new undertaking, and previous research provides important findings in the early grades.[44] However, we know far less about what factors contribute to the college completion gap. Our findings suggest that the factors influencing this gap are not limited to the postsecondary level—that is, colleges and universities alone are not responsible for this gap. In fact, students enter college with background factors that account for nearly two-thirds of the racial college completion gap, factors that are well beyond the control of colleges and universities. This finding by no means excuses the accountability responsibilities to students at colleges and universities. However, understanding these factors and what mechanisms are most likely to help close the achievement gap at all stages of the K–20 pipeline is key to increasing the college completion rates for all students, but particularly for those who lag behind their peers with higher completion rates.

In sum, given that Hispanic and Black students are less likely than White students to complete college due largely to precollege factors, it seems unfair and perhaps even inefficient to punish colleges and universities that enroll large portions of minority students, many of who are underprepared or low income, by tying select forms of state or federal funding to outcome measures such as college completion rates. Even if such an approach led to a higher completion rate, those most harmed, without significant interventions, will be students who entered college with fewer resources and academic preparation than their non-disadvantaged student counterparts. In other words, is it worth increasing our nation's college completion rates by limiting who enrolls in college at a time when the national economy demands a workforce equipped with a postsecondary degree?[45] Increasing college completion rates for all students is a laudable goal. However, current proposals to do so by tying funding to performance metrics could have grave consequences for institutions enrolling high percentages of minority students, as well as the students they serve, without considering that many Black and Hispanic students may not arrive at college as academically prepared as their White counterparts. To be clear, our data do not suggest that accountability proposals are not needed. However, they do indicate that a fair assessment and evaluation system accounting for the role of precollege factors is necessary.

Because our analysis indicates that college completion is not just a matter of postsecondary institutional response, we recommend a deeper investigation into what factors constitute metrics of achievement as well as barriers across the K–20 education landscape. A growing number of states now have longitudinal K–20 state administrative databases that could work for these purposes. While not all states (to date) have the capacity for these data systems, public officials, educators, and education advocates can work together to ensure higher data quality in all states for the purposes of implementing more effective education policies for low-income and minority students. (Indeed, this study would not have been possible without the detailed, student-level database maintained in Texas.) Our analysis indicates that attention to race, income, and the high school context in which a student is likely to form their life chances are all metrics that require attention in proposed evaluation systems. Ignoring the powerful role of these factors in evaluating institutions will lead to an inaccurate conclusion about institutional success and how we are progressing as a nation on matters of education attainment.

CHAPTER 6

Making Accountability Fair for Hispanic-Serving Institutions

ANNE-MARIE NÚÑEZ AND AWILDA RODRÍGUEZ

Now more than ever, it is critical that higher education institutions follow accountability principles to realize the ideals set forth in the 1964 Civil Rights Act, which forbids discrimination in all programs and institutions receiving federal assistance, including all colleges whose students receive federal grants and loans. Under federal civil rights law, all racial and ethnic groups must be treated fairly. These accountability principles should be used to ensure that all students have opportunities to enroll in postsecondary education options in which they are likely to obtain degrees at a reasonable cost and that institutions are enrolling and addressing the needs of students who have traditionally been underserved. But not all accountability systems are designed to promote civil rights and to acknowledge the current and historical structures of inequality, and this results in regimes that can be unfair to the very institutions that serve students of color and low-income students. This issue is particularly important in the context of Hispanic-Serving Institutions (HSIs), which now educate the majority of Latina/o college students.[1]

There is widespread concern that too many US students who go to college fail to graduate, and this problem is particularly acute for students of color, leading to policies holding colleges accountable for increasing those rates and applying pressure and sanctions on those that fall behind. In this context it is very important that these standards are appropriately designed and do not do unintended harm to key institutions. A bad standard is one that punishes institutions for things that are not their responsibility.

In this chapter we interrogate the application of regression-adjusted analysis in predicting institutional graduation rates, a central metric proposed in accountability frameworks. Regression-adjusted analysis has been proposed to account for differences across institutions that have been found to facilitate college completion, such as the students they serve and their available resources. The intention is to make measuring accountability fairer for institutions like HSIs by recognizing that they are disadvantaged on characteristics critical to increasing graduation rates, such as having fewer resources to spend on student support, while also serving students with less academic preparation and fewer financial resources. We ask whether it is possible to adjust for these inequalities via new analytical techniques. Can we leverage existing data to *estimate* and *predict* institutional performance as a means of accountability?

Answering this question is no easy task, and we compare several potential ways regression-adjusted graduation rates could be used to measure the performance of HSIs. Notably, comparing these different analyses reveals inconsistent, and sometimes contradictory, interpretations of HSIs' performance. Including different variables, or variables for which significant data are missing, often produces significantly different results across different models. Moreover, several variables critical to account for institutional performance are not available in the data set and therefore cannot be adjusted for in the model.

We conclude that regression-adjusted performance metrics (at least in the case of graduation rates) requires solid conceptual grounding coupled with the appropriate data to model how key variables are associated with performance goals. Without these conditions, measuring accountability based on either raw or regression-adjusted graduation rates risks unintended consequences that could ultimately punish the very schools that have been at the vanguard of advancing equitable access to higher education. Here we underscore the need to better leverage extant state and federal data sources and to collect more and better data elements if we are to expand our methodological toolkit to enable us to hold institutions accountable for their outcomes in a way that truly disentangles institutional performance from student inputs.

ADJUSTING GRADUATION RATES FOR INSTITUTIONAL AND STUDENT CHARACTERISTICS

The Need for Regression Adjustments

Researchers have previously documented the sizeable differences in institutional and student characteristics of HSIs and non-HSIs.[2] For example, HSIs tend to serve greater shares of low-income students.[3] Therefore, many have argued that comparing the graduation rates of institutions with different student bodies and institutional resources is unfair. Studies have also shown that the gaps in graduation rates between HSIs and non-HSIs are diminished once these observed differences are accounted for.[4] Findings from such studies underscore the importance of taking into account colleges' resources as well as the types of students they serve when comparing college outcomes.

We illustrate this important fact in figure 6.1. Here, we use Integrated Postsecondary Education Data System (IPEDS) 2012 survey data to compare six-year graduation rates in public (n=541) and nonprofit (n=1,123) US colleges and universities. The first column for each sector shows that HSIs, on average, have lower graduation rates than non-HSIs, approximately a ten-point difference at both four-year public and private nonprofit colleges.[5] The following columns use regression-adjustment analysis to show how the gap in graduation rates shrinks toward zero once we account for important factors beyond HSI status.

Once we add institutional characteristics to our regression model, including the college's geographic region, urbanicity, and size, the gap shown in the second column is smaller than the first.[6] Adding financials resources, such as tuition, academic support expenditures, and student services expenditures, reduces the graduation rate gap even further, as shown in the third column.[7] Adding data about the various campus policies that could facilitate college completion in the fourth column, which includes whether the campus provides on-campus child care, remedial services, or accepts nontraditional credits (e.g., advanced placement, dual credit), the gap rises in the public sector but shrinks in the nonprofit sector. The next column includes student characteristics, which adjusts for the share of undergraduates who are enrolled part time, those who are non-degree seekers, those exclusively enrolled in distance education, and Federal Pell Grant recipients.[8] Adding these characteristics reduces the gap in both sectors. The final column accounts for whether an institution had an open admissions policy, and we

Figure 6.1   Regression-adjusted differences in graduation rates of HSIs by sector

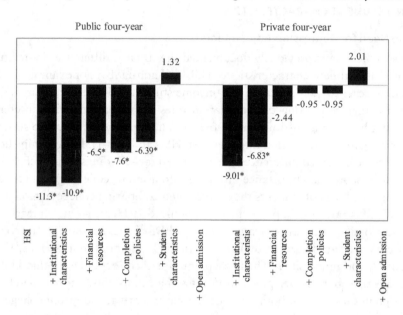

Note: * represents statistically significant differences at p-value <0.05.

see the gap now become positive (but not statistically significant) in both sectors.[9]

This figure shows how graduation rate gaps were reduced both in magnitude and significance once we controlled for institutional and especially student characteristics. These findings support the arguments that, once the differences in institutional and student characteristics are accounted for, HSIs perform on par with their non-HSI counterparts. For the public sector, financial characteristics (including tuition and how much money was spent on instruction per student) and the percentage of part-time students accounted most for reducing the graduation rate gap. At private nonprofits, the amount of tuition per student contributed the most to reducing that gap.

Regression Adjustments, a Cautionary Tale

We used multiple regression to model the relationships displayed in figure 6.1, allowing us to adjust for the average differences between HSIs and non-

HSIs and to predict colleges' graduation rates based on the information we have about them. These results should be encouraging for proponents of regression-adjustment analysis because they equalize the playing field for HSIs. But this did not come without trade-offs, such as excluding the critical academic preparation variable of ACT scores, because to do so would have resulted in a 40 percent reduction of our sample size of institutions. Additionally, computing regression-adjusted group means is not quite the same as producing regression-adjusted graduation rates for individual colleges.

Regression-adjusted graduation rates are predicted values calculated with each college's information in the regression model. To illustrate the extent of the adjustments, we plotted in the changes between the actual (original) and adjusted graduation rates for HSIs. Each line represents the difference between the actual and predicted graduation rate of an individual HSI. If the adjusted graduation rate was higher than the actual, then the particular line corresponding to that institution would tilt upward on the graph. This would also mean that, given its characteristics, a college would be predicted to have a higher graduation rate than how it actually performed (i.e., it underperformed). If the adjusted graduation rate was lower than the actual (the line sloped downward), then the opposite would be true: that institution would be performing better than expected, given the college's characteristics. If no adjustment was made, then the line between the actual and adjusted graduation rate would be flat. In order to facilitate interpretation, we separated out the colleges by deciles of graduation rate percentages (e.g., 10–19, 20–29, etc.).

The adjustments varied by colleges' actual graduation rates. Many of the HSIs with low graduation rates were adjusted upward. For example, Donnelly College in Kansas had a 12 percent graduation rate yet a predicted graduation rate of 32 percent. Under an accountability framework, institutions with higher adjusted graduation rates would be seen as underperforming. Yet, many of the higher performing colleges were adjusted downward. Boricua College, for example, actually had a 69 percent graduation rate with a 33 percent predicted graduation rate. That is, Boricua College would be expected to have a far lower graduation rate based on its largely Pell Grant-receiving student population (90 percent).

Figure 6.2 demonstrates how including potential variables in a regression-adjusted calculation changes the graduation rates of different institutions in very different directions and magnitudes. What this graph shows is

Figure 6.2 Comparison of actual and adjusted HSIs' graduation rates after controlling for student characteristics and open admission

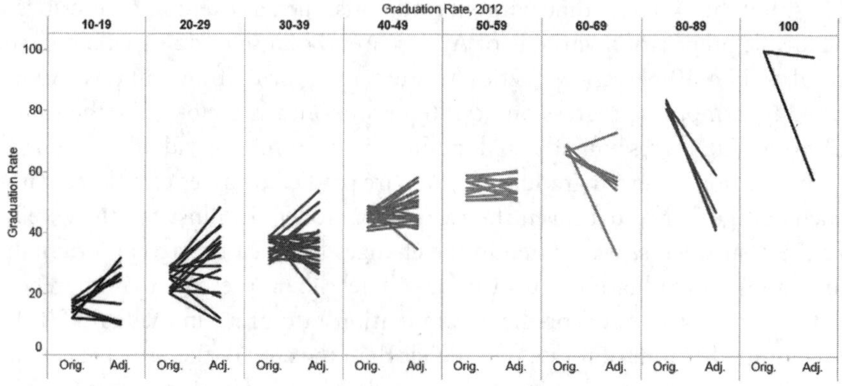

that the major issues with regression models are that they are highly sensitive to the variables included and the colleges that appear in the data set. As a result, there is potential for a lot of volatility between steps in these regression-adjusted graduation rates unless a good model is used that fits the data well and accounts for much of the variation in graduation rates.

One of the diagnostic tools to determine how well the data fit the linear model is the R^2 statistic. The R^2 is an indicator of how much variation has been accounted for within the data, based on the selected variables. Plainly stated, it is the extent to which the variables and the data tell the story of graduation rates. The closer to 1 (or 100 percent), the better the R^2. Despite our best efforts to use variables that can help explain differences in graduation rates, there is still a lot of unexplained variation in the models in column 6 of figure 6.1: 20 percent of the variance in the public four-year colleges and nearly half of the variance at private four-year nonprofit colleges have gone unexplained. Therefore, if we were to find additional data in IPEDS to put in the model that could help explain a large share of the unexplained variation, the model can adjust the predicted graduation rates for some colleges by several points. This means a college can go from being an overperformer to an underachiever, or vice versa, based on as little as one additional variable.

THE OMITTED PREDICTORS OF COLLEGE COMPLETION

The above exercise should alarm proponents who want to attach high-stakes accountability policies, whether at the state or federal level, to regression-adjusted graduation rates using the existing data. This approach has two glaring shortcomings: omitted variable bias and missing data. Excluding either colleges or variables in regression-adjusted analyses due to missing data is problematic because the data are typically not missing at random. This problem is particularly salient for private nonprofit colleges, where the variables included in our model thus far only accounted for half of the variance in graduation rates. Both shortcomings are major criticisms of using existing data such as IPEDS to craft high-stakes accountability systems. In this section we further unpack the extent of the missing data and omitted variables along with the associated implications for HSIs.

There are variables substantiated in the completion literature that should be included in our regression adjustments yet could not be for one of two reasons: either they were not collected by National Center for Education Statistics (NCES), or they had such high rates of missing data that it was not prudent to include them in the regression models. These instances of leaving out variables can help explain how the variation in graduation rates creates omitted variable bias.

Academic Preparation

Academic preparation is one of the strongest positive predictors of college completion, especially course rigor.[10] Latino students and low-income students, two populations that HSIs serve, are less likely than their Asian, White, and high-income counterparts to be enrolled in rigorous coursework, including Advanced Placement, International Baccalaureate, or advanced mathematics courses. For example, a study of a nationally representative sample of ninth graders in 2009 revealed greater shares of White (24 percent) and Asian (53 percent) students were taking precalculus or calculus than Latino students (16 percent) by eleventh grade.[11] Similarly, students in the highest socioeconomic quintile were three and a half times more likely than a student from the lowest socioeconomic quintile to take either precalculus or calculus. This also has consequences for math placement when students enroll in college. For example, one study found that 52 percent of Latino first-year college students in all four-year institutions were initially placed into developmental mathematics.[12] Another study found that students from all racial/ethnic groups in HSIs are less likely than their counterparts at non-HSIs to have taken advanced mathematics in high school.[13] These findings concerning academic preparation are consistent with research documenting that Latinos are less likely than their White or Asian counterparts to attend well-resourced high schools, meaning that they have fewer opportunities to take college preparatory coursework from more experienced teachers who are certified in their topic area.[14]

Given academic preparation's predictive power of college completion, measures of academic preparation are essential to include in the model for adjusting institutional graduation rates. Colleges that serve students who are less academically prepared are more likely to have lower graduation rates. However, we could not find measures in IPEDS that characterize the academic preparation of student populations. Therefore, one major limitation of this approach with the existing data in IPEDS is the inability to account for academic preparation.

Academic Achievement

In research on college access and outcomes, academic achievement is often operationalized as students' test scores and grades. Previous studies have shown measures of achievement prior to college, particularly high school GPA, are also highly predictive of college-going outcomes, such as end-of-first-year GPA, persistence, and college completion.[15] We also know that Latinos and low-income students are less likely than their White, Asian, and high-income peers to possess high GPAs and college entrance exam scores (e.g., ACT and SAT), largely because of inequities in high school resources.[16] Moreover, Latino and low-income students are less likely to take college entrance exams and would therefore not be eligible to enroll at institutions that require SAT or ACT scores.[17] Indeed, only 43 percent of HSIs require SAT or ACT scores as part of their admissions process.[18] Therefore, HSIs are mechanically poised to be disadvantaged in their ability to adjust for academic achievement.

How do achievement measures stack up in IPEDS? We identified variables in IPEDS that measure academic achievement and calculated their rates of missing data in table 6.1 by sector and HSI status. While NCES does not collect information about students' GPAs, the best academic predictors of college success, they do survey colleges that require the SAT and/or ACT to report the twenty-fifth and seventy-fifth percentile scores. In both sectors, there were higher rates of missing data among HSIs than non-HSIs.

Table 6.1   Percentage of missing data among key available college completion predictors in IPEDS by sector and HSI status

	Public four-year		Private four-year nonprofit	
	HSI	Non-HSI	HSI	Non-HSI
Academic achievement				
SAT math 25th percentile	31%	29%	43%	30%
SAT math 75th percentile	31%	29%	43%	30%
ACT composite 25th percentile	35%	27%	49%	32%
ACT composite 75th percentile	35%	27%	49%	32%
Admission and selectivity				
Admission rate	25%	12%	17%	11%
Yield rate	25%	12%	17%	11%

If we were to include the SAT or ACT variables in our regression, we would invariably omit one-third to one-half of HSIs.

Admissions and Selectivity

The self-sorting of students that occurs in the application and enrollment processes shapes colleges' student compositions. For example, high-achieving students might be more likely to apply to and enroll at certain colleges. Indeed, previous research has shown that controlling for the types of students who apply and enroll explains differences in college graduation rates to a significant extent.[19] However, we are limited to only the colleges' acceptance and yield rates in IPEDS. Table 6.1 suggests that data on students' prior academic performance and colleges' selectivity in IPEDS are not missing at random but, rather, are missing more frequently for HSIs than for their non-HSI counterparts.

To further explore the extent of missing data on each of these variables in IPEDS, we grouped colleges by graduation and reexamined the percent of colleges missing information on students' prior performance and colleges' selectivity. Table 6.2 shows that colleges with lower graduation rates are less likely to report data on students' prior performance and college selectivity than higher performing colleges. For example, four out of every five colleges with the lowest graduation rates (0–24 percent) are missing SAT/ACT infor-

Table 6.2 Percentage of missing data among key available college completion predictors in IPEDS by graduation rate

	Graduation rate (%)				
	0–24	25–49	50–74	75–99	100
N	120	603	683	249	9
Academic achievement					
SAT math 25th percentile	84%	36%	21%	14%	100%
SAT math 75th percentile	84%	36%	21%	14%	100%
ACT composite 25th percentile	82%	33%	22%	23%	100%
ACT composite 75th percentile	82%	33%	22%	23%	100%
Admission and selectivity					
Admission rate	46%	16%	5%	2%	56%
Yield rate	47%	16%	5%	2%	56%

mation and are six times more likely to be missing this information when compared to colleges with the highest graduation rates. This is expected, as most low performing colleges do not require SAT or ACT scores for admission, and only colleges where over 60 percent of students submit scores are asked to report their ACT or SAT percentiles to IPEDS. In reality, most US colleges below the top fifth, including most HSIs, reject few students who meet the minimum requirements and complete the application process.[20]

The amount of missing data on admission and yield rates was less drastic than that of exam scores, yet only about half of the lowest performing colleges reported this information. Therefore, trying to adjust for the variables in table 6.2 would result in omitting most of the lowest performing colleges from the model. In doing so, the sample of institutions in the model would not be representative of low performing colleges, and we would be unable to accurately regression adjust for these colleges. Arguably, these are the institutions that would stand to gain most from regression adjustments. Missing data pose a serious challenge for adjusting graduation rates. Many variables that can help explain college completion are not found in IPEDS. Moreover, because omitting colleges with missing data would cause us to lose large shares of HSIs and systematically restrict the data to higher performing colleges, any regression that adjusts for the few student achievement variables in IPEDS will be invariably limited.

Figure 6.3   Comparison of graduation rate adjustments for HSIs before and after controlling for student performance and admission rates

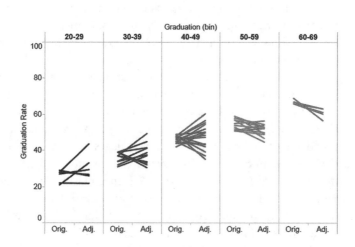

THE POWER OF PRIOR PERFORMANCE

Keeping in mind the limitations of missing data, what would have happened if we included some of the predictors for the colleges that *do* report data on students' prior achievement? In figure 6.3 we examine the extent to which regression-adjusting for student's prior achievement can further alter the predicted graduation rates. By doing so, we can begin to understand how HSIs might be adjusted by additional measures of students' prior achievement. For this final analysis, we repeated the sequential regression adjustments from earlier using only the colleges that reported SAT, ACT, and admission rates information.

Because far fewer institutions in our sample reported all these measures, this reduced our sample of institutions by 40 percent. This step also removed 47 percent of HSIs from the sample. Second, as noted above, the data were not missing at random; most of the schools that remained in the sample were higher performing. In addition, we had to drop the open admission measure from our analysis because no college that reported SAT or ACT score percentiles had an open admissions policy. We also excluded the measure that denoted whether colleges accepted Advanced Placement for public four-year colleges, because all institutions in this sample had done so. Finally, we added the twenty-fifth and seventy-fifth percentile scores for the SAT and ACT as well as the colleges' admission rate. Taken together, the differences in the models used in figures 6.2 and 6.3 rendered direct comparisons across the full models inappropriate since the sample sizes and variables were far different from one another in the models. Nonetheless, we felt it was important to show the predictive power of exam scores and admissions rates, to compare changes within the model.

What does this mean for adjusting the graduation rates of HSIs? Figure 6.3 illustrates the changes between the actual and adjusted graduation rates after accounting for the full model of institutional and student characteristics. While there is a mix of direction and magnitude of adjustments, the general trend was that lower performing colleges were adjusted up, middling colleges were quite mixed, and higher performing colleges were adjusted down, similar to the trends in figure 6.2. In other words, many of the lower performing HSIs were predicted to perform better than they actually did, given their characteristics. Also, many of the high performing HSIs had higher graduation rates than expected, considering their characteristics. The colleges in the middle (40–49 percent graduation rates), however, performed about as expected.

However, the magnitude of the adjustments, in many cases, was not as large as in figure 6.2. Holy Names University, for instance, experienced an upward adjustment of fifteen points in the first analysis, an indication that it was severely underperforming. However, after adjusting for exam scores and admission rate in this analysis, its graduation rate was adjusted up by only two points. For a third of HSIs, the difference between their raw and adjusted graduation rates was greater than five percentage points. Also, the direction of the adjustments changed for nearly 30 percent of HSIs in the sample between the first and second analysis. In the first analysis, La Sierra University, with an actual graduation rate of 53 percent, went from a five-point upward adjustment (meaning it was underperforming) to an eight-point downward reduction when adjusting for exam percentile scores and admission rate (meaning it was overperforming).

IMPLICATIONS

These results indicate that although a regression-adjusted approach may seem to be a valid way to account for student and institutional differences, there are several pitfalls to this approach that would call its outcomes into question. Our findings indicate that when unequal student and institutional inputs are accounted for, the average differences in graduation rates between four-year HSIs and non-HSIs disappear. While at first glance a regression-adjusted approach may appear to be a solution, our findings also show that the regression results for individual colleges vary quite dramatically depending on the variables included in the regression model, even at times implying *opposite* adjustments in graduation rates for the same institution. Therefore, evaluations of institutional performance using regression approaches may in fact depend more on the variables and colleges included in the analysis than on how a college is actually supporting the success of its students. This is because a regression approach can only base an adjustment on observed information. Therefore, colleges' graduation rates will not be adjusted for a variety of unobserved or immeasurable characteristics that influence completion.

The use of a regression-adjustment approach is further complicated by missing data. Less selective institutions, like most HSIs, are less likely to report data on the academic preparation or performance characteristics of incoming students as measured by standardized admissions test scores. There are many potential reasons for this, among them that many four-year HSIs do not collect these test scores as part of their admissions process and that HSIs have fewer resources than non-HSIs to collect and report these kinds of data.

Finally, we show that the inability to fully account for incoming student academic preparation or performance poses a large obstacle to accurately gauging institutional performance, particularly for HSIs. Even above and beyond other student and institutional characteristics, the admission test scores of the student body account for a significant amount of institutional performance. Therefore, if this critical piece of information is not included in regression adjustments (as will be the case with many HSIs that do not collect or report such test scores as part of the admission process), the assessment of the institutional performance of many HSIs will be distorted.

Our analysis indicates that although regression adjustment techniques may help to level the playing field in evaluating the average institutional performance of HSIs, these models are limited by missing data and the associated volatility in predicting individual institutional performance. The instability of these models calls into question the accuracy and utility of a performance-based accountability system predicated on regression analyses, particularly for HSIs. At least three implications result.

First, an accountability system that could be constructed with available data may be limited, or even distorted, in its accuracy. Historically underrepresented and underserved students and families deserve reasonably accurate assessments of institutional performance. Providing them with an accountability system based on questionable methodological premises and incomplete data would not fill their need for a useful consumer tool to make informed decisions about their postsecondary options. As for the institutions themselves, it is unjust to evaluate them according to suspect methods and data and then allocate federal or state funding according to assessments of institutional performance that might be inaccurate. Second, because HSIs tend to underperform on traditional metrics of institutional success and comparatively lack data on important predictors of success, they could suffer more adverse consequences than other institutions if funding is tied to evaluations of their institutional performance. Third, because HSIs, by definition, serve disproportionately large numbers of underrepresented and low-income students, such an accountability system could worsen the disenfranchisement of historically underserved groups.

RECOMMENDATIONS

Because data about strong influences on student performance is either missing or very limited, any accountability system predicated on these data is extremely questionable. Creating a performance-based accountability system with existing data will very likely to punish HSIs for outcomes that are caused by factors other than poor institutional performance. This would hurt the very institutions that are working to help the majority of the nation's largest minority group to attain postsecondary degrees. To minimize unintended negative consequences of such an accountability system for HSIs, we recommend three ways forward.

Resist the temptation to implement high-stakes policies that would most likely penalize the students who have had the least access to postsecondary education and the colleges that serve these students.

Collect or utilize better data to evaluate institutional performance, particularly data related to student inputs such as academic preparation, because these data are highly important in predicting graduation rates.[21] The recent release of new data from the US Department of Education is a good start, as it includes data concerning loan repayment, transfer students, and earnings after college. However, it does not necessarily assuage missing data issues.

Continue efforts like those currently underway by IPEDS to collect data on a broader range of students in enrollment and graduation measures, such as transfer students. Also consider examining other populations of nontraditional students who are currently overlooked in graduation measures, including part-time enrolled students, older students, independent students, students who are employed full-time, and English learner students.[22] Better measures of access could also include the graduation rates for students on Pell grants or first-generation students.[23] In some cases, these efforts may involve utilizing and leveraging existing data. For example, use National Student Clearinghouse data or state longitudinal data sets to incorporate precollege measures and to track student movement into and out of institutions over time.[24] The Common Data Set, a private data collection initiative from which information for college guide books and rankings is compiled, could also serve as a model for improving data collection and reporting efforts.[25] Such efforts must also involve capacity building to enhance HSIs' capacity to report accurate data. A basic problem is that many of the same forces supporting high-stakes accountability are opposed to additional data collection.[26] It is very important that policy makers realize that fair assessment of institutional performance requires better data.

Draw on the existing and voluntary efforts of higher education associations to develop appropriate outcome measures in any federal or state accountability system intended to measure the performance of higher education institutions. The Student Achievement Measure project is supported by several higher education organizations representing a wide range of institution types, including American Association of Community Colleges, American Association of State and College Universities, Association of American Universities, Association of Public and Land-Grant Universities, American Council on Education, and National Association of Independent Colleges and Universities.[27] These organizations have joined together to identify and disseminate common accountability metrics, including metrics that use National Student Clearinghouse data to measure transfer rates. Partnering with postsecondary institutions in these initiatives can reduce duplication of efforts to identify salient measures.

These efforts can also yield information on what may be useful additional outcome measures besides graduation rates, because postsecondary education provides many noneconomic and social benefits.[28] Scholars have also pointed out that, due to the extremely limited validity of existing data, it is important to avoid depicting gradations in performance that do not exist, because in reality no more than three gradations (the handful of institutions that perform the best, the handful of institutions that perform the worst, and the vast majority that perform in the middle) appear to exist.[29] Furthermore, graduation rates can also vary from year to year, which challenges the idea that any accountability regime would be stable over time.

If it is deemed absolutely necessary to proceed with a formal accountability system at the federal level or in a given state despite the formidable limitations that have been outlined, it should be phased in slowly, with careful consideration of how to minimize the extreme limitations of existing data.[30] Accountability policies should reward rather than sanction institutions effectively helping students who have not had an equal chance to prepare for college but are very eager to learn. An accountability policy that relies on flawed data or omits factors that research shows are strongly related to outcomes is likely to disproportionately punish Hispanic-serving institutions unfairly, raising serious civil rights questions.

CHAPTER 7

High-Stakes Accountability in the Context of Education Deserts

NICHOLAS HILLMAN

How do students choose where to go to college?

This simple question has no easy answers. In fact, it has been the subject of research studies for several decades, and we are still gaining new insights into the way students make education choices. One of the most promising new areas of inquiry into this topic relates to the *geography of opportunity*, where researchers study the role of community assets in shaping education destinations. Despite advances in technology and distance learning, place still matters when choosing a college, since only about one in ten undergraduates enroll in college exclusively online.[1] In the public sector of higher education, location can determine whether and where a student attends college. For policy makers who come from large metro areas where there may be dozens of colleges and a good transit system, the idea that accountability data may inform better choices and create more fruitful competition seems plausible. But when people live in thinly populated areas with limited resources and transit, the situation is fundamentally different, and standards with consequences may limit further or even end options.

For many students interested in pursuing a public college education, choices are constrained according to whatever college is located within commuting distance from home and work.[2] Considering that many students work full time, have dependents to care for, and commute to campus, the simple question about education choices becomes very complicated.[3] Instead, a more relevant question becomes, "Do place-bound students have alternative college options near home or work?" Answering this question is made even more complicated because it is entangled in the deeply rooted inequalities of our postsecondary marketplace, where communities with the greatest economic advantages are likely to be the same communities with the most robust education infrastructure. Alternatively, communities suffering from the worst forms of economic and racial inequality may have the fewest options.

In this chapter I wrestle with these issues and bring data to bear on debates about the geography of opportunity in postsecondary education. I identify education deserts, or clusters of counties where community colleges are the only public postsecondary option nearby. Approximately 34 million people live in education deserts (11 percent of the US population), and 309 community colleges operate in these communities, enrolling approximately 1.7 million students. While the definition of *education deserts* should be refined over time, the basic conclusion drawn here is enduring: students choose college based on what options are nearby, and these local markets are highly unequal.

This conclusion matters for any state or federal high-stakes accountability regime designed to reward and sanction colleges according to a number of performance measures. Such systems are often built on the assumption that students are mobile and shop around for colleges. From this vantage point, policy makers may be inclined to solve education problems by providing better information about each college's quantifiable "value." In addition to the inherent measurement problems, such an approach also fails to account for structural inequalities that exist in local communities. For any accountability system to be effective and equitable, it must be sensitive to the fact that not all students have the luxury of shopping around for a college. And not all colleges serve highly mobile students. Any accountability system that is not sensitive to the structural inequalities of place will do little to reverse them.

This chapter asks the following research questions:

1. To what extent does the number of colleges (public, nonprofit, and for-profit) vary according to a community's racial/ethnic, socioeconomic, and local labor market characteristics?
2. What are the characteristics of the communities where the fewest public higher education options exist (i.e., education deserts)?

Table 7.1   Distance from student's home to college (in miles)

	Mean	Median
Public two-year	31	8
Public four-year	82	18
Private nonprofit four-year	258	46
Total	107	13

EDUCATION DESERTS

Table 7.1 uses the 2012 National Postsecondary Student Aid Survey to document the mean and median distance between home and the place where undergraduate students enrolled.[4] Community college students tended to enroll approximately thirty miles from home, and public four-year college students were typically only about eighty miles from home.

By conceptualizing education opportunity through the lens of geography and place, we can quickly see how a community's structural environment can shape and constrain education options. As I explore later, there are several communities that have limited (and in some cases no) public options for pursuing postsecondary education. For people living in these communities, education opportunities are constrained not by their own preferences and dispositions but by their community's own education infrastructure. The phenomenon of food deserts illustrates the importance of place.[5]

The 2008 Farm Bill defines a food desert as "an area in the United States with limited access to affordable and nutritious food, particularly such an area composed of predominantly lower-income neighborhoods and communities."[6] Food deserts do not occur at random; there are systematic patterns of where these communities are located and how they have evolved. For example, predominantly Black and low-income neighborhoods have comparatively fewer supermarkets than White and higher-income neighborhoods.[7] As a result, residents of food deserts have higher probabilities of chronic illnesses related to their diets (e.g., diabetes, heart disease, and obesity) because their communities have more unhealthy or cost-prohibitive food options.[8] Structural inequalities shape individual choices, so even the most well-informed and savvy consumer living in a food desert is constrained in making healthy choices.

Figure 7.1 Number of public colleges by commuting zone (CZ) and county

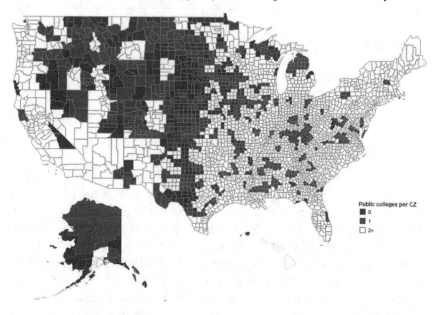

Public colleges per CZ
■ 0
■ 1
□ 2+

A corollary is true in education deserts: a prospective student may be well informed about the benefits of college yet still not enroll if there is no college nearby. I define the term *education desert* as a commuting zone that has no public colleges or has community colleges as the only public option (figure 7.1).

DATA AND RESEARCH DESIGN

To measure a local community, this study utilizes US Department of Agriculture commuting zone (CZ) classification, which is a cluster of counties sharing similar labor markets and economic activity. Charles Tolbert and Molly Sizer developed this classification scheme using journey-to-work data that measures the county-to-county flow of commuters, resulting in 708 CZs for all counties in the country.[9] Using the US Department of Education's Integrated Postsecondary Education Data System (IPEDS) for the years 2010–11 and 2012–13, each college (n=7,756) is then connected to its respective CZ.

To account for the local demographic and economic characteristics of each CZ, the analysis aggregates county-level data up to the CZ from such

Table 7.2   Variables and data sources constructed for analysis

Variable	Source
Commuting zone	US Department of Agriculture
Census regions	US Census Bureau
Rural continuum	US Department of Agriculture
Population	Census Bureau and National Center for Health Statistics
Unemployment	Bureau of Labor Statistics, Local Area Unemployment
Education attainment	US Census Bureau, American Community Survey
Income	Bureau of Economic Analysis
Manufacturing labor force	Bureau of Economic Analysis
Number of colleges	Integrated Postsecondary Education Data System

sources as the US Department of Agriculture's (USDA) Rural-Urban Continuum zones, the US Census Bureau's American Community Survey, National Center for Health Statistics, and the Bureau of Labor Statistics' Bureau of Economic Analysis (table 7.2).[10]

To answer the first research question, which examines the count of colleges per CZ, this analysis implements a Poisson regression model. The second research question, which identifies the CZ characteristics associated with being an education desert, employs a logistic regression. In both models, CZs are the unit of analysis, and the same vector of controls are included to account for observable differences between each CZ's racial/ethnic, socioeconomic, and local labor market conditions. Since each CZ is nested within its respective state, the error terms are clustered at the state level.[11] In addition, for ease of interpretation, Poisson results are displayed as incident rate ratios and the logistic results as odds ratios.

KEY FINDINGS

In the United States, half of all commuting zones are classified as education deserts, and approximately 34.2 million people (11 percent of the population) live in these areas. Education deserts contain 353 public colleges and enroll 1.7 million undergraduate students; most of these colleges (n=309) are community colleges (table 7.3 and table 7.4).

Table 7.4 shows how education desert CZs differ from other CZs on the variables included in the analysis. Education deserts differ from other

Table 7.3   Population, enrollment, and number of public colleges located in education deserts

	Number of CZs	Population (million)	Public enrollment (million)	Number of public colleges
Total	708	313.8	18.7	2,076
Education desert	405	34.2	1.7	353
Share of total	(57%)	(11%)	(9%)	(17%)

CZs in their urbanicity, where approximately 88 percent of education deserts' populations live in nonmetropolitan counties, while only 38 percent of non-desert populations live in these areas. Education deserts tend to also have smaller populations than non-deserts, but on other measures (income, unemployment rates, and manufacturing's share of the labor force) these differences are not as stark as the summary statistics displayed in table 7.4 seem to indicate. These statistics help display broad characteristics, but they do not answer the central research questions concerning the number of colleges per CZ or the odds of classifying a CZ as an education desert. For those answers, we turn to multiple regression analysis.

Research Question 1

The first research question asks how a CZ's racial/ethnic, socioeconomic, and local labor market characteristics are associated with the number of public colleges within commuting distance. The number of public options varies along racial/ethnic lines in systematic and unequal ways; namely, CZs with growing Hispanic populations are associated with having fewer public four-year and two-year college options. A 1 percent increase in Hispanic population is associated with decreasing the rate of public four-year colleges by a factor of 0.837 (83.7 percent) and 0.957 (95.7 percent). Since these rates are below 1, they suggest a negative relationship between Hispanic communities and public colleges. This relationship is statistically significant for public four-year colleges, suggesting that there are systematic inequalities around the number of public options Hispanic communities have relative to other groups. While Hispanic communities have the fewest public options, table 7.5 shows that each 1 percent rise in population increases the number of for-profit colleges by a rate of 15.4 percent.

Table 7.4   Descriptive statistics used in analysis

	Non-desert		Education desert	
	Mean	SD	Mean	SD
Northeast (New England)	4%	19%	1%	9%
Northeast (Mid-Atlantic)	7%	26%	1%	9%
Midwest (East North Central)	14%	35%	8%	27%
Midwest (West North Central)^	12%	33%	30%	46%
South (South Atlantic)	21%	41%	9%	28%
South (East South Central)	9%	28%	11%	31%
South (West South Central)	16%	36%	15%	36%
West (Mountain)	10%	30%	17%	38%
West (Pacific)	8%	27%	8%	28%
Nonmetro share of population	38%	39%	88%	28%
Asian population (logged)	9.0	1.8	5.8	1.6
American Indian population (logged)	7.8	1.4	6.0	1.6
Black population (logged)	10.3	1.9	6.9	2.2
Hispanic population (logged)	10.2	1.8	7.7	1.7
White population (logged)	12.6	1.1	10.4	1.3
Unemployment rate	9.1%	2.6%	8.5%	3.2%
Share of population with less than BA	75.7%	7.2%	81.5%	6.1%
Per-capita income (in $1,000s)	38.1	7.8	38.5	10.1
Manufacturing share of labor force	8.2%	4.5%	8.3%	7.3%

Note: ^ denotes reference group in regression analysis.

   In addition to these patterns in Hispanic communities, CZs with larger Black populations tend to have more private colleges: a 1 percent increase in Black population is associated with a greater number of private for-profit and nonprofit colleges—18.6 percent and 16.8 percent more institutions, respectively. This relationship is likely driven by the demographic trend of Blacks migrating back to the South, where many private Historically Black Colleges and Universities (HBCUs) are located. But further research is necessary to disentangle this relationship. Many of these private colleges are likely HBCUs that have a mission of serving their local communities. These patterns tell different stories according to different racial/ethnic

Table 7.5 Poisson and logistic regression estimates for number of colleges and education deserts

	RQ1: number of colleges per CZ (incident rate ratios)				RQ2: education deserts (odds ratios)
	Public 4-year	Public 2-year	Nonprofit	For-profit	
Northeast (New England)	2.132***	1.710**	1.239	0.705***	0.364
	(0.392)	(0.456)	(0.218)	(0.076)	(0.421)
Northeast (Mid-Atlantic)	1.987***	1.006	1.116	0.546***	0.121
	(0.385)	(0.179)	(0.179)	(0.085)	(0.182)
Midwest (East North Central)	1.192	0.833	0.772**	0.835	0.877
	(0.219)	(0.182)	(0.092)	(0.112)	(0.354)
South (South Atlantic)	1.222	0.858	0.546***	0.629***	1.070
	(0.200)	(0.190)	(0.075)	(0.067)	(0.620)
South (East South Central)	1.069	0.673*	0.688**	0.821	1.266
	(0.204)	(0.150)	(0.112)	(0.126)	(0.538)
South (West South Central)	1.437***	0.911	0.378***	0.862	0.580
	(0.191)	(0.231)	(0.059)	(0.175)	(0.231)
West (Mountain)	1.187	1.101	0.332***	1.184	1.250
	(0.276)	(0.223)	(0.071)	(0.241)	(0.601)
West (Pacific)	1.097	1.570*	0.951	0.873	3.212*
	(0.277)	(0.392)	(0.228)	(0.159)	(1.977)
Non-metro share of population	0.998	1.007***	1.003*	0.992***	1.005
	(0.002)	(0.002)	(0.002)	(0.002)	(0.004)
Asian population (logged)	1.321***	0.982	0.980	0.969	0.393***
	(0.108)	(0.087)	(0.085)	(0.070)	(0.113)
American Indian population (logged)	1.088**	1.124*	0.944	0.933	0.819**
	(0.047)	(0.067)	(0.051)	(0.059)	(0.080)
Black population (logged)	1.100	1.254***	1.168***	1.186***	0.779*
	(0.068)	(0.061)	(0.063)	(0.078)	(0.117)
Hispanic population (logged)	0.837***	0.957	1.088	1.154*	1.450**
	(0.050)	(0.051)	(0.065)	(0.095)	(0.237)
White population (logged)	1.290*	1.870***	2.499***	2.536***	1.041
	(0.182)	(0.194)	(0.292)	(0.307)	(0.290)
Unemployment rate	0.970	0.962*	0.938**	0.966**	1.051
	(0.023)	(0.020)	(0.030)	(0.016)	(0.079)

Table 7.5, *continued*

	RQ1: number of colleges per CZ (incident rate ratios)				RQ2: education deserts (odds ratios)
	Public 4-year	Public 2-year	Nonprofit	For-profit	
Share of population with less than BA	0.994 (0.011)	1.042*** (0.010)	0.990 (0.008)	1.014** (0.007)	1.108*** (0.036)
Per-capita income (in $1000s)	0.829 (0.187)	1.128 (0.184)	0.661*** (0.053)	0.771 (0.224)	5.419 (9.291)
Manufacturing share of labor force	0.983 (0.011)	0.992 (0.009)	1.008 (0.012)	0.984* (0.009)	1.066*** (0.024)
Observations	708	708	708	708	708
Bayesian information criterion (BIC)	1398.4	2002.7	1934.6	2176.7	626.0
Akaike information criterion	1311.7	1916.0	1847.9	2090.0	539.3
Wald Chi Square	2183.0	2061.5	5098.7	4342.2	217.8
Pseudo-R^2	0.422	0.469	0.746	0.844	0.489

Note: Clustered standard errors in parentheses. * $p<0.1$. ** $p<0.05$. *** $p<0.01$.

groups; Hispanic communities tend to have fewer public options (and more for-profit options), while Black communities tend to have both more private colleges and more community colleges, but not more public four-year colleges.

The patterns found with Hispanic and Black communities do not hold for other minority communities. CZs with large Asian populations have a large number of public four-year colleges, and American Indian CZs tend to have more public options and fewer private options (though the differences in the latter were statistically insignificant). Many of the public colleges near communities with a large share of American Indian populations are likely to be tribal colleges and universities (TCUs), but this needs to be confirmed. Unlike institutions that serve Blacks and American Indians, however, there are very few colleges founded with—and federally recognized for—the distinct mission of serving Hispanic students. The only group that consistently has more colleges (public or private) per CZ is the White population: a 1 percent increase in the White population, after controlling for other factors, is associated with increasing the rate of colleges operating in the CZ by 29 percent to 153 percent.

In addition to these racial/ethnic differences, there are inequalities with respect to local education attainment rates and the number of public colleges per CZ. Communities where a larger share of the population has less than a bachelor's degree (i.e., low education attainment levels), tend to have larger numbers of community colleges and for-profit colleges to choose from. These same communities have fewer (though not statistically significant) public four-year colleges. Structural inequalities perpetuate in CZs with low education attainment levels; they have greater access to sub-baccalaureate rather than baccalaureate degrees.

Research Question 2

In communities where public options are the most constrained, education deserts, the data show unequal patterns that cut along lines of race/ethnicity, socioeconomics, and local labor market conditions even after controlling for a number of important variables. Still, as the share of a CZ's Hispanic population rises, so does its odds of being an education desert. For each additional 1 percent increase in Hispanic population, the odds of being an education desert increase approximately 1.4 times.[12]

Consistent with findings from the count models (Research Question 1), the odds of living in an education desert decline as the numbers of American Indians and Asians rise. This is not surprising since Asians are very strongly concentrated in a few large metropolitan areas that likely have more colleges nearby, and many TCUs are public. Interestingly, a CZ's White population is no longer a systematic factor associated with being an education desert; changes in the White population are not associated with having constrained public alternatives. As the Black population increases for a CZ, the odds of it being an education desert decline. This is additional evidence that public college options are not equal across lines of race/ethnicity.

Also consistent with the count models, CZs with lower education attainment levels are more likely to be located in education deserts. As the share of a CZ with low education attainment levels rises by 1 percent, its odds of being a desert increase 1.1 times. Related, CZs with high shares of the labor force working in manufacturing industries are also more likely to be in an education desert and have the most constrained public options. A 1 percent increase in manufacturing's share of the labor force is associated with having 1.1 times greater odds of being an education desert.

Findings

When using CZs to represent local communities where people live, work, and pursue formal education, this study finds inequalities in terms of the number of public colleges and universities available to their residents. These findings should be considered in light of national demographic trends, particularly as a growing number of Hispanics are moving to nonmetropolitan communities, where low-wage work is available, and as many Blacks are migrating back to southern states.[13] Non-metropolitan communities experiencing these demographic shifts may not have the education infrastructure in place to respond to these demographic changes (e.g., Alabama and Georgia). Likewise, communities that have long been home to minority groups may not be providing an adequate education infrastructure for these groups (e.g., South Texas). In either event, local higher education markets are unequal and are drawn along lines of race and class.

One of the more striking patterns found in this study is that communities with rising shares of Hispanics tend to have fewer public (and more private) options, while Whiter communities tend to have more alternatives, public and private. Communities with growing Hispanic populations not only have fewer options, but they are the most likely to be classified as education deserts, having the fewest public options nearby. In addition to these racial/ethnic differences, a community's education attainment rate is systematically related to the number of nearby colleges. Communities with low attainment rates are characterized as having more public two-year and for-profit colleges that often do not offer bachelor's degrees. Similarly, when the share of the labor force employed in manufacturing rises, the odds of being an education desert also rises.

POLICY IMPLICATIONS

Geography of opportunity is largely missing from college access and college choice research. Not surprisingly, the importance of place has not played a significant role in ongoing federal and state policy debates concerning the potential consequences of rationing federal aid or state appropriations based on college performance. Instead, the underlying policy logic is that college choices are made independent of place and that accountability systems like the proposed federal rating system "can empower students and families to make good choices" about where to attend college.[14] This is a market-based logic that assumes students are either mobile or that they live in communities where there are several public higher education options.

This study shows the limitations of this line of thinking and demonstrates how geography and place matter in the college choice process. Building the capacity for these colleges to better serve their communities, many of which are rural and experiencing demographic and workforce changes, is likely the best way to help the nation reach its college completion goals. And failing to account for these geographic differences is a surefire way for policy makers to design high-stakes policies systems that are likely to reinforce rather than reverse structural inequalities.

If federal and state policy makers assume that all students are mobile, that they live in communities with several public alternatives, or that online education is an adequate alternative to place-based education, then the findings reported here do not bear on education equity or opportunity. However, there is a growing body of evidence to refute these claims. This study contributes to this body of evidence by exploring the geography of opportunity. It raises important implications for high-stakes accountability policies that could disproportionately burden people who live in minority communities or in communities that already have low education attainment levels.

An example illustrates the implications of these findings. The cities of Uvalde and Eagle Pass, Texas, are in the same four-county commuting zone located between San Antonio and the border town of Piedras Negras, Mexico. The Uvalde–Eagle Pass CZ has approximately 100,000 residents, most (87 percent) of whom are Hispanic. The CZ's unemployment rate is 13 percent, and approximately 87 percent of its residents have less than a bachelor's degree. Rural areas in South Texas have a long history of education inequality, and there are several communities where public colleges are either underresourced or simply unavailable to students.

The Uvalde–Eagle Pass community is serviced by Southwest Texas Junior College (STJC), which enrolls approximately six thousand undergraduate students. The only other college within a one-hundred-mile radius is Southwest School of Business and Technical Careers, a small for-profit college specializing in cosmetology certificates.[15] Sul Ross State College, a public four-year institution, offers upper-level courses at satellite locations in the CZ; however, these are not full academic degree programs, nor are they reported in US Department of Education search tools.

One of the accountability measures originally proposed in the federal rating system was a college's cohort default rate, the percent of borrowers who default on their federal loans within three years of entering repayment. Another was related to annual changes in net price, which is the cost of attendance (tuition, books, supplies, room, and board) minus all grant aid. At STJC, the cohort default rate is high (23.7 percent), its graduation rate low (21 percent), and its net price ($6,805) moderate. Depending on what measures were included in the ratings system, this college could have easily received a poor federal rating and consequently lost eligibility to federal financial aid. If this were to occur, prospective students living in this CZ would have seen their education opportunities become less affordable and more inaccessible, effectively hurting the exact students and institutions policy makers should be helping.

This policy dilemma is not unique to the Uvalde–Eagle Pass community; it can be observed in hundreds of communities across the United States. One in ten citizens live in an education desert not too dissimilar from Uvalde–Eagle Pass, Texas. Though these problems are far more prevalent in low-density communities, it is useful to realize that a combination of family economic circumstances (the need to live at home during college) and the admissions and aid policies of individual campuses can gravely limit the choices even in metro areas. Because of this, we need to think about standards that create risks for what may be the only real options for many students in other settings.

If federal or state officials are going to pursue accountability systems like those described in this volume, then they should consider geographic factors, such as whether the college is the only public option within commuting distance. Doing so might result in policy solutions that are sensitive to the differences in local education markets. For example, state or federal officials may find it advantageous to offer waivers to colleges located in education deserts so they are not disproportionately affected by high-stakes accountability regimes. Alternatively, policy makers could help build the capacity of education deserts by investing in or helping expand opportunities among the colleges located in designated areas (similar to enterprise zones).[16]

Regardless of how policy makers ultimately proceed with their policy solutions, it is important to consider the unequal geographic opportunities many students face when pursuing higher education. High-stakes accountability regimes that address this inequality are likely to avoid unintended consequences while promoting efforts to reverse structural inequalities in our nation's higher education marketplace.

CHAPTER 8

The Impact of Financial Aid Limits

A View from a Leading HBCU

WILLIE KIRKLAND

Student financial aid is a key component in providing access to Dillard University for a vast majority of its students. Dillard, a private historically black college in New Orleans, founded shortly after the Civil War, educates many low-income students. Annually, nearly all (90 percent) of Dillard students have financial need, yet only one in four receives enough aid to cover their full need. This means many students face financial pressure that can ultimately affect their progress toward earning a degree. To cover this unmet need, students often turn to loans; yet, even after taking out the maximum amount, they still have need. This is where the Parent Loans for Undergraduate Students (PLUS loan) program plays a critical role in filling the unmet financial need gap for many students.

Once a student has exhausted all other aid, namely Federal Pell Grants and guaranteed student loans, many Dillard students fall well short of having enough to cover the full cost of their education. To fill this gap, the institution's Office of Financial Aid usually recommends PLUS loans, unsubsidized high-risk loans that cannot be expunged in bankruptcy and can too often result in elderly parents' pensions being garnished. But for some families, it is the only way to financially support their child's higher education.

However, the federal government has faced significant default rates on these loans. And so when the Obama administration instituted more stringent credit worthiness requirements in an attempt to address this problem, it became harder for applicants to secure funding. The impact of high-rate loan denial during the 2012 and 2013 academic years was evident at Dillard, when 80 percent of parents seeking PLUS loans had their applications denied. Though the denial numbers improved somewhat in 2013–14, dropping to 73 percent, this meant that many students still were not getting the financial help they needed.[1]

This chapter examines what loan denial means for students as well as its implications for a leading HBCU, where tighter PLUSs loan restrictions contribute to a widening of the affordability gap. Less access to any form of financial aid in a school with many students of limited means has consequences for the institution: a lower retention rate in the short run, a lower graduation rate in the long run, smaller enrollment, and reduced revenues.

DILLARD UNIVERSITY'S HISTORY AND MISSION
AND THE KATRINA CRISIS

Founded in 1869, Dillard University has, throughout its history, touted itself as being an "avenue of opportunity" for thousands of underprivileged youth seeking to improve their lives. Its mission statement reads: "True to its heritage, Dillard University's mission is to produce graduates who excel, become world leaders and are broadly educated, culturally aware and concerned with improving the human condition. Through a highly personalized and learning centered approach, Dillard's students are able to meet the competitive demands of a diverse, global and technologically advanced society."[2] Dillard enjoys a reputation for producing world leaders. Prior to the end of segregation, Dillard was hailed as being a member of the "Black Ivy League." Among its outstanding alumni are Ruth Simmons, emeritus president of Brown University and the first African American president of an Ivy League institution; Carl Stewart, chief judge of the US Fifth Circuit Court of Appeals; and Sheila Tlou, the former health minister of Botswana and current director of UNAIDS Regional Support Team for Eastern and Southern Africa.

Currently, there are approximately 1,200 students enrolled at Dillard, and 98 percent of the student body is African American. The institution attracts students from thirty-one states and the District of Columbia (65 percent are from Louisiana) and nine foreign countries (the largest share from Brazil). The cost of attendance at Dillard is modest compared with other private HBCUs located in large to medium-sized cities and far below the overall private school average. Using criteria and data collected by the

National Center for Education Statistics (NCES), Dillard developed a peer list of nine private HBCUs it uses for comparison, among them Spelman College (Georgia), Morehouse College (Georgia), and Johnson C. Smith University (North Carolina).[3] Dillard's 2013 report shows that, for academic year 2012–13, tuition and fees amounted to $14,770, while the peer average was $17,150. In terms of the net cost of attendance, Dillard's costs were, again, lower than its peers: $15,804 compared to $17,309.[4]

Further illustrating the modest costs of attending Dillard is a comparison of its tuition and fee expenses with thirty-one other colleges and universities identified as peer institutions by NCES. This group is made up of institutions with similar characteristics, such as similar Carnegie classifications, private nonprofit status, and similar enrollment size, and includes Hanover College (Indiana), Maryville College (Tennessee), Oglethorpe College (Georgia), and Claremont McKenna College (California). Importantly, this list does not include any HBCUs. Data from 2012–13 show that the average annual tuition and fees for the comparison group is $30,522 compared to $14,770 for Dillard. The average tuition and fees charged by the comparison group schools is twice what Dillard charges.[5] Yet, despite the school's relatively modest cost, many of its students face financial challenges: 40 percent of its students are first generation and 39 percent come from families with annual incomes below $40,000. For families in this income range, even Dillard's modest net costs, even after aid, present a very real financial challenge.

In 2005, Hurricane Katrina struck New Orleans and devastated Dillard's campus. In Katrina's wake, freshmen retention declined sharply from 73 percent to 45 percent, and overall enrollment declined 44 percent, from 1,993 to 1,124. There was also a significant decline in the number of out-of-state students, from 48 percent in 2005 to 35 percent in 2012.[6]

Parents from outside the state, hearing reports of a lack of essential city services, were afraid to send their children to New Orleans. Even after most services had been restored, the perception persisted around the country. The university's infrastructure was damaged by the catastrophe. Some dormitories remained closed for a few years, the library was offline for nearly a year, and many classrooms were unusable due to flood damage. Further, many families who lived in the area did not move back after the hurricane. This was especially critical, since at that time nearly one-third of Dillard's student body came from New Orleans and the surrounding area.

The first post-Katrina freshmen cohort arrived in the fall of 2006. It had only 222 students, far below the 500-plus freshmen who matriculated in

2005. The first-to-second-year retention rate for that cohort was 61 percent. This meant that the entering class had been cut by more than half, and two-fifths of those who did come left at some point during their first year. Over the next two years, the cohorts remained small, with 175 in 2007 and 173 in 2008. But in the fall of 2009, for the first time since the storm, the institution enrolled more than 300 new freshmen, a threshold that was met for the next four years. However, during 2010 and 2011, the first-to-second-year retention rate dropped to 65 percent and 61 percent, respectively. By 2012, the rate rose to 67 percent, though it fell back to 58 percent in the fall of 2013. Despite these declines, the size of the new freshman cohorts stabilized above 300 (save for 2013, when fewer than 250 enrolled). This stabilized environment made planning easier, as consistent enrollment patterns emerged.[7]

ACCOUNTABILITY PRESSURES AND STUDENT SUCCESS

Since the 2000s, there has been increasing external environmental pressure on higher education institutions centered on student retention and graduation rates, among other issues. The Spellings Commission became the impetus for reforming how colleges and universities prepare students.[8] With prodding from regional accreditation bodies, which, in turn, are responding to pressure from the US Department of Education, Dillard and many other institutions have become more vigilant in monitoring their retention and graduation rates since they now must report their retention, graduation, and placement rates, among other things, to the public. Many private colleges were susceptible to these pressures due to their reliance on federal funding.

Pressure has also come from internal stakeholders taking note of the link between attrition and budget woes. In the case of Dillard, declining enrollment and lower freshman retention rates have combined to reduce revenues derived from tuition and fees, resulting in increased fiscal stress on the institution. Both administrators and trustees understand that increasing retention will alleviate financial pressures and that there are likely some key factors driving retention.

Institutional leaders operate in an environment where constraints are numerous. Where an institution focuses its attention is often influenced by external as well as internal pressures. External pressures emanate from various stakeholders, such as accreditation bodies, parents, the business community, alumni, and government officials. Internal pressures often originate from faculty, students, staff, and trustees. At Dillard, the declining retention rate exacerbated the institution's financial stability.

In the face of financial pressure brought on by declining or static enrollment, in 2009 the institution embarked on a sustained austerity strategy. As revenues fell below expenditures, administrators reduced spending, and thus forcing some very difficult cuts. One area that came under intense scrutiny was the size of the faculty. In 2008, Dillard employed 104 full-time faculty members; by 2009 that number dropped to 92 and by 2010 to 82. Currently, there are 58 full-time faculty members. While there has been a rapid decline in full-time faculty, there has also been a rapid rise in part-time faculty. In 2009 there were 23 part-time faculty, and currently, there are 86 part-time faculty, representing a 274 percent increase over four years. In 2011, full-time faculty taught over 80 percent of all sections; however, by 2013 they were teaching less than 60 percent of all sections.[9] Changes on this scale threaten the institution's character, and an inadequate full-time faculty also has the potential to affect accreditation.

In this context, at Dillard and so many other institutions, any policy that significantly restricts student access to financial aid is likely to contribute to greater student attrition, as many students will have to find work, and thereby attend school only part time, in order to fill the gap or look to another institution or even abandon a college education altogether.

According to NCES, nationally, about 41 percent of traditional students are employed; 16 percent work fewer than 20 hours per week and 17 percent work more than 20 hours per week.[10] In October 2014, 59 percent of Dillard students were employed (a rate 18 percent higher than the national average), and 52 percent of these students indicated that they work to pay for college expenses. Of those who work, 80 percent work off-campus jobs, with 63 percent working three to five days a week, 38 percent working 21 or more hours per week, and 24 percent working 16–20 hours per week.[11]

Since 94 percent of Dillard's students are enrolled full time and carry an average load of fifteen hours per semester, work demands can be particularly troublesome for many students and, according to the vice president for Student Success, jeopardize their academic success.[12] Even those able to keep up with the demands of both work and school suffer emotional distress, and some require counseling.

Not just limited to tuition and fees, students' financial hardships extend to housing and food. The director of Residential Life noted cases of students who are homeless, living house to house or in a car, all the while worried about running out of the money necessary to continue their studies.[13]

FINANCIAL AID AND STUDENT RETENTION

In turning its focus to retention, Dillard's senior leadership challenged various offices to find ways to assist in increasing retention. While administrators knew about the retention rate and the way it was trending, no one at the institution had an inkling about which factors may be driving the phenomenon. Accordingly, the director of Institutional Research designed a retention study specific to Dillard.

Much of what we know about financial aid and retention at HBCUs is limited to subjective assessments by leaders of individual institutions.[14] For instance, according to James Scannell, "Variables such as amount of borrowing, unmet need, and level of grant sometimes emerge as statistically significant variables in predictive models, but their influence on behavior is minor."[15] In its study, Dillard found unmet need to be a major influence on retention, even though Dillard's student body differs from those institutions cited by Scannell. In examining the 2010, 2011, and 2012 cohorts, William Kirkland found that the influence of this variable was subject to changes in the first-year matriculation cycle.[16] These findings drew attention to establishing reliability by building on and expanding the time frame of the initial study.

Analysis from the Office of Institutional Research showed that reduced access to financial aid harmed retention. To reinforce this, it was critical to establish a long-term linkage. Confirming the relationship and acting on it could greatly enhance enrollment and budgetary planning by infusing more reliability into the planning process. It could also provide key information to help students understand the importance of financial literacy.

ANALYSIS AND RESULTS

Data for this study are drawn from the records of Dillard University's Offices of Records and Registration, Admissions, and Financial Aid. The focus is the 2010, 2011, and 2012 first-time freshmen cohorts.

For the purpose of this study, a *returnee* is defined as an individual who entered the university as part of a cohort group in a given fall semester and who reenrolled in the fall semester of the next year. A *nonreturnee* is a student from that cohort who did not reenroll. In aggregate, the study tracked 1,046 cohort members during the first to second years. Table 8.1 summarizes this data, showing average levels of financial need and need that goes unmet by gift aid across each cohort. Here we see that students who left

Table 8.1   Average financial aid differences between returnees and non-returnees

	2010 cohort group		2011 cohort group		2012 cohort group	
	Need	Unmet need	Need	Unmet need	Need	Unmet need
Returnees	$21,386	$2,527	$22,693	$3,452	$24,112	$4,212
Non-returnees	$22,765	$6,355	$22,412	$7,034	$23,762	$7,692
Difference		–$3,828		–$3,582		–$3,480

Table 8.2   Cross-tabulation of PLUS loan application status by retention status

		Applied	
	Did not apply	Approved	Denied
Returnees	63%	60%	52%
Non-returnees	37%	40%	48%
Total	100%	100%	100%

after their sophomore year tended to have $3,500 more in unmet need than those who persisted.

This unmet need could have been covered by a PLUS loan, but table 8.2 shows students who did not return and who also did not have their loan applications approved. The table also shows that students whose parents' loan application was denied were less likely to return for the second year than either those whose parents were approved for a loan and those whose parents did not apply. There is little difference between the return rate of students whose parents did not apply and those whose parents applied and were approved. Based on these results, it can be argued that new freshmen whose parents are denied a PLUS loan tend leave the institution at a higher rate than other new freshmen. Moreover, the results imply that the loan may equalize access for students whose parents qualify for those loans to a rate comparable with students whose parents do not need access to that loan. It stands to reason that if loan requirements were made less stringent, more parents would be approved for the loan, which may result in a higher retention rate for the institution.

Table 8.3 Regression estimates of student retention

	2010 cohort	2011 cohort	2012 cohort
Original need	0.001	0.036	0.121***
Unmet need	−0.230***	−0.136***	−0.155***
Percent unmet need	0.002	−0.815	0.273
PLUS loan Denial			−0.704*
Observations	341	354	351

Note: Estimates control for student academic background, hours attempted, and residency status (*p<.05, **p<.01, ***p<.001).

The analysis goes one step further by implementing a logistic regression model to see if PLUS loan denial is still significantly related to leaving college. The model includes nine independent variables:

- in-state student versus out-of-state student
- first semester GPA
- course hours taken first semester
- on-campus resident versus commuter
- high school GPA
- ACT composite score
- original financial aid need amount
- unmet financial aid need amount
- percent of unmet financial aid need

Unmet need and original amounts represent first-year aid packages. The loan denial data is limited to the 2012 cohort; nevertheless, comparing this cohort to previous cohorts can reveal helpful patterns. Table 8.3 shows that PLUS loan denial was the strongest predictor of leaving college, even after controlling for the variables.

Results from table 8.3 also show how unmet need is negatively related to retention. This is consistent with the earlier finding that, at Dillard, students with high unmet need leave at disproportionately higher rates. That this pattern holds even after accounting for several important controls illustrates the strong relationship between finances and enrollment. Ultimately, the combination of high unmet need and PLUS loan denial likely reinforce one another, effectively pushing students out of college when more money could help them stay enrolled.

IMPLICATIONS FOR POLICY AND PRACTICE

This study of the impact certain factors have on student retention attempts to answer the question of whether unmet financial need is predictive of first-to- second-year retention at Dillard University. It concludes that the answer is yes. Unmet need is a consistent predictor of retention, and the strength of its influence varies during the first-year matriculation cycle. The study also finds that denial of PLUS loan applications is negatively related to student retention. Given that many students are dependent on financial aid to obtain as well as maintain access to the university, it is imperative to understand the consequences of denying aid to students and to leaving them with unmet need. Quality planning, buttressed by meaningful assessment, is essential for Dillard as it seeks to determine the extent to which it is achieving its mission. Administrators, staff, faculty, and students from other higher education institutions can also benefit from the knowledge explicated in this research.

Forces beyond the control of college administrators often impinge on plans and strategies for managing their institutions. Yet, many are held accountable for negative outcomes that emanate from their institutions. In the case of budget shortfalls, there may be external factors that negatively affect outcomes, the availability of financial aid to disadvantaged students being one such factor. This study demonstrates a clear link between unmet financial aid need and student retention. Government policies that restrict access to financial aid may have an indirect negative impact on the budget of institutions serving a large disadvantaged population. If access to aid becomes more restrictive for those who need it for access to Dillard, it is expected to have a negative impact on the institution's budget.

Like many minority-serving institutions, Dillard also recruits and enrolls a sizeable share of first-generation and low-income students, further compounding its ability to obtain a high graduation rate. For institutions that enroll a sizeable number of low-income students, the ability to retain and graduate those students is often compromised by the students' family resources. According to David Deming, "In the U.S., more so than in other countries, you as a family are making a larger and riskier investment in your own future."[17]

Dillard and other minority-serving institutions will be disadvantaged by an accountability standard like the crude graduation rate. It seems unfair that an institution that offers an avenue for social mobility for numerous disadvantaged students could be subject to withdrawal of federal funds for enrolling students who need assistance the most. In fact, one wonders whether such a policy would be counterproductive and lead to fewer opportunities for upward mobility for low-income students who do not have outstanding precollegiate credentials and therefore have little chance of attending highly selective institutions.

In addition to negatively impacting the budget, there are accountability issues institutions will have to grapple with. As colleges and universities are expected to post their graduation and retentions rates for prospective students, lower retention and graduation rates may impact their ability to attract new students, thus compounding the ability to grow or maintain enrollment. Although this study focuses on Dillard, the findings have implications for other HBCUs, as well as the majority of institutions with a sizeable minority population that depends on financial aid. If such institutions focus on disaggregating their student bodies, they may identify groups of students who are negatively impacted by a reduction in access to aid, and the implication is that their budgets, retention rates, and graduation rates may decline.

Finally, this research indirectly highlights the problem of using a one-size-fits-all accountability metrics such as retention or graduation rates as accountability measures when it is clear that the makeup of the student body, in terms of disadvantaged students, affects the rates at some institutions more than others. Many institutions, especially those serving large numbers of minority students, have little control over the financial challenges or future employment of (or wages paid to) their students. Yet, institutions that serve primarily middle-to-upper-income students may not face such challenges. The nature of the students served may be enough of an advantage for those types of schools to meet accountability standards with greater ease.

This research is intended to be a catalyst for other HBCUs to study the impact of unmet need on their ability to retain students. A further expansion of this research to include a larger number of minority-serving institutions could potentially give more credence to the voices of HBCU administrators who have been critical of government policies that result in retrenchment of financial aid opportunities for the disadvantaged students they serve.

CHAPTER 9

Student Debt Accountability and Its Unintended Racial Consequences

SARA GOLDRICK-RAB AND JASON HOULE

Students are deeply concerned with rising student loan debt levels and the risks associated with repaying loans long into the future. Yet, federal loans are now a common experience in US higher education. Half of all first-year undergraduates accept federal loans, with the median debt among college seniors amounting to about $20,000 in 2011–12.[1] In 2014, total outstanding student loan debt recently surpassed $1.11 trillion, up more than 10 percent in one year, and more than 10 percent of students are currently at least ninety days delinquent, a rate that has nearly doubled over the last decade.[2] With this, policy makers are increasingly vocal about their concerns with the size of loans, their purposes, and the likelihood that they will not be repaid, along with the potential impact of student loan debt on the economic, psychological, and social well-being of young American adults.

The high price of college, even at public colleges and universities, renders loans a necessity for many cash-strapped students and their families.[3] But the recent wave of high-stakes accountability policies from the federal government aimed at reducing student debt threatens to curtail access to loans, thus making a very bad situation far worse. These efforts include

- institutional accountability for student borrowing via close scrutiny of default rates
- risk-sharing proposals that ask colleges to "put some skin in the game" by directly covering part of the cost for making student loans

- tightened eligibility for loans borrowed by parents on behalf of their students, which is meant to prevent parents from taking on debt that they cannot afford to repay
- calls for additional data from the US Department of Education on delinquencies and defaults to provide better information and put serious pressure on colleges.

These are well-intentioned efforts, but they suffer from a basic problem: they misdiagnose the drivers of debt and default. Student debt is growing so fast largely because of state disinvestment from public higher education, the long growth of the for-profit industry (until the recent past), real declines in family income, and massive decreases in family wealth among critical populations, including African Americans and Latinos. Default rates are rising because of low college completion rates, debt held by low-income families, and jobs not providing income sufficient to pay off debt. These efforts are intended to wage war on student debt, but it is war that is deeply flawed and misguided. Its approach threatens the positive benefits of the student loan program while failing to address its very real problems. Students of color and those from economically vulnerable backgrounds will bear the consequences of this war, as their ability to pay for college will diminish as their rates of participation shrink. Instead of fixing these problems, current efforts will result in the underwriting of student loans by colleges, which will only make current problems worse. because the job of underwriters at banks and insurance companies is to assess risks and reject loans or insurance where the risk is too high. Their fundamental job is to protect the lender, not to equalize opportunity.

Such a move will violate the basic premise of the federal student loan program: students have a right to a loan because they enrolled in college and show financial need. The information gained from analyses of default rates will be used in Congress or conservative administrations to introduce credit checks of the types installed for the Parent Loans for Undergraduate Students (PLUS loans) program in 2011. The evidence suggests that as a result of those tightened restrictions, college enrollment rates fell for African Americans because borrowing by their parents was their only way to meet high college prices. Trying to fix price problems with means that unintentionally harm those who are most vulnerable and least likely to attain college credentials will exacerbate inequality.

Let's be clear about the politics of the current situation. At this time, the Republican Party (and the president) seeks to end access to federally backed student loans and weaken or close the Department of Education, which could make it nearly impossible for many low-income people and people of color to pay for college. Colleges and universities must seek to do well on accountability metrics in order to protect essential access to federal aid. Many are fearful of being penalized for cohort default rates and are thus willing to restrict access to federal loans to avoid risk. Witness the growth in concerns expressed by financial aid officers and even Congress about "overborrowing"—the idea that students are borrowing more money than they need to for college. There is no evidence to support the claim of overborrowing, nor is there any evidence which suggests that overborrowing is a driver of loan default. Instead, this is an indication that institutions are grasping for ways to comply with accountability and blaming the students. Financial literacy and loan counseling are popular, but borrowing in an era of such high prices is rarely a choice, and treating it as such can be seriously misleading. On this front, recent research finds no correlation between financial literacy and outstanding student loan debt.[4]

In this chapter, we explain why these discussions must take into account a critical issue conspicuously absent from most public debate about reforming higher education financing, and student loans in particular. There is a severe racial disparity in families' needs to borrow for college, such that Black students depend much more heavily on access to loans and leave college with a great deal more in student loan debt than do their White counterparts. Research indicates that family wealth has powerful impacts on college opportunities, exhibiting effects even stronger than those played by family income. Moreover, racial disparities in wealth are large, growing, and unlikely to disappear anytime soon. Black students—whose families disproportionately do not own homes or have retirement accounts and who cannot rely on intergenerational transfers for support—are far more likely to not only borrow federal subsidized and unsubsidized loans but also to have fewer alternative sources of credit beyond PLUS loans. Indeed, our analyses indicate that differences in parental net worth and home ownership explain a substantial portion of the Black-White gap in student loan debt among young adults.

Therefore, policies that penalize students and/or schools for borrowing, or make it harder to borrow, will likely have severe unintended consequences for education opportunities overall and racial equity in particular. Simply put, restricting borrowing for college without first substantially reducing the price of attending college has great potential to disproportionately harm the college opportunities of Black and Latino students. Ironically, while the federal student loan program aims to expand choice, these restrictions will effectively limit Black students' college choices by undermining the financial security of colleges and universities where they comprise the majority of undergraduates. Historically Black Colleges and Universities (HBCUs) will be disproportionately affected by proposed reforms, primarily due to the lack of family wealth among students they serve and their historical underfunding when compared to predominantly White institutions. Extending college opportunities to all Americans is critical to sustaining the national economy and providing hope for future generations. Efforts to deal with current student debt problems must be careful to address the root causes of debt to avoid inadvertently limiting the college prospects of any group.

BACKGROUND

At the inception of the federal financial aid system, participation in higher education was much less robust than it is today, and the choice of colleges and universities far less plentiful. College was the privilege of the few rather than the domain of the many. Over the next forty years, the landscape dramatically shifted. People from all walks of life made their way to college, convinced by economic and political arguments that a postsecondary education was no longer optional—even if it never truly became affordable.[5] Since 1974, the number of students in postsecondary education has doubled.[6]

A change in college financing accompanied that swing in college attendance.[7] When college enrollment was largely confined to students with stronger academic backgrounds and from families with more resources, grant aid was viewed as the appropriate way to help a small number of lower-income individuals afford college.[8] Even so, debates over the best way to achieve that goal kept the focus on college choice front and center, shaping the decision to invest in student-centered grants as vouchers rather than institutional grants.[9] Over time, the emphasis on grant aid eroded, and loan programs became the primary mechanism to make it possible for families to aid students.[10]

The Middle Income Student Assistance Act of 1978 expanded federal student loan programs to all students by removing the income cap for unsubsidized loans made to students.[11] The government did not pay the cost but did provide a guarantee of repayment, which could be very costly. Then, during the 1980 reauthorization of the Higher Education Act, the PLUS loan program was created to enable parents to more easily borrow money to help their children pay for college, shifting the costs of subsidizing loans from government to parents.[12] The program originally limited borrowing to $3,000 per year (about $8,600 in 2014 dollars), with a total lifetime limit of $15,000.[13] The idea was to prevent excessive, sometime unpayable, parent indebtedness. In 1986, however, those loan limits were increased to $4,000 per year (about $8,700 in 2014 dollars) and a total limit of $20,000.[14] In 1992 the borrowing limit increased again to be equivalent to the amount of a student's unmet financial need (as measured by the total cost), enabling large loans, and the lifetime loan limit was removed entirely.[15]

As the list price of attending college rose at 4–5 percent above the rate of inflation in the 1980s, with the largest increases occurring in the private sector, more families took out loans to cover those costs.[16] The percentage of students borrowing federal subsidized or unsubsidized loans increased from 27 percent in 1989–90 to 52 percent in 2011–2012.[17] Similarly, while only 2.5 percent of students had PLUS loans in 1995–96, with an average value of about $8,700 (in 2011 dollars), this rose to 4.5 percent of students in 2011–12, whose parents took an average loan of nearly $12,100.[18]

LOAN PROGRAMS UNDER SCRUTINY

Positive feelings about student loans and the choices they engendered eroded during the Great Recession. As the cost of attending college remained high, while incomes declined, more American families turned to federal and state grant aid—and found it insufficient. Today, net price (the difference between the cost of attendance minus a family's expected contribution and all grant aid received) is substantial for middle-, moderate-, and low-income families. Dependent students in the lowest income quartile face an average net price of $12,300 per year, 59 percent of the typical family income. Even students in the third quartile face a net price of 25 percent of their family income.[19] While the Federal Pell Grant is available to every qualified student, its purchasing power has been so severely diminished that it effectively serves as a gateway to student loans for most families, not a solution.[20] State aid programs are overtaxed, with long waiting lists of eligible students and high barriers to qualification. Under these circumstances, many families feel that they *need* loans to exercise any sort of college choice.

Today, about half of students borrow the maximum annual subsidized loan of $3,500 for first-year students, $4,500 for second-year students, and

$5,500 for all other students.[21] About 60 percent of students who take out a loan borrow the maximum subsidized and unsubsidized loans of $5,500 for first-year dependent students or $9,500 for first-year independent students, $6,500 or $10,500 for second-year students, and $7,500 or $12,500 for all other students up to a lifetime limit of $31,000 for dependent students or $57,500 for independent students.[22] But students who borrow federal loans are still left with unmet need. After taking all grant, loan, and work-study aid into account, they have to come up with an average of $7,900 more to pay for college. Between 2003–04 and 2008–09, the proportion of students borrowing private loans grew from 5 percent to 14 percent, before falling back to 6 percent in 2011–12. Rates of borrowing are higher among Black students than White or Hispanic students.[23] Private loans are widely considered "one of the riskiest ways to finance a college education," given their higher and variable interest rates and limited protections for borrowers.[24]

Policy makers have become concerned about the use of federal loans for several reasons and have even begun to talk about restricting access to those loans. Chief among these reasons are high and rising rates of student default, which have increased in spite of the introduction of income-based repayment plans designed to eliminate the need to default in tough economic times. Ten percent of students who left college with loans in 2011 defaulted on those loans within two years, up for the sixth consecutive year and double the average default rate from 2000 to 2006.[25] Seventeen percent of federal loans are at least thirty-one days delinquent, representing at least two million borrowers.[26] Many others defer repayment and may default much later. These numbers have led to concerns about the ability of borrowers to ever repay federal loans. This is particularly the case for PLUS loans, which do not have income-based repayment options and sometimes cannot be paid off by aging parents.

In addition, some have pointed to the low college graduation rates of students taking federal loans and raised questions about the types of institutions where borrowing is more common.[27] Borrowers often have lower rates of graduation than nonborrowers, and students who take loans are substantially overrepresented at for-profit colleges and universities and somewhat overrepresented at HBCUs.[28] But these descriptive trends can be misleading, since such statistics do not prove that borrowing harms students' chances of graduating from college or that attending certain institutions causes students to borrow.

In fact, there is very limited empirical evidence to support either of those claims in general and only some evidence to buttress them for specific schools and populations. It is difficult to ascertain the causal impacts of loans, since borrowing is often conditional based on factors that are not observed by researchers, and decisions about loan *taking* may precede decisions about college attendance or persistence. Policy makers do not know who did not come to college because of the price.[29] The strongest available evidence at the institutional level exists for the for-profit sector, where studies indicate that availability of federal student aid drives up the cost of attendance, forcing students to borrow more.[30] No such evidence exists for HBCUs or other types of colleges and universities. At the student level, reviews of research examining the impact of loan programs in the United States show mixed results, with most studies estimating null effects for White and minority students alike.[31] However, some studies have found that Black students who borrow are more likely to graduate or persist than Black students who do not borrow, although the estimates in these studies likely suffer from selection bias.[32] The PLUS loan program itself has never been systematically evaluated.

Given a lack of evidence on how loans impact college attainment, the media has instead focused on the evidence that debt—and particularly PLUS loan debt—is detrimental for postcollege life. Policy analyst Kevin Carey called the PLUS loan the "Federal Parent Rip-Off Loan," asserting that many families will never be able to repay those loans and that the terms are unfavorable to students.[33] Two analysts suggested that the federal government should make it more difficult for families to obtain PLUS loans, even going so far as to call for the elimination of the program in favor of increasing loan limits and/or income-based repayment plans for subsidized loans.[34]

The federal government took actions to tighten the definition of *adverse credit*, again reducing access to PLUS loans. In October 2011, without public announcement, the Department of Education amended the definition to include accounts in collections or written off in the last five years.[35] This is particularly problematic, given that the number of families with adverse credit under this definition grew substantially during the Great Recession. Students who had previously been approved for PLUS loans were denied them, leaving some scrambling for additional resources.[36] Although the Department of Education does not make available PLUS loan denial (or default) data by college, it did release denial data by broad sector for the first time in early 2014 in response to demands from a rulemaking committee. The percentage of credit checks that resulted in loan denials rose from 22 percent in 2010–11 to 28 percent in 2011–12 and 42 percent in 2012–13.[37]

On the one hand, these restrictions might be sensible, since "the downside to the growth in PLUS loans is that some families have borrowed more than they can repay."[38] The growing fraction of students attending college but not completing a degree and leaving with debt is certainly a cause for concern. On the other hand, the impacts of loans are likely heterogeneous, helping some students attend college and complete degrees while exerting no effect for others.[39] Thus, eliminating loans entirely could have two impacts leading in different directions: postcollege outcomes might be improved for one group of students who fail to finish at the cost of reducing possible college attainment for another group of students. For this reason, policy makers need to pay careful attention to the color of student debt.

THE COLOR OF STUDENT DEBT

Despite the fact that most PLUS loan borrowers are White, Black students and their families are *disproportionately* reliant on student loans for college access. This fact must be considered when weighing the consequences of changing student loan programs. According to the 2010 Survey of Consumer Finances, Black adults are about twice as likely to have student debt as White adults (34 percent compared to 16 percent), and an analysis of the National Longitudinal Study of Youth 1997 data reveal that Black young adults carry substantially more debt than White young adults while receiving lower incomes after completion.[40] According to data from the National Postsecondary Student Aid Study (displayed in table 9.1), 52 percent of Black students took out a student loan in 2011–12, compared to 42 percent of White students, 36 percent of Hispanic students, and 28 percent of Asian students.[41]

Not only have Black students historically borrowed more than White students, but the growth in take-up rates of federal student loans in recent decades is also greater for Black students than White students. This is especially true for unsubsidized loans: over that period, the take-up rate tripled for White students and quadrupled for Black students. Moreover, while the average size of the loan taken by a Black or a White student is nearly the same (~$8,000 in 2011–12), that amount represents a much larger fraction

Table 9.1   Federal loan take-up rates and amounts borrowed by institution type and race/ethnicity, 1995–96 to 2011–12

	Percent with any loan					Amount of total loan ($, among borrowers)				
	1995–96	1999–2000	2003–4	2007–8	2011–12	1995–96	1999–2000	2003–4	2007–8	2011–12
Race/ethnicity										
White	25.5	28.8	34.2	39.0	41.9	6,529	7,542	7,817	9,015	8,590
Black	31.3	35.6	41.9	49.5	52.3	5,894	6,875	6,861	8,091	8,047
Hispanic	22.0	25.0	29.5	34.5	35.6	5,717	6,720	6,983	8,314	7,970
Asian	22.7	21.8	24.1	25.8	28.4	6,510	7,274	7,687	8,546	8,650
Native American	23.5	23.4	30.0	35.9	43.0	5,805	6,097	6,539	6,641	7,051
Institution type										
Non-HBCU	25.0	28.1	33.9	38.7	41.6	6,362	7,339	7,528	8,705	8,356
HBCU	58.0	62.2	40.5	65.9	65.3	6,175	7,154	8,435	9,074	10,164
4-year public	37.9	40.6	46.0	47.8	50.2	6,282	6,661	7,308	8,406	8,615
4-year private nonprofit	47.7	52.1	56.7	61.0	62.6	7,606	9,394	9,758	11,902	11,292
2-year public	4.4	5.5	9.4	13.2	17.6	3,635	4,466	4,173	4,429	4,731
For-profit	56.8	75.4	77.4	85.1	73.0	6,123	7,427	7,620	9,148	8,430
Overall	25.5	28.6	34.1	39.1	41.9	6,355	7,333	7,553	8,714	8,397

Source: National Postsecondary Student Aid Study.

Notes: (1) All values adjusted for inflation to 2011–12 dollars using the Consumer Price Index.
(2) No private loan receipt data were available in the 1995–96 NPSAS.

of Black students' family income and their own future earnings. Analysts believe that the Black/White disparities in federal loan taking would be even larger if more community colleges serving minority students opted to participate in federal student loan programs.[42]

With the dearth of available grant aid, federal loans are especially important to Black students, who are still much more likely than White students to leave college without a degree because of financial problems.[43] At the same time, Blacks are much more likely to worry about paying off their debt and more likely to default on their loans, mainly because they are less likely to be employed (partly due to labor market discrimination) and more likely have lower earnings than Whites (partly due to wage discrimination).[44] They are also discriminated against when it comes to securing credit outside of the federal student loan system and face higher borrowing costs in the form of subprime and higher-interest loans.[45]

THE RACIAL WEALTH GAP

Disparities in student debt are closely related to the stark racial disparities in wealth characterizing American society. A long history of economic and political disadvantages has generated enormous Black/White disparities in wealth, which, in turn, affect education attainment and intergenerational mobility.[46] While the federal financial aid system focuses on family income, research shows that parental net worth is a stronger determinant of postsecondary outcomes.[47]

The racial wealth gap is extraordinarily large. Estimates vary, but most suggest that White families hold at least about eight times as much wealth as Black families (one estimate puts the figure at closer to twenty times).[48] Between 1984 and 2009, the absolute racial gap in wealth increased by $151,000.[49] Moreover, the racial wealth gap increased dramatically during the recessionary period, as minority families lost more wealth (in percentage terms) than their White counterparts.[50] Today, the median wealth of White families is $124,000, compared to $16,000 for Black families.[51] The racial wealth gap is three times larger than the racial income gap and more unequal than ever before, and it exists among families of all income levels.[52]

Consider Min Zhan and Deirdre Lanesskog's analysis of students in the National Longitudinal Survey of Youth young adult sample that enrolled in college for the first time between 2000 and 2004.[53] While the annual family income of White students outstripped that of Black students by $23,000, their wealth advantage was almost $134,000. The debt-to-assets ratio for Black families was nearly 50 percent higher than that for White families. The authors note, "Debt looms larger for black families, so they are less able to pay it off"—yet, at the same time, their lack of assets makes it more likely that they will need to go further into debt to obtain a college education.[54]

Racial disparities in wealth are largely due to disparities in rates of employment, years of home ownership, levels of education, and differences in inheritances, as well as variation in income.[55] While the Great Recession destroyed the wealth of some White families, it virtually "hammered out" the wealth of the majority of Black middle-class families.[56] The wealth of white families declined by 11 percent, while the wealth of Black families declined by 31 percent.[57] Compared to Whites, Black families were 38 percent more likely to have fallen into debt during the Great Recession and 74 percent more likely to have lost at least $250,000.[58]

What Melvin Oliver and Thomas Shapiro call "asset poverty," the lack of economic resources to support one's household in the absence of income, can make it extraordinarily difficult not only to begin college but also to persist and graduate.[59] With income volatility on the rise and fewer social support programs, family wealth helps ensure the continuity and momentum of education trajectories.[60] Some evidence indicates that if Black and White families had similar levels of wealth, Blacks would attend college at higher rates and Black and Whites would graduate from college at the same rate.[61]

FINANCIAL AID ELIGIBILITY AND FAMILY WEALTH

The way that eligibility for federal student financial aid is calculated may exacerbate racial disparities in borrowing. Despite a paradigmatic shift in focus from income to wealth in most other areas of social policy, higher education policy continues to emphasize family income as the way to understand a family's available resources for college.

The Free Application for Federal Student Aid (FAFSA), which determines federal financial aid eligibility, does not take into account many assets, including: money invested in qualified retirement accounts, such as individual retirement accounts (IRAs), 401(k) plans, 403(b)s, Simplified Employee Pension IRAs, and pension plans; equity in the primary home; and small businesses that a family owns and controls. These assets do not reduce a family's eligibility for financial aid despite demonstrable evidence that families secure education advantages using this wealth. For example, Michael Lovenheim finds that, for lower-income families, each $10,000 in home equity raises the prospect of college enrollment by about 5.7 percentage points.[62]

Families can further enhance their ability to qualify for financial aid (particularly grant aid) by putting savings in the names of other relatives, delaying gifts to students, reducing or repositioning assessable assets (e.g., by making large purchases before the child begins college), and timing income correctly (e.g., avoiding capital gains, maximizing retirement plan contributions, and minimizing withdrawals). To the extent that wealthier families more often possess nonassessable assets and are better equipped to know about and take advantage of these strategies, they secure more federal grant support and depend less heavily on loans, more readily obtaining a college education for their children.[63]

The omission of most family assets in the calculation of federal student aid is the result of policy changes that began in the early 1990s. More recently, Congress has continued toward disregarding assets, coming close to eliminating the remaining six asset questions in 2009. These changes would have simplified the application for financial aid, possibly improving access to aid for students for low-income families, but they may also have reserved somewhat more funding for low-income families with assets.[64]

Perhaps even more importantly for minority students, the federal student aid application overlooks debt. Without accounting for a family's debt-to-asset ratio, Black students are disproportionately likely to receive less financial aid than they need. Not only are White families more likely than Black families to have positive net worth, but they are also far less likely to have negative net worth.[65] In fact, nearly one-third of all Black families reported having zero or negative wealth in 2009.[66] Students whose families have negative wealth are likely to need more help than those whose families have low incomes but have at least some assets. Students whose families have more moderate incomes may also have no wealth or even negative wealth and yet be expected to pay an Estimated Family Contribution (EFC) similar to that calculated for a moderate-income family owning a $2 million small business. But the federal needs analysis does not allow these students to receive any additional financial assistance beyond the stated cost of attendance, even when it is needed not only to pay for that EFC but also to help ensure that the family stays afloat while the child is in college.[67]

The evidence suggests that a portion of the racial disparity in student loan debt can be traced back to family background, and particularly family wealth. To more directly test this claim, we used data from a nationally representative longitudinal data set of young adults (the National Longitudinal Study of Youth 1997 cohort) and examined racial disparities in outstanding student loan debt at age twenty-five.[68] We find that Black young adults report 130 percent more debt than their White counterparts in young adulthood. Moreover, regression analyses indicate that racial disparities in parents' socioeconomic status and wealth account for over a third (35 percent) of the Black-White student loan debt in young adulthood.[69]

Clearly, many Black students face a catch-22. Given their lack of wealth, which stems from the "sedimentation of racial inequality," they are far more likely to need loans in order to attend and complete college.[70] Indeed as Brandon Jackson and John Reynolds note, loans could help ameliorate inequality if they equally benefit Black and White students' persistence in college.[71] With the current constraints on Black families, it is unsurprising that between 2007–08 and 2011–12, the composition of PLUS loan borrowers shifted from 10.3 percent Black to 15.2 percent Black.[72]

Unfortunately, among Black students who began college for the first time in 1995–96, fully 13.2 percent borrowed a federal loan, did not complete a bachelor's degree, and defaulted on that loan by 2001, compared to just 2.4 percent of White students.[73] This rate of growth was higher for PLUS loans than for other types of loans primarily because federal loan limits make it difficult to increase take-up of those loans. And yet research suggests that the Black-White gap in college completion might be even larger if loans were restricted and not replaced by grant aid.[74]

INSTITUTIONAL DISPARITIES IN STUDENT DEBT

If institutions are held accountable for student debt and repayment, and the accountability system and financial aid rules are not adjusted for differences in the students the institutions serve and the resources they have, those most vulnerable to sanctions will be the colleges and universities that serve the most disadvantaged students and have the fewest resources to help them. The United States is a racially and economically stratified society substantially segregated by area, and the higher education system is large, complex, profoundly decentralized, and stratified by student background. The

Table 9.2   PLUS loan take-up rates and amounts borrowed by institution type and race/ethnicity, 1995–96 to 2011–12

	Percent with a PLUS loan					Amount of PLUS loan ($, among borrowers)				
	1995–96	1999–2000	2003–4	2007–8	2011–12	1995–96	1999–2000	2003–4	2007–8	2011–12
Race/Ethnicity										
White	2.7	3.4	4	4.3	4.9	8,875	9,539	11,097	11,811	12,267
Black	2.6	2.7	2.6	2.7	4.3	7,889	9,305	10,602	10,641	11,438
Hispanic	1.5	2.1	2.5	3	3.3	7,496	9,225	10,301	11,318	11,634
Asian	2.4	1.9	2.6	2.6	3.6	9,612	10,579	11,453	12,204	13,497
Native American	NA	NA	NA	NA	3.3	NA	NA	NA	NA	9,346
Institution type										
Non-HBCU	2.4	3	3.5	3.6	4.4	8,717	9,552	10,924	11,682	12,066
HBCU	7.5	6.1	5.5	9.9	12.8	8,688	8,555	11,742	10,126	12,625
4-year public	3.6	3.7	5.2	5.8	7	7,769	8,301	9,450	10,381	11,103
4-year private nonprofit	6.2	7.7	8.2	8.5	11.9	11,076	11,727	13,815	15,221	14,861
2-year public	0.1	0.1	0.2	0.2	0.1	NA	NA	6,697	5,087	5,656
For-profit	5.2	7.9	6	5.2	4.6	6,565	8,016	10,634	9,842	10,198
Overall	2.5	3.1	3.5	3.7	4.5	8,716	9,522	11,622	11,622	12,089

HBCUs represent a system that diverges significantly and intentionally from national averages and that is extremely dependent on federal aid.

The HBCUs owe their founding to the passionate support of churches and other institutions that strove to offer some form of higher education opportunity to former slaves after the Civil War. Their mission was clear and unique in a society that was still extremely segregated and where very few Blacks had ever graduated from White colleges. A major set of supporting institutions arose from the initiative by the federal government, in the two Morrill Land-Grant Acts, to found state universities with gifts of public land and federal dollars. In the seventeen states that instituted rigid education segregation after the war, the federal government required separate colleges for Blacks, though they were far from equal. Two northern states also founded separate Black colleges. These colleges have, by and large, continued to pursue their distinctive mission. Although White colleges were more or less open to Black students after the *Brown* decision and the 1964 Civil Rights Act, most HBCUs continued to operate. Their mission became even more focused on the disadvantaged portion of the Black population, as many of the best-prepared students went to the more prestigious formerly all-White campuses or to northern and western schools that adopted affirmative action policies in the civil rights era.

HBCUs have traditionally had low tuition but have been severely affected by rising costs. While the overall percentage of students borrowing for college rose from 26 percent to 42 percent between 1995–96 and 2011–12, table 9.1 shows significant variation by institution type. In that most recent year of data, 2011–12, fully 73 percent of students at for-profit colleges took federal loans, compared to 65 percent of students attending HBCUs, 63 percent of students at non-HBCU four-year private nonprofit colleges, 50 percent of students at four-year public colleges, and 17 percent of students at community colleges. The vast majority of the growth was concentrated in unsubsidized loans, where usage swelled from 35 percent to 66 percent in the for-profit sector, 17 percent to 59 percent at HBCUs, and 1.5 percent to 11 percent in community colleges. Private loan receipt fluctuated, driven mainly by for-profit colleges (where 39 percent of students took out private loans) and private nonprofit colleges (where 25 percent took out loans).

Private four-year nonprofit and for-profit colleges receive more loan revenue per student than do public colleges, mainly because of their higher costs of attendance. But the proposed changes in student loans will have a disproportionate impact on smaller colleges and universities serving a larger number of Black students (specifically, HBCUs and some for-profit colleges). Table 9.2 shows that the average PLUS loan (among borrowers) amount has risen faster for Black students and students at HBCUs than for White students and students at non-HBCUs. The average total amount borrowed at HBCUs rose from $6,175 in 1995–96 to $10,164 in 2011–12 after adjusting for inflation, while the average PLUS loan rose from $8,688 to $12,625 during this period.[75]

HBCUs have long been a central component of African American cultures of social mobility, providing a distinctly useful pathway into the middle class.[76] It is therefore unsurprising that recent efforts curtailing access to PLUS loans have sparked great controversy in the Black community and created a moment of significant crisis for HBCUs. As Theodore Cross and Robert Slater note, "In the past, many black families eased the financial burden by sending their children to the relatively inexpensive HBCUs. These institutions continue to be a cost-effective alternative for black families. However, tuition and fees have risen at these schools at an even higher rate than at the elite private universities or at the large state universities."[77] This is primarily because HBCUs have far smaller endowments and benefit from less alumni giving, due to the far lower rates of wealth among their students, yet exhibit no differences in financial management practices compared to other institutions.[78] Moreover, they serve students who are both less likely to graduate and less likely to be able to hold on to their financial aid during college.[79]

Despite the outsized attention paid to them in debates over PLUS loans, HBCUs are a tiny but critical fraction of the higher education landscape. With just ninety-nine four-year institutions nationwide, they serve just 2 percent of all undergraduates, and their students comprise less than 4 percent of all PLUS loan borrowers.[80] But they differ from other colleges and universities in several critical ways. These differences are an integral part of the mission of HBCUs, which aim to offer a more intimate and racially diverse setting than their counterparts. On average, a public HBCU enrolls about 4,000 students, 80 percent of whom are Black; a public non-HBCU enrolls about 10,000 students, only about 10 percent of whom are Black. Private HBCUs are about half the size of their non-HBCU counterparts, and representation of Black students at private non-HBCUs ranges from 9 percent to 14 percent.

One of the most important differences between HBCUs and non-HBCUs is the fraction of students depending on Federal Pell Grant aid to support their college attendance. Pell grant recipients comprise 70 percent of students attending public HBCUs, 69 percent of students attending private HBCUs with large endowments, and 83 percent of students attending private HBCUs with smaller endowments. In contrast, among non-HBCU schools, the corresponding fractions are 37 percent at public schools, 31 percent at well-endowed private schools, and 44 percent at private schools with smaller endowments. In part because their students have fewer family resources, HBCUs have historically tried to charge less as well. While the differences among public schools are not substantial, non-HBCU private schools charge about $12,000–$13,000 more than HBCUs, despite having more resources from endowments and bigger enrollments. But because non-HBCUs have less than half as many impoverished students (from families earning less than $30,000 a year), they are able to discount the cost of attendance more for those students, offering them a lower net price compared to HBCUs. At HBCUs, between 61 percent and 67 percent of FAFSA filers have a family income below $30,000 per year; that percentage ranges from 23 percent to 36 percent at non-HBCUs.[81]

HBCUs receive substantially less revenue per student than non-HBCUs. Net tuition revenue at public HBCUs is just $4,081 per student, $6,160 at private lower-endowment HBCUs, and $10,304 at private higher-endowment HBCUs; each of these values is about two-thirds of what similar non-HBCUs collect in revenue. Public and private lower-endowment HBCUs have slightly higher expenditures per student (excluding auxiliary enterprises) than non-HBCUs, while higher-endowment HBCUs spend about $4,000 less per student.[82] HBCUs spend a higher percentage of their resources on institutional support, which includes administrative services, technical support for student services, and some facilities maintenance, than non-HBCUs; this is likely a reflection of the greater need for student services and deferred maintenance costs at their facilities.

Table 9.3 displays some additional characteristics of HBCUs and non-profit non-HBCUs that offer bachelor of arts (BA) degrees and participate in the federal student loan programs as independent entities.[83] This analysis examines 82 of the nation's 99 BA-granting HBCUs: 39 public HBCUs (average endowment of $3,466 per full-time equivalent [FTE] student), 22 private lower-endowment HBCUs (average endowment of $6,160 per student), and 21 private higher-endowment HBCUs (average endowment $31,470 per student).

Public HBCUs and private HBCUs with small endowments are substantially dependent on tuition paid by students and families, which is increas-

Table 9.3   Descriptive statistics of HBCUs

| | Public | Private non-profit | |
		High endowment	Low endowment
Admissions and demographics			
Percent of students admitted	50.6	59.6	49.3
Percent full-time students	84.3	93.7	94.5
Percent Black students	80.3	90.1	93.3
Percent minority students	83	92.8	95.2
Percent zero EFC (NPSAS)	52.5	NA	44.4
ACT composite score	17.8	19.2	16.7
Undergraduate fall enrollment	4,420	1,774	1,346
Undergraduate 12-month FTE	4,121	1,761	1,298
ACT composite score	17.8	19.2	16.7
Financial aid			
Percent Pell recipients	69.9	69.3	82.8
Percent receiving federal loan	74.2	81.8	83.6
Percent receiving any grant	81.5	86.8	94.3
Cost of attendance ($)	18,067	28,566	22,474
Tuition/fees ($)	5,891	16,044	11,629
Net price of attendance ($)	10,660	18,791	14,051
Observations	39	21	22

Notes: All data are for the 2011–12 academic year.

"Higher endowment" HBCUs are those private HBCUs with endowments of at least $10,000 per FTE student in each year 2010–12; all other private HBCUs are "lower endowment."

Only four-year HBCUs are shown; this excludes eight historically Black community colleges.

The "percent minority" measure does not count Asian students as minorities.

SAT scores converted to ACT equivalents using the ACT-SAT concordance guide, College Board, ACT and SAT Concordance Tables, https://research.collegeboard.org/publications/content/2012/05/act-and-sat-concordance-tables.

This only includes colleges that participated in federal student loan programs as independent entities.

NPSAS measures are calculated using "very selective" as a proxy for higher-endowment colleges and all other categories as a proxy for lower-endowment colleges; not enough HBCUs are very selective to allow for point estimates or standard errors.

ingly covered by loans. Only about one in five HBCUs appears capable of devoting significant resources to students without leaning heavily on tuition. Since their families more often qualify for financial aid, HBCUs frequently have to depend on the federal government to cover students' cost of attendance. Public HBCUs received $3,563 per FTE student in federal grant aid in the 2011–12 academic year, while private higher-endowment HBCUs got $3,909 and lower-endowment HBCUs got $4,466. Federal loans covered $7,869 of the cost of attendance at public HBCUs, $8,639 at lower-endowment HBCUs, and $10,924 at higher-endowment colleges. Most of this difference was driven by PLUS loans. Public and private lower-endowment HBCUs had PLUS loan revenues of about $1,300 per FTE, but higher-endowment private colleges got nearly $3,900 per FTE in PLUS loan revenue. This meant that federal aid contributed 56–66 percent of the total cost of attendance across HBCUs, compared to 37 percent at non-HBCU public comprehensive colleges and just 19 percent at private higher-endowment non-HBCUs.[84]

While the percent of costs covered by financial aid at HBCUs does not approach the level of the for-profit sector (which often clusters around the maximum of 90 percent allowed by the federal government), the data clearly indicate the importance of federal funds for the survival of HBCUs. Much of this reliance on federal funds at public HBCUs is due to historic and current inadequacies of state funding compared to other public colleges and universities.[85] For example, a court ruled in 2002 that Mississippi public HBCUs were owed $503 million due to inadequate funding in the past; however, that money has been slow to reach the colleges.[86]

UNINTENDED CONSEQUENCES OF LOAN ACCOUNTABILITY

It is easy to write about the reform of federal student loan programs in technocratic terms, raising questions about their costs and implications while ignoring the political economy of the discussion. But such an approach skirts a critical issue that shapes policy effectiveness and efficiency: while federal student aid programs have long claimed to be about addressing a shortfall in family income, loans in particular address a shortfall in family wealth. And, in turn, given the extensive ways in which Black families in the United States have been kept from effectively accruing wealth, discussions about student loans are fundamentally about race as well.[87]

It is remarkable that HBCUs have attracted so much attention in debates over student loans, despite receiving only about 4 percent of all PLUS loan funds. For example, Rachel Fishman at the New America Foundation questioned the value of allowing students to choose where they use PLUS loans, suggesting that parents are mistaken in their "implicit assumption" that, with a PLUS loan in hand, "the extra debt will help their child earn a degree."[88] She arrived at this analysis by examining the unadjusted graduation rates of institutions where PLUS loans are often used and discovering that most PLUS loan borrowers attending four-year institutions are attending "middle or low performing" schools with graduation rates under 75 percent over six years. Notably, Fishman's report does not mention race or consider what could happen to students' college choices if PLUS loans are unavailable.

This is an important omission given that loan programs have long been intended to facilitate college access and choice. Indeed, the proclivity of contemporary higher education policy makers to prioritize choice above all other possible goals (including equity) is part of why it is difficult to exert additional accountability on institutions making loans without doing real and significant damage to the college prospects of minority students. It is clear that student loans contribute to the financial stability of many colleges and universities, facilitating a broader range of college choices for all undergraduates. While research over many decades has concluded that *where* a student attends college makes a relatively small difference in the odds of college completion, those college choices appear to matter far more for minority students. Attending a well-resourced, selective institution—which, for the most part, in today's system means a private school with a large endowment or an elite flagship public university—seems to generate sizable returns for minorities, both in terms of postgraduation earnings and graduation rates.[89] There are about 550 such institutions in the country, and they are overwhelmingly White; at those that are not HBCUs, just under 10 percent of the student body on average is Black (90 percent at HBCUs).

Of course, Black students are also more likely than White students to attend for-profit colleges, many of which have actively recruited them. For profit colleges are far more costly than public community colleges, and the labor market returns are mixed and sometimes clearly negative, compared to attending community colleges. While Stephanie Cellini and Latika Chaudhary and Kevin Lang and Russell Weinstein both found similar earnings gains (or a lack thereof in some cases) between for-profit and community colleges, David Deming and colleagues showed that for-profit students had lower earnings, higher unemployment rates, and worse debt and default outcomes than community college students even though completion rates were somewhat better in the for-profit sector.[90] The cost differential of attending a for-profit college (often in the tens of thousands of dollars for an associate degree) makes similar earnings after graduation decidedly dissimilar.

There are several ways to think about the returns of college choices for Black students. The positive return they receive from attending elite private schools may mean that they benefit more from these environments, but it could also mean that their alternative options are worse than those enjoyed by White students. In other words, a White student who is unable to borrow money to attend a better-resourced, more selective institution is still likely to attend a reasonably well-resourced, fairly selective school and face good graduation prospects. But a Black student faced with the same challenge may encounter extremely limited choices given the lower density of quality postsecondary options in minority communities and the continued prevalence of racial discrimination in both public and private institutions. And the only remaining option is likely to provide far fewer advantages when it comes to graduation prospects. Thus, while college choice is not the margin that matters for non-Hispanic White students, it is a very important margin for Black students, and college choice is impacted by the availability of loans.[91]

What this also suggests is that Black students face a number of disadvantages when they set out for college, which, in turn, has a profound impact on the amount of student loan debt they need to take out in pursuit of a college degree. First, Black students face a legacy of disadvantage, whereby the Black-White wealth gap mirrors and produces large racial disparities in student loan debt.[92] Second, Black students face limitations in the colleges that they enroll in and are often funneled into for-profit institutions and institutions that are underfunded, which then leads them to take on more debt. Because of the limited resources of their families, they are often under great pressure to help pay their education costs and even provide funds to their family during their college experience.

Our analysis of the National Longitudinal Study of Youth, 1997 Cohort, data support such a narrative and suggest that these factors account for over half of the Black-White disparity in student loan debt. Table 9.4 extends the earlier National Postsecondary Student Aid Study analyses to examine the contributors to the racial debt gap, suggesting five key findings:

- Young adults who attend for-profit institutions leave with far more debt compared those who attended nonprofit institutions, adjusted for confounders.
- Attending a HBCU does not appear to increase debt among young adults.
- The disproportionate enrollment of Black students in for-profit colleges and universities contributes to the racial debt gap, but the disproportionate enrollment of Black students in HBCUs does not.
- The disproportionate enrollment of Black students in colleges and universities with less financial support (as proxied by the proportion of the total cost that is covered by state, federal, and institutional aid) also contributes to the racial debt gap.
- The racial debt gap exists within and between schools and is largest at colleges and universities with less financial support.[93]

The issues we present here cannot be remedied through proposed federal loan accountability reforms. If federal loan reforms restrict college access for Black students, it may reduce the debt held by these students in the short term (or it may not if they simply turn to private loans), but over the longer term it could make it harder for them to use education as a way out of the racial wealth gap. Of course, if grants are substituted for loans, college enrollment and choices for minority students are unlikely to suffer. But in the far more likely scenario that current federal loan reforms reduce the ability of minority students to afford college, history suggests that enrollment and graduation rates among these students will drop. This has happened before. In the 1970s, Black college-going rates declined as need-based grant aid became less available.[94] And as loans became the dominant form of college financing in the 1980s (never making up for the diminished support from grant aid), enrollment among Blacks further declined, even as enrollment for all other groups of students remained stable or increased.[95]

Of course, restrictions on loans will not affect all Black students, or all HBCUs, in the same manner. It is likely that students currently enrolled in smaller private HCBUs, where declining enrollment is creating financial struggles, will be the most affected.[96] The financial stability of these institutions is difficult to separate from the needs of their students, given that many students attend these schools because of a lack of other options that are as welcoming, accessible, and affordable. The implications are perhaps even more significant, because, as Pamela Bennett writes, "The role of HBCUs in

Table 9.4   Differences in outstanding (logged) student loan debt in young adulthood

	Base model	Add institution type	Full model
Student's race			
Black	0.845***	0.638**	0.597**
	(0.198)	(0.213)	(0.212)
Institution type			
Attended HBCU		0.559	0.582
		(0.347)	(0.346)
Attended for-profit		0.977***	0.905***
		(0.232)	(0.232)
Institutional finances			
Total aid/Total cost			−0.096***
			(0.025)
R^2	0.294	0.299	0.302

Notes: * $p<.05$; ** $p<.01$; *** $p<.001$, N=3008. All models adjust for family background (parents' wealth, education, income), postsecondary education attendance (years enrolled, % years enrolled full time, % years enrolled in a private institution; degree pursued and attained; current enrollment status), region, and age at debt measurement. Referent for race is non-Hispanic White.

Source: NLSY-97 respondents who ever attended a postsecondary institution.

the social mobility of African Americans remains strong even though other options for postsecondary education are available to them . . . [They have accomplished this] even while maintaining a long history of educating students from disadvantaged backgrounds . . . [including those] . . . at risk for downward mobility."[97] Punishing these colleges on the basis of their lower completion rates is much like punishing hospitals that take on and succeed with a substantial share of patients many hospitals would not have tried to treat.

RECOMMENDATIONS

Current discussions about reforming federal loan programs are conspicuously silent on the issue of race. But as we have demonstrated, student debt, like family wealth, has a color. Compared to White students, Black,

Hispanic, and Native American undergraduates enjoy much less security from family assets and far more often have to turn to the federal government and private loans to finance college enrollment. This issue has been neglected, even in recent reports describing problems with PLUS loans at HBCUs.[98] HBCUs are said to constitute a tiny fraction of the loan issue and yet have received disproportionate attention for the borrowing practices of their students, their low unadjusted graduation rates, and their financial aid practices—even though such problems also exist at non-HBCU public and private colleges across the country.[99] HBCUs are so unusually reliant on federal loans because of the lack of wealth of their students and historical funding inequities that their very existence may be at stake—factors that are often omitted in policy discussions.

The assumption of accountability efforts is that institutions which take on students who pose great challenges to completion and to securing jobs that make payback possible are acting inefficiently. Wise policy making must consider the history which shows that these decisions are intentional, that they are fundamental to the institutional missions, and that they are addressing a population of lower-income black families that badly need more opportunities for higher education.

Policy makers seeking to improve the national economy by extending opportunities to all Americans need to proceed cautiously when it comes to reforming student financial aid programs so as to avoid doing untold harm to the college prospects of Black students. Obviously, the extremely unequal resources of these families call for more generous federal funding, but until and unless that is accomplished, the wise policy is to avoid additional harm to these families and the institutions that serve them. PLUS loans are not a good solution, but exclusion of students on financial grounds is far worse.

Finally, income-based repayment should be provided for undergraduate PLUS loans. It makes very little sense to apply separate rules for loans made to students and parents, who are often part of the same family economic unit and pursuing a common goal—the child's education. All families should be supported in their choice to support their children into adulthood, and current PLUS loan policies fall short of that goal.

Accountability and Racial Fairness to Advance Civil Rights—A Way Forward

NICHOLAS HILLMAN

Accountability is a powerful idea but is much more complicated than it sounds and is often a double-edged sword. It can cut through obfuscation but can also do a great deal of unintended damage to vulnerable colleges and students, as the studies in this book demonstrate. Yet, in higher education policy, the accountability movement is here to stay and will only become more central to federal and state policy debates about improving college access, affordability, and outcomes with limited funds. This is no surprise, since modern governments now demand a degree of accountability in order to achieve their policy goals and justify their investment in public goods. This press for better accountability sounds promising and conveys the idea of systematically measuring and improving institutional performance. Policy makers can then justify giving more resources to those colleges that appear to use them better and less to those falling behind. But most accountability systems are not designed to address deeply rooted racial injustices, which in turn cannot help this nation advance civil rights.

Because of this, accountability systems themselves can be part of the problem when they ignore differences in opportunities and resources, which, in turn, reinforces education inequality. This does not mean we should abandon accountability efforts or that inequality is an intractable problem that accountability cannot address. Without accountability, it would be impossible to diagnose or address education inequalities because we would not have access to timely and relevant data. A better way forward would be to build an accountability system that plays a central role in reversing inequality. This would require significant investments in improving the nation's current higher education data infrastructure, a point raised in each chapter in this book. It would also require a degree of policy maintenance where state and federal officials update the way they approach accountability with an eye toward reversing inequality. Doing this well will require better data and careful thought about what share of the outcome can reasonably be attributed to the institutions as opposed to social, economic, or education inequality occurring outside the campus.

Yet, higher education accountability efforts continue to be fraught with poor data quality and designed in ways that overlook or oversimplify root problems related to inequality. Under the Obama administration, we saw several new accountability reforms, including the College Scorecard, Financial Aid Shopping Sheet, enhanced gainful employment regulations, and efforts to improve consumer protection in for-profit colleges. It is unclear what is in store for the Trump administration, but early signs indicate a desire to roll back these efforts while possibly introducing its own ideas into federal higher education policy. States are also expanding their accountability efforts primarily through performance-based funding policies. Chapters in this book speak to these policy areas and identify where accountability can be improved by focusing on racial justice and inequality. Doing so should not only improve education outcomes for students but also advance civil rights by putting colleges on a more equal playing field, where Black, Latino, and poor students attending unequally resourced colleges have a better chance at securing upward mobility while equalizing education opportunities.

Designing such an accountability system would require a new way of thinking about accountability altogether and a willingness to collect the data needed for better measures. Designing a new system of accountability is not impossible; in fact, chapters in this book point to a number of policy solutions that can result in a fairer accountability system. Using input-adjusted performance metrics, accounting for differences in campus resources, rewarding colleges for serving underrepresented students well, and building capacity where inequalities exist—these design features would be a departure from current accountability systems that focus on simple outcomes that fail to account for inequality.

Take state performance-based funding, for example, which uses high-stakes financial incentives to reward and penalize colleges for their performance. To measure "performance," states often count the number of credit hours completed, degrees conferred, and job placement rates and monitor growth on these measures over time. Minority-serving institutions (MSIs) and broad-access colleges have fewer resources, yet they enroll disproportionate numbers of students who attended economically and academically disadvantaged high schools. They also enroll disproportionate shares of Black and Latino students, groups experiencing the greatest labor-market discrimination and wage inequality. Rewarding and penalizing colleges based on these simple performance metrics will only worsen inequality by unfairly disadvantaging colleges that serve students of color and low-income students.

A growing number of states have embedded into their accountability systems bonus funding for colleges "prioritizing underrepresented students" as an attempt to acknowledge and address inequality. For example, Tennessee gives a performance premium to colleges enrolling and graduating adult and low-income students. Unfortunately, add-ons and bonuses are insufficient mechanisms to help reverse inequality. And when they fail to engage directly with racial inequality, their impact will be even more muted. Given the growing body of evidence on the negative consequences current and proposed accountability systems have on colleges serving Black, Latino, and poor students, it is past time for change. If we are committed to making progress on advancing racial justice and civil rights, then state and federal accountability systems are a key mechanism for facilitating those goals.

When looking to reform, future accountability systems do not need to follow past models. In fact, if we are to make progress toward racial justice and civil rights, they *cannot* follow these past models. Instead, future models should apply the recommendations outlined throughout this book. Doing so should create a fairer system where underresourced colleges serving the nation's Black, Latino, and low-income students are not disproportionately harmed by poorly designed accountability systems. Instead, an accountability system that adjusts and accounts for inequality while rewarding (rather than penalizing) colleges for serving underrepresented students is better positioned to reverse inequality and expand opportunity.

Such a system would be a positive force in advancing racial justice and civil rights. But reforming accountability with an eye toward these ends would not on its own be a sufficient means for reversing inequality. It is a minimal expectation of all state and federal accountability policies. Doing so will help state and federal governments start to close inequality gaps that have for too long persisted in higher education. With a fairer accountability system in place, resources can be better targeted to help build the capacity and close equity gaps between colleges that have been unfairly penalized by systems blind to inequality. With colleges now judged and held accountable on an equal playing field, scarce financial resources can be targeted in fairer and more equitable ways.

Far too many MSIs and broad-access institutions serving our nation's Black, Latino, and low-income students have unequal capacity when compared to predominantly White institutions. With fewer financial resources, students will have higher student-to-faculty ratios, which has been found to reduce time-to-degree. With fewer technological resources, it is challenging for campuses to adopt promising interventions like predictive analytics and other tools to help keep students on track to graduating. And with unequal access to professional staff who can support students' academic pursuits, students attending underresourced institutions may be more likely to not persist to completion. A fairer accountability system would help reverse these inequalities by prioritizing and uplifting colleges with the fewest resources and, as a result, will improve education outcomes for Black, Latino, and low-income students. MSIs, those serving traditionally underserved students, and colleges located in education deserts doing their best to meet local needs stand to gain the most from new accountability systems. A poorly designed accountability system will deepen inequality, but one that is well designed and appropriately used will prioritize and remedy these resource inequalities first.

With an eye toward civil rights, we can envision a new accountability system that uses carefully designed input-adjusted performance measures, accounts for baseline differences across institution types, differentiates goals by each institution's mission, takes into account the major differences in precollege preparation for most students of color, and focuses on performance outcomes that are under the direct and unambiguous control of the college. Doing this should provide a fairer baseline from which to judge colleges and hold them accountable for their outcomes. These features represent the minimal conditions under which we can expect to ever make progress toward racial justice and civil rights in higher education.

Doing so should reduce the unintended consequences of current accountability efforts. It should also increase the chances that colleges will equalize opportunities for students. These accountability features are necessary for equalizing opportunity in higher education. There is surely a long way to go, and the challenges we face are not with the goal of accountability, per se, but are with poorly conceptualized accountability systems that offer simple solutions to complex problems.

Many of these accountability reforms discussed in this book originated under the Obama administration and during one of the most polarized Congresses in our nation's history.[1] This polarization made it difficult, if not impossible, to advance a policy agenda through the legislative process. Congress typically reauthorizes the Higher Education Act (HEA) every few years, yet the last reauthorization occurred in 2008. With delays in the reauthorization process, the Obama administration often turned to regulation as a vehicle for reform, resulting in the College Scorecard, gainful employment rules, and the simplification of financial aid and loan repayment.[2] But regulatory reform is not as permanent as legislated reform, and it does not create needed data or target funds to address preexisting inequalities. New federal and state policies could undo these efforts and take "accountability" in a very different direction.

Under the Trump administration, we can anticipate that these regulatory reforms to be scaled back or removed altogether. Rather than working to improve and update existing policies and regulations to better meet accountability goals, it is likely the administration and Republican-controlled 115th Congress will adopt changes that simplify, deregulate, and destabilize civil rights goals in these areas. In this process, we might expect to see the emergence of "risk-sharing" policies similar to the accountability efforts described in this book. The basic logic behind risk-sharing is that colleges with poor student loan repayment rates and high default rates will be penalized and required to repay the federal government a share of those debts. In so doing, proponents believe colleges will have "skin in the game" and better incentives to help students succeed. This, of course, hinges on the belief that colleges are not currently exhausting their resources to serve students well. It also believes that low performance outcomes are due to the way colleges are managed, not to the complexities of racial and economic inequality that colleges are working to reverse. Much discussion assumes that, for example, MSIs currently have "skin" to put in the game. If this assumption is wrong, then they will face pressure to respond by excluding the very students who need the most support, thereby perpetuating inequality.

Not surprisingly, current risk-sharing proposals are likely to disproportionately affect MSIs. Lessons from this book should help us avoid these outcomes while advancing accountability policies aimed at reversing inequality. Instead of penalizing these institutions for outcomes that are complex and not under the direct and unambiguous control of the colleges, policies should seek out ways to build colleges' capacity to prevent these outcomes in the first place. For example, if Black and Latino college graduates face labor-market discrimination, wage inequality, and economic segregation, why should a college be held responsible for these outcomes? What can a college do to avoid or reverse them? Judging a college for these simple outcomes that ignore the realities of racial and economic injustice will only worsen the exact inequalities higher education is designed to reverse.

With federal action focused on HEA reauthorization and deregulation, we can expect states to become even more important sources of policy change affecting civil rights. States are adopting and expanding performance-based funding efforts, which is effectively merit-based aid to colleges. States are also tying more funds to financial aid programs that require students to enroll full time or to graduate "on time." In both cases, these policies would likely favor students from White and upper-income families who do not have to work while enrolled (thus can attend full time) and who are less sensitive to college costs (thus able to graduate sooner). State policy makers who would like to avoid these predictable outcomes should consider new accountability models that are input-adjusted and address the root causes of the perceived poor performance. They will likely find that problems are far more complex than initially expected; consequently, so too will new policy solutions. A policy initiative that is simple and has good political optics but does not protect and advance civil rights is a failure. Failing to come to terms with this complexity risks shrinking opportunity and reinforcing inequality. In higher education policy making, we need sophisticated systems and not political sound bites. Policy makers at the state and federal levels cannot afford poorly designed accountability systems if they truly want a society where all students have a fair chance and where colleges that help those whose lives can be most transformed get the recognition and support they deserve.

Notes

Introduction

1. William G. Bowen and Derek Bok, *The Shape of the River: Long-Term Consequences of Considering Race in College and University Admissions* (Princeton, NJ: Princeton University Press, 1998), 4–7.
2. Eric Kelderman, "State Spending on Higher Education Has Grown but More Slowly Than Before the Recession," *Chronicle of Higher Education*, May 6, 2016, A15.
3. *Regents of the University of California v. Bakke*, 438 U.S. 265 (1978).
4. Gary Orfield and Susan Eaton, *Dismantling Desegregation: The Quiet Repeal of Brown v. Board of Education* (New York: New Press, 1996).
5. *Schuette v. Coalition to Defend Affirmative Action*, 134 S.Ct. 1623 (2014).
6. Liaison Committee of the State Board of Education and the Regents of the University of California, *A Master Plan for Higher Education in California, 1960–1975* (Sacramento: California Department of Education, 1960).
7. John F. Hale, "The Making of the New Democrats," *Political Science Quarterly* 11, no. 2 (1995): 207–35; Bill Clinton and Al Gore, *Putting People First: How We Can All Change America* (New York: Times Books, 1992).
8. Donald Heller and Patricia Marin, *Who Should We Help? The Negative Social Consequences of Merit Scholarships* (Cambridge, MA: Civil Rights Project, 2002).
9. Mary Martinez Wenzl and Rigoberto Marquez, *Unrealized Promises: Unequal Access, Affordability, and Excellence at Community Colleges in Southern California* (Los Angeles: Civil Rights Project, 2012).
10. Rakesh Kochhar and Richard Fry, "Wealth Inequality Has Widened Along Racial, Ethnic Lines Since the End of the Great Recession" (report, Pew Research Center, Washington, DC, December 2014), http://www.pewresearch.org/fact-tank/2014/12/12/racial-wealth-gaps-great-recession/; Tanzina Vega, "Minorities Fall Further Behind Whites During Economic Recovery," New York Times, January 26, 2015, A11; Dionne Searcey, "More Fall Out as Middle Class Shrinks Further, *New York Times*, January 26, 2015, B1.
11. Richard Fry, "Wealth Inequality Has Widened Along Racial, Ethnic Lines Since End of Great Recession," *Fact Tank*, Pew Research, December 12, 2014, http://www.pewresearch.org/fact-tank/2014/12/12/racial-wealth-gaps-great-recession/.
12. Michael Stratford, "GOP Would Freeze Pell," *Inside Higher Education*, March 20, 2015.

13. College Board, *Trends in College Pricing, 2015* (New York: College Board, 2015), https://trends.collegeboard.org/sites/default/.../2015-trends-college-pricing-final-508.pdf.

14. Stephen Burd, *The Out-of-State Student Arms Race: How Public Universities Use Merit Aid to Recruit Nonresident Students* (Washington, DC: New America, 2015).

15. Less than 7 percent of colleges claimed to meet full student need. Farran Powell, "Colleges That Claim to Meet Full Financial Need," *U.S. News and World Report*, September 19, 2016.

16. Affirmative action was ended in California by referendum and in Florida by an action by Governor Jeb Bush.

17. Adam Liptak, "What the Trump Presidency Means for the Supreme Court," *New York Times*, November 9, 2016.

18. College Board, *Trends in Student Aid, 2016* (New York: College Board, 2016).

19. See Vincent Tinto, *Completing College:Rethinking Institutional Action* (Chicago: University of Chicago Press, 2012).

20. David Leonhardt, "Upward Mobility Has Not Declined, Study Says," *New York Times,* January 23, 2014, B1.

21. Gary Orfield and Erica Frankenberg, Brown *at 60: Great Progress, a Long Retreat, and an Uncertain Future* (Los Angeles: Civil Rights Project, 2014).

22. Ibid.

23. Gary Orfield and Jongyeon Ee, *Segregating California's Future* (Los Angeles: The Civil Rights Project, 2014).

24. Lyndon B. Johnson, *The Vantage Point: Perspectives on the Presidency, 1963–1969* (New York: Popular Library, 1971), 166.

25. Philip D. Tegeler, "The Persistence of Segregation in Government Housing Programs," in *The Geography of Opportunity: Race and Housing Choice in Metropolitan America*, ed. Xavier de Souza Briggs (Washington, DC: Brookings Institution, 2005), 197–216.

26. Gail L. Sunderman, James S. Kim, and Gary Orfield, *NCLB Meets School Realities: Lessons from the Field* (Thousand Oaks, CA: Corwin Press, 2005).

27. "Gallup Review: Black and White Differences in Views on Race," news release, December 12, 2014, http://www.news.gallup.com/poll/180107/gallup-review-black-white-differences-views-race.aspx.

28. "Changes in State Appropriations for Higher Education per Student Since the Great Recession," *Chronicle of Higher Education: Almanac 2016–17* 62, no. 43 (2016): 56.

Chapter 1

1. Health Care and Education Reconciliation Act of 2010 (Pub.L. 111–152, 124 Stat. 1029).

2. Dick Morris, *Behind the Oval Office: Winning the Presidency in the Nineties* (New York: Random House, 1997), 85–86, 214–15.

3. Internal Revenue Service, "American Opportunity Tax Credit," https://www.irs.gov/newsroom/american-opportunity-tax-credit-questions-and-answers.

4. More than 70 percent of the tax-sheltered benefits in these plans are held by families with incomes over $200,000, far more than three times the average national income. Tara Siegel Bernard, "White House Proposals on 529 College Plans Would Reduce Benefits," *New York Times*, January 23, 2015, B3. The median 2014 income was $53,900. Tami Luhby, "Income Is on Rise—Finally," *CNN Money*, August 20, 2014.

5. Ron Lieber, "Taxing 529 Accounts: A Plan That Went Away," *New York Times*, January 31, 2015, B1.

6. Caroline M. Hoxby and George B. Bulman, "The Effects of the Tax Deduction for Postsecondary Tuition: Implications for Structuring Tax-Based Aid,"*Economics of Education Review* 51 (2016): 23–60.

7. Michael Stratford, "Net Price Rising," *Inside Higher Education*, October 23, 2013; College Board, *Trends in Student Aid, 2016* (New York: College Board, 2016).

8. Elizabeth J. Akers and Matthew M. Chingos, *Are College Students Borrowing Blindly?* (Washington, DC: Brookings Institution, 2014).

9. A. J. Angulo, *Diploma Mills: How For-Profit Colleges Stiffed Students, Taxpayers, and the American Dream* (Baltimore: Johns Hopkins University Press, 2016).

10. Hearing, US Senate, Committee on Health, Education, Labor, and Pensions, "For-Profit Higher Education: The Failure to Safeguard the Federal Investment and Ensure Student Success," 112th Cong., 2d Sess., July 2012; *New York Times*, March 26, 2015; *Association of Private Sector Colleges and Universities v. Duncan*, Civ. Action No. 14-1870 (D.D.C.), June 21, 2015.

11. Angulo, *Diploma Mills.*

12. Karen Weise, "The For-Profit College That's Too Big to Fail," *Bloomberg Businessweek*, September 25, 2014.

13. "ITT Barred from Taking Students on U.S. Aid," *New York Times*, August 26, 2016, B3.

14. Douglas Belkin, "DeVos Appointee to Head Student-Loan Program Has Done His Homework," *Wall Street Journal*, June 20, 2017; Stacy Cowley and Patricia Cohen, "U.S. Halts New Rules Aimed at Abuses by For-Profit Colleges," *New York Times*, June 14, 2017.

15. Jennifer Steinhauer, "House and Senate Approve Compromise 2011 Budget," *New York Times*, April 14, 2011.

16. Kelly Field, "Obama Proposes a 'Student Aid Bill of Rights': Here's What It Will—and Won't—Do," *Chronicle of Higher Education*, March 20, 2015, A18.

17. Barack Obama, State of the Union Address, February 12, 2013. All of the Obama documents were taken from the White House website https://obamawhitehouse.archives.gov; they can no longer be found there. In time, they will appear in published presidential papers.

18. Barack Obama, State of the Union Address, January 28, 2014.

19. Michael Stratford, "The Second Summit," *Inside Higher Education*, December 4, 2014.

20. Barack Obama, "A New College Scorecard," weekly address, September 12, 2015.

21. Michael Stratford, "Counting Students Equally?" *Inside Higher Education,* January 30, 2015. There were scores of critical comments on the draft regulations proposed

by the US Department of Education. Ryan Leou, "UC Still Skeptical of Proposed Federal College Ratings System," *Daily Bruin*, January 5, 2015, 3.

22. Julie Peller, "Obama Administration's Ratings Proposal" (Lumina Issues Paper, Lumina Foundation, Indianapolis, September 1, 2014), 2, http://www.luminafoundation.org/resources/obama-administrations-ratings-proposal.

23. Jamienne Studley, conference comments, September 2, 2014. The Civil Rights Project Conference on Accountability in Higher Education, Washington, DC.

24. Jamienne Studley, conference comments, September 2, 2014.

25. *A Test of Leadership Charting the Future of U.S. Higher Education: A Report of the Commission Appointed by Secretary of Education Margaret Spellings* (Washington, DC: US Department of Education, 2006), 4.

26. James S. Coleman, Earnest Q, Campbell, Carol J., Hobson, James McPartland, Alexander M Mood, Frederick D. Weinfeld, and Robert L. York, *Equality of Educational Opportunity* (Washington, DC: Government Printing Office, 1966).

27. Orfield and Frankenberg, Brown *at 60*; Gary Orfield and Chungmei Lee, *Why Segregation Matters: Poverty and Educational Inequality* (Cambridge, MA: The Civil Rights Project, 2005).

28. Economic Policy Institute, "Unemployment Rate of Young College Graduates, by Race and Ethnicity, 1989–2014." Data for 2014 represent a twelve-month average from April 2013 to March 2014. Data are for college graduates aged 21–24 who did not have an advanced degree and were not enrolled in further schooling. Authors' analysis of US Bureau of the Census current population survey microdata in Heidi Shierholz, Alyssa D. Avis, and Will Kimall, "The Class of 2014: The Weak Economy Is Idling Too Many Young Graduates" (Briefing Paper No. 377, Economic Policy Institute, Washington, DC, May 2014), 11–12.

29. Devah Pager and David S. Pedulla, "Race, Self-Selection, and the Job Search Process," *American Journal of Sociology* 120, no. 4 (2015): 1005–54; Roland G. Fryer Jr., Devah Pager, and Jörg L. Spenkuch, "Racial Disparities in Job Finding and Offered Wages," *Journal of Law and Economics* 56 (August 2013): 633–89.

30. Shierholz et al., "The Class of 2014."

31. "Survey of Admission Officers on Federal Regulations," National Association of College Admissions Counseling, January 2015, https://www.nacacnet.org/search/.

32. Some scholars note that the severe debt problem affects a small share of all households.

Chapter 2

1. "Higher Education: State Funding Trends and Policies on Affordability," Government Accountability Office, 2014, http://www.gao.gov/products/GAO-15-151.

2. Mark Huelsman, *The Debt Divide: The Racial and Class Bias Behind the "New Normal" of Student Borrowing* (New York: Demos, 2015), http://www.demos.org/publication/debt-divide-racial-and-class-bias-behind-new-normal-student-borrowing.

3. Martha Snyder, *Driving Better Outcomes: Typology and Principles to Inform Outcomes-Based Funding Models* (Washington, DC: HCM Strategists, 2015), http://hcmstrategists.com/drivingoutcomes.

4. Stan Jones, "The Game Changers: Strategies to Boost College Completion and Close

Attainment Gaps," *Change: The Magazine of Higher Learning* 47, no. 2 (2015): 24–29, doi: 10.1080/00091383.

5. Bruce D. Johnstone, "Cost-Sharing and the Cost-Effectiveness of Grants and Loan Subsidies to Higher Education," in *Cost-Sharing and Accessibility in Higher Education: A Fairer Deal*, ed. Pedro Teixeira, D. Bruce Johnstone, Maria Rosa, and Hans Vossensteyn (Dordrecht, the Netherlands: Springer, 2008), 51–77.

6. Jennifer Delaney and William Doyle, "State Spending on Higher Education: Testing the Balance Wheel over Time," *Journal of Education Finance* 36, no. 4 (2011): 343–368; Harold Hovey, "State Spending in Higher Education in the Next Decade: The Battle to Sustain Current Support," National Center for Public Policy and Higher Education, 1999, http://www.nchems.org/pubs/docs/State_Spending_Hovey.pdf.

7. Don Hossler, "Students and Families as Revenue: The Impact on Institutional Behaviors," in *Privatization and Public Universities*, ed. Douglas Priest and Edward St. John (Bloomington: Indiana University Press, 2006), 109–28; "Higher Education."

8. Kevin Dougherty, Kevin Dougherty, Sosanya Jones, Hana Lahr, Rebecca Natow, Lara Pheatt, and Vikash Reddy, "Implementing Performance Funding in Three Leading States: Instruments, Outcomes, Obstacles, and Unintended Impacts," *Community College Research Center* 74 (November 2014): 1–61.

9. David Tandberg and Nicholas Hillman, *State Performance Funding for Higher Education: Silver Bullet or Red Herring?* (Madison: Wisconsin Center for the Advancement of Postsecondary Education, 2013), https://wiscape.wisc.edu/docs/WebDispenser/wiscapedocuments/pb018.pdf?sfvrsn=4.

10. "Performance Funding for Higher Education," National Conference of State Legislatures, 2015, http://www.ncsl.org/research/education/performance-funding.aspx.

11. Ibid.

12. "State Higher Education Finance," State Higher Education Executive Officers, 2017, http://www.sheeo.org/projects/shef-%E2%80%94-state-higher-education-finance.

13. Nancy Shulock and Colleen Moore, *Invest in Success: How Finance Policy Can Increase Student Success at California's Community Colleges* (Sacramento: Institute for Higher Education Leadership and Policy, 2007).

14. Snyder, *Driving Better Outcomes*.

15. "Using Federal Data to Measure and Improve the Performance of U.S. Institutions of Higher Education," Executive Office of the President of the United States Council of Economic Advisors, 2017, https://collegescorecard.ed.gov/assets/UsingFederalDataToMeasureAndImprove Performance.pdf.

16. Dougherty et al., "Implementing Performance Funding in Three Leading States."

17. David Tandberg, Nicholas Hillman, and Mohamed Barakat, "State Higher Education Performance Funding for Community Colleges: Diverse Effects and Policy Implications," *Teacher's College Record* 116, no. 12 (2015); David Tandberg and Nicholas Hillman, "State Higher Education Performance Funding: Data, Outcomes and Policy Implications," *Journal of Education Finance* 39, no. 3 (2014): 222–42.

18. Amanda Rutherford and Thomas Rabovsky, "Evaluating Impacts of Performance Funding Policies on Student Outcomes in Higher Education," *Annals of the American Academy of Political and Social Science* 655 (2014): 185–208.

19. Snyder, *Driving Better Outcomes*.

20. Mark Umbricht, Frank Fernandez, and Justin Ortagus, "An Examination of the (Un) intended Consequences of Performance Funding in Higher Education," *Educational Policy* 31, no. 5 (2015): 643–73.

21. Nicholas Hillman, David Tandberg, and Jacob Gross, "Performance Funding in Higher Education: Do Financial Incentives Impact College Completions?" *Journal of Higher Education* 85, no. 6 (2014): 826–57.

22. Nicholas Hillman, David Tandberg, and Alisa Fryar, "Evaluating the Impacts of 'New' Performance Funding in Higher Education," *Educational Evaluation and Policy Analysis* 37, no. 4 (2015): 501–19.

23. Thomas Sanford and James Hunter, "Impact of Performance-Funding on Retention and Graduation Rates," *Education Policy Analysis Archives* 19, no. 33 (2011): 1–30.

24. Ed Gerrish, "The Impact of Performance Management on Performance in Public Organizations: A Meta-Analysis," *Public Administration Review* 76, no. 1 (2015): 48–66.

25. Gwyn Bevan and Christopher Hood, "What's Measured Is What Matters: Targets and Gaming in the English Public Health Care System," *Public Administration* 84, no. 3 (2006): 517–38; Yujing Shen, "Selection Incentives in a Performance Contracting System," *Health Services Research* 38, no. 2 (2003): 535–52; Robert M. Wachter, Scott Flanders, Christopher Fee, and Peter Pronovost, "Public Reporting of Antibiotic Timing in Patients with Pneumonia: Lessons from a Flawed Performance Measure," *Annals of Internal Medicine* 149, no. 1 (2008): 29–32; James A. Welker, Michelle Huston, and Jack McCue, "Antibiotic Timing and Errors in Diagnosing Pneumonia," *Archives of Internal Medicine* 168, no. 4 (2008): 351–56.

26. Brian Jacob, "Accountability, Incentives and Behavior: The Impact of High-Stakes Testing in the Chicago Public Schools," *Journal of Public Economics* 89 (2005): 761–96, http://www.sciencedirect.com/science/article/pii/S0047272704001549.

27. James Heckman, Carolyn Heinrich, and Jeffrey Smith, "The Performance of Performance Standards," *Journal of Human Resources* 37, no. 4 (2002): 778–811.

28. Steven Craig, Scott Imberman, and Adam Perdue, "Do Administrators Respond to Their Accountability Ratings? The Response of School Budgets to Accountability Grades," *Economics of Education Review* 49 (December 2015): 55–68; Matthew Steinberg and Lauren Sartain, "Does Teacher Evaluation Improve School Performance? Experimental Evidence from Chicago's Excellence in Teaching Project," *Education Finance Policy* 10, no. 4 (2015): 535–72; Rachel Werner, Jonathan Kolstad, Elizabeth Stuart, and Daniel Polsky, "The Effect of Pay-for-Performance in Hospitals: Lessons for Quality Improvement," *Health Affairs* 30, no. 4 (2011): 690–98.

29. Jeannette Colyvas, "Performance Metrics as Formal Structures and Through the Lens of Social Mechanisms: When Do They Work and How Do They Influence?" *American Journal of Education* 118, no. 2 (2012): 167–97; David Himmelstein, Miraya Jun, Reinhard Busse, Karine Chevreul, Alexander Geissler, Patrick Jeurissen, Sarah Thomson, Marie-Amelie Vinet, and Steffie Woolhandler, "A Comparison of Hospital Administrative Costs in Eight Nations: U.S. Costs Exceed All Others by Far," *Health Affairs* 33, no. 9 (2014): 1586–94.

30. Edward Layzear, "Performance Pay and Productivity," *American Economic Review* 90, no. 5 (2000): 1346–61.
31. Avinash Dixit, "Incentives and Organizations in the Public Sector: An Interpretative Review," *Journal of Human Resources* 37, no. 4 (2002): 696–727; Richard Rothstein, *Holding Accountability to Account: How Scholarship and Experience in Other Fields Inform Exploration of Performance Incentives in Education* (Nashville: National Center on Performance Incentives, 2008).
32. Dougherty et al., "Implementing Performance Funding in Three Leading States."
33. For more information, see Ozan Jaquette and Edna Parra, "Using IPEDS for Panel Analyses: Core Concepts, Data Challenges, and Empirical Applications," in *Higher Education: Handbook of Theory and Research*, ed. Michael Paulsen (Dordrecht, the Netherlands: Springer, 2014), 467–533.
34. Joshua Angrist and Jörn-Steffen Pischke, *Mastering Metrics: The Path from Cause to Effect* (Princeton, NJ: Princeton University Press, 2015).
35. Marianne Bertrand, Esther Duflo, and Sendhil Mullainathan, "How Much Should We Trust Differences-in-Differences Estimates?" *Quarterly Journal of Economics* 119, no. 1 (2004): 249–75.

Chapter 3

1. National Center for Education Statistics, "High School and Beyond Longitudinal Study of 1980 Sophomores," 2012; and "High School Transcript Study," 1990, 1994, 1998, 2000, 2005, 2009. See http://nces.ed.gov/programs/digest/2012menu_tables.asp.
2. There are also more than 100 Asian American, Native American, and Pacific Islander Serving Institutions, which have greater than 10 percent Asian American or Pacific Islander students. Although Asian Americans, as an aggregate, are a more successful subpopulation in terms of college access, there are subgroups that experience serious problems. And while those issues deserve attention, they are not part of this analysis.
3. Marybeth Gasman, *Envisioning Black Colleges: A History of the United Negro College Fund* (Baltimore: Johns Hopkins University Press, 2007); Marybeth Gasman, Valerie Lundy-Wager, Tafaya Ransom, and Nelson Bowman, *Unearthing Promise and Potential: Historically Black Colleges and Universities* (San Francisco: Jossey-Bass, 2010); Bryan Brayboy, Amy Fann, A. Castagno, and J. Solyom, *Postsecondary Education for American Indians and Alaskan Natives: Higher Education for Nation Building and Self-Determination* (San Francisco: Jossey-Bass, 2012).
4. Marybeth Gasman, Benjamin Baez, and Caroline Sotello Turner, eds., *Understanding Minority-Serving Institutions* (Albany: State University of New York Press, 2008); Marybeth Gasman and Clifton Conrad, *Minority Serving Institutions: Educating All Students.* (Philadelphia: Penn Center for Minority Serving Institutions, 2013); Clifton Conrad and Marybeth Gasman, *Educating a Diverse Nation: Lessons from Minority-Serving Institutions* (Cambridge, MA: Harvard University Press, 2015).
5. American Association of Community Colleges, 2014, www.aacu.org; IPEDS, 2013, https://nces.ed.gov/ipeds.

6. We are excluding Asian American and Native American Pacific Islander Serving Institutions; Native American Serving Nontribal Colleges; Alaskan Native/Native Hawaiian Serving Institutions; and Predominantly Black Institutions.
7. Gasman and Conrad, *Minority Serving Institutions*; Conrad and Gasman, *Educating a Diverse Nation*; Marybeth Gasman and Thai-Huy Nguyen, *HBCUs as Leaders in STEM* (Philadelphia: Penn Center for Minority Serving Institutions, 2014).
8. Gasman, *Envisioning Black Colleges*; Gasman et al., *Understanding Minority-Serving Institutions*; Gasman and Conrad, *Minority Serving Institutions*; Conrad and Gasman, *Educating a Diverse Nation*.
9. Marybeth Gasman and Heather Collins, "The Historically Black College and University Community and the Obama Administration: A Lesson in Communication," *Change* 46, no. 5 (2014): 39–43.
10. *My Brother's Keeper Task Force Report to the President* (Washington, DC.: Department of Education, 2014), https://obamawhitehouse.archives.gov/sites/default/files/docs/053014_mbk_report.pdf.
11. Edward Fergus, Pedro Noguera, and Margary Martin, *Schooling for Resilience: Improving the Life Trajectory of Black and Latino Boys* (Cambridge, MA: Harvard Education Press, 2014).
12. Kathryn Edin and Timothy Nelson, *Doing the Best I Can: Fatherhood in the Inner City* (Berkeley: University of California Press, 2013).
13. *My Brother's Keeper Task Force Report.*
14. Alisa Cunningham, Eunkyoung Park, and Jennifer Engle, *Minority-Serving Institutions: Doing More with Less* (Washington, DC: Institute for Higher Education Policy, 2014).
15. Laura Perna, Valerie Lundy-Wagner, Noah Drezner, Marybeth Gasman, Susan Yoon, Enashi Bose, and Shannon Gary, "The Contribution of HBCUs to the Preparation of African American Women for STEM Careers: A Case Study," *Research in Higher Education* 50, no. 1 (2009): 1–23.
16. Anthony Carnevale, N. Smith, and M. Melton, *Expanding Underrepresented Minority Participation: America's Science and Technology Talent at the Crossroads*, Consensus Study Report (Washington, DC: National Academies Press, 2011).
17. Doug Massey, Camille Charles, Garvey Lundy, and Mary Fischer, *The Source of the River: The Social Origins of Freshmen at America's Selective Colleges and Universities* (Princeton, NJ: Princeton University Press, 2011).
18. Adam Maltese and Robert Tai, "Pipeline Persistence: Examining the Association of Educational Experiences with Earned Degrees in STEM Among US Students," *Science Education* 95, no. 5 (2011): 877–907; Will Tyson, Reginald Lee, Kathryn Borman, and Mary Hanson, "Science, Technology, Engineering, and Mathematics (STEM) Pathways: High School Science and Math Coursework and Postsecondary Degree Attainment," *Journal of Education for Students Placed at Risk* 12, no. 3 (2007): 243–70.
19. National Center for Education Statistics, "High School and Beyond Longitudinal Study"; and "High School Transcript Study," 1990, 1994, 1998, 2000, 2005, 2009.

20. National Science Foundation, 2013, www.nsf.gov. Due to data reliability issues on American Indians or Alaska Natives and Native Hawaiians and Pacific Islanders, the results of our analysis are less conclusive.

21. Robert Teranishi, *Asians in the Ivory Tower: Dilemmas of Racial Inequality in American Higher Education,* Multicultural Education Series (New York: Teachers College Press, 2010).

22. Catherine Riegle-Crumb and Barbara King, "Questioning a White Male Advantage in STEM: Examining Disparities in College Major by Gender and Race/Ethnicity," *Educational Researcher* 39, no. 9 (2010): 656–64.

23. Catherine Alexander, Ellzabeth Chen, and Katherine Grumbach, "How Leaky Is the Health Career Pipeline? Minority Student Achievement in College Gateway Courses," *Academic Medicine* 84, no. 6 (2009): 797–802; Elaine Seymour and Nancy Hewitt, *Talking About Leaving: Why Undergraduates Leave the Sciences* (Boulder, CO: Westview Press, 1997).

24. Oren McClain, "Negotiating Identity: A Look at the Educational Experiences of Black Undergraduates in STEM Disciplines," *Peabody Journal of Education* 89, no. 3 (2014): 380–92; Seymour and Hewitt, *Talking About Leaving.*

25. Kenneth Maton and Freeman Hrabowski III, "Increasing the Number of African American PhDs in the Sciences and Engineering: A Strengths-Based Approach," *American Psychologist* 59, no. 6 (2004): 547.

26. Gasman et al., *Understanding Minority-Serving Institutions*; Perna et al., "The Contribution of HBCUs."

27. Asian American, Native American, and Pacific Islander institutions were not included in this discussion, as STEM-related data are not available.

28. Instead of "Hispanic-serving institution," the National Science Foundation uses "high Hispanic enrollment," because only enrollment of 25 percent or more Hispanics was used as the criteria for inclusion. HSIBoth terms are not equal, since "high Hispanic enrollment" does not have Pell grant criteria.

29. Jeff Berger and Jeff Milem, "Exploring the Impact of Historically Black Colleges in Promoting the Development of Undergraduates' Self-Concept," *Journal of College Student Development* 41, no. 4 (2001): 381–94; Robert Palmer and Marybeth Gasman, "It Takes a Village to Raise a Child": The Role of Social Capital in Promoting Academic Success for African American Men at a Black College," *Journal of College Student Development* 49, no. 1 (2008): 52–70.

30. Conrad and Gasman, *Educating a Diverse Nation*; Palmer and Gasman, "It Takes a Village to Raise a Child."

31. McClain, "Negotiating Identity."

32. Sylvia Hurtado, Chris Newman, C. Tran, & Mith Chang, "Improving the Rate of Success for Underrepresented Racial Minorities in STEM Fields: Insights from a National Project," *New Directions for Institutional Research* 148 (2010): 5–15; Perna et al., "The Contribution of HBCUs."

33. See www.ed.gov/teaching.

34. Richard Ingersoll and Henry May, "The Minority Teacher Shortage: Fact or Fable?" *Phi Delta Kappan* 93, no. 1 (2011): 62–65.

Chapter 4

1. US Department of Education, "Undergraduate Retention and Graduation Rates," National Center for Education Statistics, https://nces.ed.gov/fastfacts/display.asp?id=40.
2. *A Stronger Nation Through Higher Education* (Indianapolis: Lumina Foundation, 2013).
3. Linda DeAngelo, Ray Franke, Sylvia Hurtado, John H. Pryor, and Serge Tran, *Completing College: Assessing Graduation Rates at Four-Year Institutions* (Los Angeles: Higher Education Research Institute, 2011).
4. Office of the Press Secretary, the White House, "Fact Sheet on the President's Plan to Make College More Affordable: A Better Bargain for the Middle Class," August 23, 2014, http://www.whitehouse.gov/the-press-office/2013/08/22/fact-sheet-president-s-planmake-college-more-affordable-better-bargain-.'
5. Steve Olson and Donna Gerardi Riordan, *Engaged to Excel: Producing One Million Additional College Graduates with Degrees in Science, Technology, Engineering, and Mathematics* (Washington, DC: Executive Office of the President of the United States, 2012), https://obamawhitehouse.archives.gov/sites/default/files/microsites/ostp/pcast-engage-to-excel-final_2-25-12.pdf.
6. Nicole M. Stephens, Maryam G. Hamedani, and Mesmin Destin, "Closing the Social-Class Achievement Gap: A Difference-Education Intervention Improves First-Generation Students' Academic Performance and All Students' College Transition," *Psychological Science* 25, no. 4 (2014): 943–53.
7. Chris Wilson, "Obama Thinks He Can Rate Colleges: Can You Do Better?" *TIME*, April 22, 2014, http://time.com/71782/make-your-own-college-ranking/.
8. Alexander W. Astin, *Assessment for Excellence: The Philosophy and Practice of Assessment and Evaluation in Higher Education* (Phoenix: Oryx Press, 1991).
9. Alexander W. Astin and Leticia Oseguera, *Degree Attainment Rates at American Colleges and Universities,* rev. ed. (Los Angeles: Higher Education Research Institute, 2005); Alexander W. Astin, Lisa Tsui, and Juan Avalos, *Degree Attainment Rates at American Colleges and Universities: Effects of Race, Gender, and Institutional Type* (Los Angeles: Higher Education Research Institute, 1996); DeAngelo et al., *Completing College.*
10. Sylvia Hurtado, Adriana Ruiz Alvarado, Abigail K. Bates, Joseph John Ramirez, and Theresa Jean Stewart, "Closing the Gap for First Generation, Underrepresented Minority Students" (presentation, Annual Forum of the Association for Institutional Research, Orlando, FL, May 2014).
11. Mark Kevin Eagan, "An Examination of the Contributors to Production Efficiency of Undergraduate Degrees in STEM" (presentation, Annual Meeting of the Association for the Study of Higher Education, Vancouver, BC, Canada, November 2009).
12. See websites for these data-based organizations, including: https://heri.ucla.edu/cirp-freshman-survey/ for CIRP Freshman Survey; http://www.studentclearinghouse.org/.snf for the National Student Clearinghouse; and https://nces.ed.gov/ipeds/Home/UseTheData for the IPEDS data bases.
13. Eagan, "An Examination of the Contributors to Production Efficacy"; Mark Kevin Eagan, Sylvia Hurtado, Tanya Figueroa, and Bryce Hughes, "Making Future Sci-

entists: Campuses' Efficiency in STEM Degree Production" (presentation, Annual Forum of the Association for Institutional Research, Orlando, FL, May 2014).

14. The details of the procedures for these analyses can be found in papers cited online at the http://heri.ucla.edu/nih.

15. DeAngelo et al., *Completing College*.

16. Sylvia Hurtado, Mark Kevin Eagan, and Bryce Hughes, "Priming the Pump or the Sieve: Institutional Contexts and URM STEM Degree Attainments" (presentation, Annual Forum of the Association for Institutional Research, New Orleans, May 2012).

Chapter 5

The data used in this paper include administrative records from the Texas Education Agency and the Texas Higher Education Coordinating Board. The conclusions of this research do not necessarily reflect the opinions or the official position of the Texas Education Agency, the Texas Higher Education Coordinating Board, or the State of Texas. An earlier version of this work can be found in Stella M. Flores, Toby J. Park, and Dominique J. Baker, "The Racial College Completion Gap: Evidence from Texas," *Journal of Higher Education* 88, no. 6 (2017): 894–921.

1. John Bound, Michael F. Lovenheim, and Sarah Turner, "Why Have College Completion Rates Declined? An Analysis of Changing Student Preparation and Collegiate Resources," *American Economic Journal: Applied Economics* 2, no. 3 (2010): 129–57; William G. Bowen, Matthew M. Chingos, and Michael S. McPherson, *Crossing the Finish Line* (Princeton, NJ: Princeton University Press, 2009); Sarah Turner, "Going to College and Finishing College: Explaining Different Educational Outcomes," in *College Choices: The Economics of Where to Go, When to Go, and How to Pay for It*, ed. Caroline Hoxby (Chicago: University of Chicago Press, 2004).

2. Michal Kurlaender and Erika Felts, "*Bakke* Beyond College Access," in *Realizing Bakke's Legacy: Affirmative Action, Equal Opportunity, and Access to Higher Education*, ed. Patricia Marin and Catherine L. Horn (Sterling, VA: Stylus, 2008).

3. We use interchangeable terms for some race and ethnic identifications. For example, while the terms *Latino* and *Hispanic* are both used currently and often interchangeably to describe people of Latin American and/or Spanish/Spanish colonial origins, we primarily use *Hispanic* to be consistent with the prevalence of this term in federal US policy documentation and in the nomenclature of the federal higher education funding program serving this population: Hispanic-Serving Institutions. We use *Black* and *African American* interchangeably in this analysis.

4. Katherine Hughes, "The College Completion Agenda: 2012 Progress Report" (report, Advocacy and Policy Center, College Board, New York, 2012), http://media. collegeboard.com/digitalServices/pdf/advocacy/policycenter/college-completion-agenda-2012-progress-report.pdf.

5. Richard Fry and Mark H. Lopez, "Hispanic Student Enrollments Reach New Highs in 2011" (report, Pew Hispanic Center, Washington, DC, 2012), http://assets.pew research.org/wp-content/uploads/sites/7/2012/08/Hispanic-Student-Enrollments-Reach-New-Highs-in-2011_FINAL.pdf.

6. Stella M. Flores and Justin C. Shepherd, "Pricing Out the Disadvantaged? The Effect of Tuition Deregulation in Texas Public Four-Year Institutions," *ANNALS of the American Academy of Political and Social Science* 655, no. 1 (2014): 99–122.

7. Edward M. Telles and Vilma Ortiz, *Generations of Exclusion: Mexican-Americans, Assimilation, and Race* (New York: Russell Sage Foundation, 2008).

8. Anthony P. Carnevale, Nicole Smith, and Jeff Strohl, "Help Wanted: Projections of Job and Education Requirements Through 2018" (report, Center on Education and Workforce, Georgetown University, Washington, DC, 2010), https://cew.george town.edu/wp-content/uploads/2014/12/fullreport.pdf.

9. Connor Dougherty and Miriam Jordan, "Minority Births Are New Majority," *Wall Street Journal*, May 17, 2012, https://www.wsj.com/articles/SB100014240 52702303879604577408363003351818; Morgan Smith, "At Some Schools, the Demographic Future Is Now," *New York Times*, August 31, 2011, http://www. nytimes.com/2012/08/31/us/hispanic-student-population-swells-at-texas-schools. html?pagewanted=all; Valerie Strauss, "For the First Time, Minority Students Expected to Be Majority in U.S. Public Schools," *Washington Post*, August 21, 2014, http://www.washingtonpost.com/blogs/answer-sheet/wp/2014/08/21/for-first-time-minority-students-expected-to-be-majority-in-u-s-public-schools-this-fall/.

10. Nicholas W. Hillman, David A. Tandberg, and Jacob P. K. Gross, "Performance Funding in Higher Education: Do Financial Incentives Impact College Completions?" *Journal of Higher Education* 85, no. 6 (2014): 826–57; Nicholas W. Hillman, David A. Tandberg, and Alisa H. Fryar, "Evaluating the Impacts of 'New' Performance Funding in Higher Education," *Educational Evaluation and Policy Analysis* 37, no. 4 (2015): 501–19; Kevin J. Doughtery, Sosanya M. Jones, Hana Lahr, Rebecca S. Natow, Lara Pheatt, and Vikash Reddy, *Performance Funding for Higher Education* (Baltimore: Johns Hopkins University Press, 2016).

11. Hillman et al., "Evaluating the Impacts."

12. "Developing Hispanic-Serving Institutions Program: Title V," US Department of Education, http://www.ed.gov/programs/idueshsi/legislation.html; Marybeth Gasman, Benjamin Baez, and Caroline S. V. Turner, eds., *Understanding Minority-Serving Institutions* (Albany: State University of New York Press, 2008).

13. Emily C. Galdeano and Deborah A. Santiago, "Hispanic-Serving Institutions (HSIs): 2012–2013" (report, Excelencia in Education, Washington, DC, 2013), http://www. edexcelencia.org/research/hsis-2012-13; Gasman et al., *Understanding Minority-Serving Institutions*; Noel Harmon, "The Role of Minority-Serving Institutions in National College Completion Goals" (report, Institute for Higher Education Policy, Washington, DC, 2012), http://www.ihep.org/sites/default/files/uploads/docs/pubs/ the_role_of_msis_final_january_20121.pdf.

14. William Boland and Marybeth Gasman, "America's Public HBCUs: A Four State Comparison of Institutional Capacity and State Funding Priorities" (report, Center for Minority-Serving Institutions, University of Pennsylvania, Philadelphia, 2014), http://www.gse.upenn.edu/pdf/cmsi/four_state_comparison.pdf; Carla Fletcher and Jeff Webster, "Profile of Minority-Serving Institutions in Texas: A Study of Historically Black Colleges and Universities and Hispanic-Serving Institutions" (report, Texas Guaranteed Student Loan Corporation, Round Rock, Texas, 2010); Christine

M. Matthews, "Federal Research and Development Funding at Historically Black Colleges and Universities" (report, Congressional Research Service, Library of Congress, Washington, DC, 2011), http://research.policyarchive.org/18821.pdf.

15. Xiaojie Li, "Characteristics of Minority-Serving Institutions and Minority Undergraduates Enrolled in These Institutions" (Postsecondary Education Descriptive Analysis Report, NCES 2008-156, National Center for Education Statistics, Washington, DC, 2007), https://nces.ed.gov/pubs2008/2008156.pdf.

16. Ibid.

17. David A. R. Richards and Janet T. Awokoya, "Understanding HBCU Retention and Completion" (report, Frederick D. Patterson Research Institute, United Negro College Fund, Fairfax, Virginia, 2012), http://files.eric.ed.gov/fulltext/ED562057.pdf.

18. Ronald L. Oaxaca and Michael Ransom, "Calculation of Approximate Variances for Wage Decomposition Differentials," *Journal of Economic and Social Measurement* 24, no. 1 (1998): 55–61; Tom D. Stanley and Stephen B. Jarrell, "Gender Wage Discrimination Bias? A Meta-Regression Analysis," *Journal of Human Resources* 33, no. 4 (1998): 947–73; Bound et al., "Why Have College Completion Rates Declined?"

19. Clifford Adelman, "The Toolbox Revisited: Paths to Degree Completion from High School Through College" (report, US Department of Education, Washington, DC, 2006), https://www2.ed.gov/rschstat/research/pubs/toolboxrevisit/toolbox.pdf; Bound et al., "Why Have College Completion Rates Declined?"; Laura W. Perna, "Studying College Access and Choice: A Proposed Conceptual Model," *Higher Education: Handbook of Theory and Research* 21 (2006): 99–157.

20. Stella M. Flores and Toby J. Park, "Race, Ethnicity, and College Success Examining the Continued Significance of the Minority-Serving Institution," *Educational Researcher* 42, no. 3 (2013): 115–28.

21. Gary S. Becker, *Human Capital: A Theoretical and Empirical Analysis* (New York: Columbia University Press, 1964); Bound et al., "Why Have College Completion Rates Declined?"; Jacob Mincer, *Schooling, Experience, and Earnings* (New York: Columbia University Press, 1974).

22. Flores and Park, "Race, Ethnicity, and College"; Stella M. Flores and Toby J. Park, "The Effect of Enrolling in a Minority-Serving Institution for Black and Hispanic Students in Texas," *Research in Higher Education* 56, no. 3 (2015): 247–76.

23. Becker, *Human Capital.*

24. Bound et al., "Why Have College Completion Rates Declined?"

25. Tatiana Melguizo, "Are Students of Color More Likely to Graduate from College if They Attend More Selective Institutions? Evidence from a Cohort of Recipients and Nonrecipients of the Gates Millennium Scholarship Program," *Educational Evaluation and Policy Analysis* 32, no. 2 (2010): 230–48; Anne-Marie Nunez and Alex J. Bowers, "Exploring What Leads High School Students to Enroll in Hispanic-Serving Institutions: A Multilevel Analysis," *American Educational Research Journal* 48, no. 6 (2011): 1286–313; Perna, "Studying College Access."

26. Clifford Adelman, "Principal Indicators of Student Academic Histories in Postsecondary Education, 1972–2000" (report, US Department of Education, Washington, DC, 2004), http://files.eric.ed.gov/fulltext/ED483154.pdf.

27. Adelman, "Principal Indicators"; Patrice Iatarola, Dylan Conger, and Mark C. Long, "Determinants of High Schools' Advanced Course Offerings," *Educational Evaluation and Policy Analysis* 33, no. 3 (2011): 340–59; Philip M. Sadler, Gerhard Sonnert, Robert H. Tai, and Kristin Klopfenstein, *AP: A Critical Examination of the Advanced Placement Program* (Cambridge, MA: Harvard Education Press, 2010).

28. Eric A. Hanushek, John F. Kain, and Steven G. Rivkin, "New Evidence About *Brown v. Board of Education*: The Complex Effects of School Racial Composition on Achievement," *Journal of Labor Economics* 27, no. 3 (2009): 350.

29. Gary Orfield, ed., *Dropouts in America: Confronting the Graduation Rate Crisis* (Cambridge, MA: Harvard Education Press, 2004); Gary Orfield, Erica Frankenberg, Jongyeon Ee, and John Kuscera, Brown *at 60: Great Progress, a Long Retreat and an Uncertain Future* (report, Los Angeles: The Civil Rights Project, 2014), https://www.civilrightsproject.ucla.edu/research/k-12-education/integration-and-diversity/brown-at-60-great-progress-a-long-retreat-and-an-uncertain-future/Brown-at-60-051814.pdf.

30. Sunny X. Niu and Marta Tienda, "High School Economic Composition and College Persistence," *Research in Higher Education* 54, no. 1 (2013): 30–62.

31. James D. Bachmeier and Frank D. Bean, "Ethnoracial Patterns of Schooling and Work Among Adolescents: Implications for Mexican Immigrant Incorporation," *Social Science Research* 40, no. 6 (2011): 1579–95.

32. Bachmeier and Bean, "Ethnoracial Patterns."

33. Alison P. Hagy and J. Farley Ordovensky Staniec, "Immigrant Status, Race, and Institutional Choice in Higher Education," *Economics of Education Review* 21, no. 4 (2002): 381–92; Charles F. Manski and David A. Wise, *College Choice in America* (Cambridge, MA: Harvard University Press, 1983); J. Farley Ordovensky, "Effects of Institutional Attributes on Enrollment Choice: Implications for Postsecondary Vocational Education," *Economics of Education Review* 14, no. 4 (1995): 335–50; Cecilia E. Rouse, "Democratization or Diversion? The Effect of Community Colleges on Educational Attainment," *Journal of Business & Economic Statistics* 13, no. 2 (1995): 217–24.

34. Michael N. Bastedo and Ozan Jacquette, "Running in Place: Low-Income Students and the Dynamics of Higher Education Stratification," *Educational Evaluation and Policy Analysis* 33, no. 3 (2011): 318–39; Bowen et al., *Crossing the Finish Line*; Stacy B. Dale and Alan B. Krueger, "Estimating the Payoff to Attending a More Selective College: An Application of Selection on Observables and Unobservables," *Quarterly Journal of Economics* 117, no. 4 (2002): 1491–528; Mark C. Long, "College Quality and Early Adult Outcomes," *Economics of Education Review* 27, no. 5 (2008): 588–602; Tatiana Melguizo, "Are Community Colleges an Alternative Path for Hispanic Students to Attain a Bachelor's Degree?" *Teachers College Record* 111, no. 1 (2009): 90–123; Melguizo, "Are Students of Color More Likely to Graduate."

35. Bound et al., "Why Have College Completion Rates Declined?"

36. Alan S. Blinder, "Wage Discrimination: Reduced Form and Structural Estimates," *Journal of Human Resources* 8, no. 4 (1973): 436–55; Robert W. Fairlie, "An Extension of the Blinder-Oaxaca Decomposition Technique to Logit and Probit Models," *Journal of Economic and Social Measurement* 30, no. 4 (2005): 305–16; Ronald

Oaxaca, "Male-Female Wage Differentials in Urban Labor Markets," *International Economic Review* 14, no. 3 (1973): 683–709; Mathias Sinning, Markus Hahn, and Thomas K. Bauer, "The Blinder-Oaxaca Decomposition for Nonlinear Regression Models," *Stata Journal* 8, no. 4 (2008): 480–92.

37. Sandy et al., "Alternative Paths"; Melguizo, "Are Community Colleges an Alternative Path."
38. Flores et al., "The Racial College Completion Gap."
39. Flores and Park, "Race, Ethnicity, and College."
40. Sandy et al., "Alternative Paths."
41. Flores and Park, "The Effect of Enrolling."
42. Tanya I. Garcia and Hans P. L'Orange, *Strong Foundations: The State of State Postsecondary Data Systems* (Boulder, CO: State Higher Education Executive Officers, 2010).
43. Susan Dynarski and Judith Scott-Clayton, "Financial Aid Policy: Lessons from Research," *The Future of Children* 23, no. 1 (2013): 67–91.
44. Sean F. Reardon and Claudia Galindo, "The Hispanic-White Achievement Gap in Math and Reading in the Elementary Grades," *American Educational Research Journal* 46, no. 3 (2009): 853–91.
45. Carnevale et al., "Help Wanted."

Chapter 6

1. Emily Calderón Galdeano and Deborah Santiago, "Hispanic-Serving Institutions (HSIs) Fact Sheet: 2012–13," *Excelencia in Education*, February 2014, http://www.edexcelencia.org/hsi-cp2/research/hispanic-serving-institutions-hsis-fact-sheet-2012-13.
2. M. Benítez and Jessie DeAro, "Realizing Student Success at Hispanic-Serving Institutions," in *Serving Minority Populations*, ed. B. V. Laden (San Francisco: Jossey-Bass, 2004), 35–48; Anne-Marie Núñez, "Hispanic Higher Education Research Collective (H3ERC) Research Agenda: Impacting Education and Changing Lives Through Understanding," Hispanic Association of Colleges and Universities, 2012, http://www.hacu.net/hacu/ H3ERC_Research_Initiative.asp.; A. Rodríguez and E. Calderón Galdeano, "The Incomparable HSI? Using Propensity Score Matching to Find Comparison Groups for Hispanic Serving Institutions," in *Hispanic-Serving Institutions: Advancing Research and Transformative Practice*, ed. A. Nuñez, S. Hurtado, and E. Calderón Galdeano (New York: Routledge, 2015).
3. Awilda Rodríguez and Emily Calderón Galdeano, "Do Hispanic-Serving Institutions Really Underperform? Using Propensity Score Matching to Compare Outcomes of Hispanic-Serving and Non-Hispanic Serving Institutions," in *Hispanic-Serving Institutions: Advancing Research and Transformative Practice*, ed. A. Nuñez, S. Hurtado, and E. Calderón Galdeano (New York: Routledge, 2015).
4. Ibid.
5. See http://www.edexcelencia.org/research/term/hispanic-serving-institutions.
6. Gregory Kienzl, Mariana Alfonso, and Tatiana Melguizo, "The Effect of Local Labor Market Conditions in the 1990s on the Likelihood of Community College Students' Persistence and Attainment," *Research in Higher Education* 48, no. 7 (2007): 751–

74, doi: 10.1007/s11162-007-9050-y; Johnelle Sparks and Anne-Marie Núñez, "The Role of Postsecondary Institutional Urbanicity in College Persistence," *Journal of Research in Rural Education* 29, no. 6 (2014): 1–19; Soo-Yong Byun, Matthew Irvin, and J. L. Meece, "Predictors of Bachelor's Degree Completion Among Rural Students at Four-Year Institutions," *Review of Higher Education* 35, no. 3 (2012): 463–84; Soo-Yong Byun, J. L. Meece, and Matthew Irvin, "Rural-Nonrural Disparities in Postsecondary Educational Attainment Revisited," *American Educational Research Journal* 49, no. 3 (2012): 412–37; Ernest Pascarella and Patrick Terenzini, *How College Affects Students* (San Francisco: Jossey-Bass, 2005).

7. John Bound, Michael Lovenheim, and Sarah Turner, "Why Have College Completion Rates Declined? An Analysis of Changing Student Perception and Collegiate Resources," *American Economic Journal: Applied Economics* 2, no. 3 (2010): 129–57; Marvin Titus, "Understanding College Degree Completion of Students with Low Socioeconomic Status: The Influence of the Institutional Financial Context," *Research in Higher Education* 47, no. 4 (2006): 371–98; Marvin Titus, "Understanding the Influence of the Financial Context of Institutions on Student Persistence at Four-Year Colleges and Universities," *Journal of Higher Education* 77, no. 2 (2006): 353–75; Marvin Titus, "The Production of Bachelor's Degrees and Financial Aspects of State Higher Education Policy: A Dynamic Analysis," *Journal of Higher Education* 80, no. 4 (2009): 439–68.

8. Anne-Marie Núñez, "Counting What Counts for Latinas/os and Hispanic-Serving Institutions: A Federal Ratings System and Postsecondary Access, Affordability, and Success" (policy briefing, President's Advisory Commission on Educational Excellence for Hispanics, New York, 2014); Titus, "Understanding College Degree Completion"; Titus, "Understanding the Influence of the Financial Context."

9. Sigal Alon and Marta Tienda, "Assessing the 'Mismatch' Hypothesis: Differences in College Graduation Rates by Institutional Selectivity," *Sociology of Education* 78, no. 4 (2005): 294–315; A. Astin and A. Antonio, *Assessment for Excellence: The Philosophy and Practice of Assessment and Evaluation in Higher Education*, 2nd ed. (Lanham, MD: Rowman & Littlefield, 2012).

10. C. Adelman, *The Toolbox Revisited: Paths to Degree Completion from High School Through College* (Washington, DC: US Department of Education, 2006).

11. Steven Ingels and Ben Dalton, "High School Longitudinal Study of 2009 (HSLS:09) First Follow-Up: A First Look at Fall 2009 Ninth-Graders in 2012," National Center for Education Statistics, October 2013, https://nces.ed.gov/pubs2014/2014360.pdf.

12. Amaury Nora and Gloria Crisp, "Hispanic Student Success and Participation in Developmental Education," Hispanic Association of Colleges and Universities, July 2012, http://www.hacu.net/images/hacu/OPAI/H3ERC/2012_papers/Nora%20 crisp%20-%20developmental%20education%20-%202012.pdf.

13. Anne-Marie Núñez and Alex J. Bowers, "Exploring What Leads High School Students to Enroll in Hispanic-Serving Institutions: A Multilevel Analysis," *American Educational Research Journal* 48, no. 6 (2011): 1286–313.

14. Patricia Gandara and Frances Contreras, *The Latino Educational Crisis* (New York: Teachers College Press, 2009); Jeannie Oakes, John Rogers, David Silver, Siomara Valladares, Veronica Terríquez, Patricia McDonough, Michelle Renée, and

Martin Lipton, "Removing the Roadblocks: Fair College Opportunities for All California Students," UC All-Campus Consortium for Research on Diversity and UCLA Institute for Democracy, Education, and Access, November 2006, http://collegetools.berkeley.edu/documents/cat_1-7/Removing_Roadblocks_to_College_(Oakes_et_al__07).pdf; Gary Orfield and Jongyeon Ee, "Segregating California's Future: Inequality and Its Alternative 60 Years After *Brown v. Board of Education*," *UCLA Civil Rights Project,* May 2014, https://www.civilrightsproject.ucla.edu/research/k-12-education/integration-and-diversity/segregating-california2019s-future-inequality-and-its-alternative-60-years-after-brown-v.-board-of-education/orfield-ee-segregating-california-future-brown-at.pdf.

15. Adelman, "The Toolbox Revisited"; Astin and Antonio, *Assessment for Excellence.*
16. Xianglei Chen, Joanna Wu, and Shayna Tasoff, "Academic Preparation for College in the High School Senior Class of 2003–04," National Center for Education Statistics, January 2010, https://nces.ed.gov/pubs2010/2010170rev.pdf.
17. Xianglei Chen, Joanna Wu, and Shayna Tasoff, "The High School Senior Class of 2003–04: Steps Toward Postsecondary Enrollment," National Center for Education Statistics, February 2010, https://nces.ed.gov/pubs2010/2010203.pdf.
18. Analysis of IPEDS data based on 171 four-year HSIs in 2012. Admissions Data File, National Center for Education Statistics, 2012, https://nces.ed.gov/ipeds/datacenter/login.aspx?gotoReportId=1.
19. Jesse Cunha, "Measuring Value-Added in Higher Education: Possibilities and Limitations in the Use of Administrative Data," *Economics of Education Review* 42 (2014): 64–77.
20. Anthony Carnevale and Jeff Strohl, "Separate and Unequal: How Higher Education Reinforces the Intergenerational Reproduction of White Racial Privilege," Center of Education and the Workforce, Georgetown Public Policy Institute, July 2013, https://cew.georgetown.edu/wp-content/uploads/2014/11/SeparateUnequal.FR_.pdf.
21. S. M. Flores and T. J. Park, "The Effect of Enrolling in a Minority-Serving Institution for Black and Hispanic Students in Texas," *Research in Higher Education 56,* no. 3 (2015): 247–76; Stella Flores, Toby Park, and Dominique Baker, "The Racial College-Completion Gap: Evidence from Texas" (paper, UCLA Civil Rights Conference Washington, DC, September 2014).
22. The limitation in the current graduation measure is germane to assessing HSIs' and MSIs' performance. For example, HSIs serve far larger numbers of students who transfer into or out of the institution. Because current graduation rate measures only examine who begins and finishes at the same institution, institutions that transfer students to other institutions are penalized, because students who later transfer are included in the denominator of graduation rate calculations. Tracking students longitudinally, as is done by the National Student Clearinghouse, would capture the progress of more students. L. L. Espinosa, J. R. Crandall, and M. Tukibayeva, *Rankings, Institutional Behavior, and College and University Choice: Framing the National Dialogue on Obama's Ratings Plan* (Washington, DC: American Council on Education, 2014), http://www.acenet.edu/news-room/Documents/Rankings-Institutional-Behavior-and-College-and-University-Choice.pdf.

23. Robert Kelchen, *Moving Forward with Federal College Ratings: Goals, Metrics, and Recommendations* (Madison: Wisconsin Center for the Advancement of Postsecondary Education, 2014), 2; Andrew Nichols, "The Pell Partnership: Ensuring a Shared Responsibility for Low-Income Student Success," Education Trust, September 2015, https://edtrust.org/wp-content/uploads/2014/09/ThePellPartnership_EdTrust_20152.pdf.

24. Flores and Park, "The Effect of Enrolling"; Flores et al., "The Racial College-Completion Gap."

25. See http://www.commondataset.org.

26. See http://education.newamerica.net/sites/newamerica.net/files/policydocs/College BlackoutFINAL.pdf.

27. See http://www.studentachievementmeasure.org.

28. Howard R. Bowen, *Investment in Learning: The Individual and Social Value of American Higher Education* (San Francisco: Jossey-Bass, 1977); Marcella Cuellar, "The Impact of Hispanic-Serving Institutions (HSIs), Emerging HSIs, and Non-HSIs on Latina/o Academic Self-Concept," *Review of Higher Education* 37, no. 4 (2014): 499–530. One of the first studies to outline the full range of social benefits of higher education in addition to individual benefits was H. R. Bowen, *Investment in Learning: The Individual and Social Value of American Higher Education* (San Francisco: Jossey-Bass, 1977). M. Cuellar has documented that Latino students in HSIs demonstrate higher academic self-concept and community engagement than students in non-HSIs; see "The Impact of Hispanic-Serving Institutions (HSIs), Emerging HSIs, and Non-HSIs on Latina/o Academic Self-Concept," *Review of Higher Education* 37, no. 4 (2014): 499–530. These are the kinds of outcomes that voluntary efforts could help develop, and these outcomes could vary among distinctive kinds of institutions.

29. Kelchen, "Moving Forward with Federal College Ratings"; Awilda Rodríguez and Andrew Kelly, "Access, Affordability, and Success: How Do America's Colleges Fare and What Could It Mean for the President's Ratings Plan?" American Enterprise Institute, February 2015, http://www.aei.org/publication/access-affordability-and-success-how-do-americas-colleges-fare-and-what-could-it-mean-for-the-presidents-ratings-plan.

30. For more specific suggestions about developing the least unsound potential measures of access, affordability, and institutional performance using existing data, see Kelchen, "Moving Forward with Federal College Ratings."

Chapter 7

An earlier version of this work is Nicholas Hillman, "Geography of College Opportunity: The Case of Education Deserts," *American Educational Research Journal* 53, no. 4 (2017): 987–1021.

1. National Center for Education Statistics, "Digest of Education Statistics, 2013, Table 303.70," in *Total Undergraduate Fall Enrollment in Degree-Granting Postsecondary Institutions, by Attendance Status, Sex of Student, and Control and Level of Institution: Selected Years, 1970 through 2012* (Washington, DC: Department of Education, 2013), http://nces.ed.gov/programs/digest/d13/tables/dt13_303.70.asp.

2. Ruth N. Lopez Turley, "College Proximity: Mapping Access to Opportunity," *Sociology of Education* 82, no. 2 (2009): 126–46.

3. Dongbin Kim and John L. Rury, "The Rise of the Commuter Student: Changing Patterns of College Attendance for Students Living at Home in the United States, 1960–1980," *Teachers College Record* 113, no. 5 (2011): 1031–66; Laura Perna, "Understanding the Working College Student," *Academe* 96, no. 4 (2010): 30–32; Mary Ziskin, Mary Ann Fischer, Vasti Torres, Beth Pallicciotti, and Jacquelyn Player-Sanders, "Working Students' Perceptions of Paying for College: Understanding the Connections Between Financial Aid and Work," *Review of Higher Education* 37, no. 4 (2014): 429–67.

4. This excludes all students who enroll exclusively online. The variable names from PowerStats include DISTANCE, SECTOR4, and ALTONLN2. WTA000 weight is used. National Center for Education Statistics, *2011–12 National Postsecondary Student Aid Study* (Washington, DC: Department of Education, 2012).

5. Daniel Block and Joanne Kouba, "A Comparison of the Availability and Affordability of a Market Basket in Two Communities in the Chicago Area," *Public Health Nutrition* 9, no. 7 (2006): 837–45; Renee E. Walker, Christopher R. Keane, and Jessica G. Burke, "Disparities and Access to Healthy Food in the United States: A Review of Food Deserts Literature," *Health & Place* 16, no. 5 (2010): 876–84.

6. P.L. 110-246, "2008 Farm Bill," US Senate Committee on Agriculture, Nutrition, and Forestry, 2008, http://www.ag.senate.gov/issues/2008-farm-bill.

7. Walker, Keane, and Burke, "Disparities and Access to Healthy Food"; Whelan et al., "Life in a 'Food Desert,'" *Urban Studies* 39, no. 11 (2002): 2083–100.

8. Block and Kouba, "A Comparison of the Availability and Affordability of a Market Basket"; Archana Lamichhane, Joshua Warren, Robin Puett, Dwayne Porter, Matteo Bottai, Elizabeth Mayer-Davis, and Angela Liese, "Spatial Patterning of Supermarkets and Fast Food Outlets with Respect to Neighborhood Characteristics," *Health & Place* 23 (September 2013): 157–64, doi:10.1016/j.healthplace.2013.07.002; Michael J. Widener et al., "Using Urban Commuting Data to Calculate a Spatiotemporal Accessibility Measure for Food Environment Studies," *Health & Place* 21 (2013): 1–9, doi:10.1016/j.healthplace.2013.01.004.

9. Charles M. Tolbert and Molly Sizer, *US Commuting Zones and Labor Market Areas: A 1990 Update* (Washington, DC: Department of Agriculture, 1996), http://trid.trb.org/view.aspx?id=471923.

10. "Rural-Urban Continuum Codes," US Department of Agriculture, 2014, http://www.ers.usda.gov/data-products/rural-urban-continuum-codes/documentation.aspx#.U9uaNGNZbZc. The Bureau of Economic Analysis data are measured as a mean of 2008–12 educational attainment levels.

11. If a CZ spans multiple states, the CZ is attributed to the state in which the largest population share resides. For example, the Memphis CZ spans three states: Tennessee, Mississippi, and Arkansas. Since the majority of this CZ's population resides in Tennessee, it is clustered around Tennessee.

12. This is calculating by taking the exponent of the log odds: exp(0.378) and exp(0.346).

13. Flavia C. D. Andrade and Edna A. Viruell-Fuentes, "Latinos and the Changing Demographic Landscape: Key Dimensions for Infrastructure Building," in *Creat-*

ing Infrastructures for Latino Mental Health (New York: Springer, 2011), 3–30, http://link.springer.com/chapter/10.1007/978-1-4419-9452-3_1; Marta Tienda and Norma Fuentes, "Hispanics in Metropolitan America: New Realities and Old Debates," *Annual Review of Sociology* 40 (2014), http://www.annualreviews.org/doi/abs/10.1146/annurev-soc-071913-043315.

14. Barack Obama, "Remarks by the President on College Affordability," Office of the President, August 22, 2013, http://www.whitehouse.gov/the-press-office/2013/08/22/remarks-president-college-affordability-buffalo-ny.

15. See, using ZIP Code 78852, http://nces.ed.gov/collegenavigator/?s=all&zc=78852&zd=100&of=3.

16. The idea of enterprise zones, equity funding, or similar policies as Title I in the Elementary and Secondary Education Act are rarely explored in higher education finance. Thanks to Greg Kienzl for providing helpful feedback.

Chapter 8

1. William Kirkland, "Predictors of First to Second Year Retention at a Private Historically Black College and University" (paper, Annual Symposium on Student Retention, San Diego, November 4–6, 2013).

2. Mission statement, *2013–2014 Dillard University Catalog*, http://www.dillard.edu/images/pdfs/Dillard%20University%202013-14%20Academic%20Catalog%20Web%20Version%20Animated%20MR%202102014%20Summer%20Sched%20Change.pdf.

3. "Integrated Postsecondary Education Data System Data Feedback Report," National Center for Education Statistics. https://nces.ed.gov/ipeds/.

4. William Kirkland, "Predictors of First to Second Year Retention at a Private Historically Black College and University" (paper, Annual Symposium on Student Retention, San Diego, November 4–6, 2013).

5. "Integrated Postsecondary Education Data System Data Feedback Report," National Center for Education Statistics. https://nces.ed.gov/ipeds/.

6. "Integrated Postsecondary Education Data System Data Feedback Report," National Center for Education Statistics. https://nces.ed.gov/ipeds/.

7. William Kirkland, "Predictors of First to Second Year Retention at a Private Historically Black College and University" (paper, Annual Symposium on Student Retention, San Diego, November 4–6, 2013).

8. Lewis Sullivan, "Accessibility, Affordability, and Accountability: A Discussion of Recommendations of the Spellings Commission Report" (speech, Institute on Quality Enhancement and Accreditation, Louisville, KY, July 23, 2007).

9. William Kirkland, "Predictors of First to Second Year Retention at a Private Historically Black College and University" (paper, Annual Symposium on Student Retention, San Diego, November 4–6, 2013).

10. "Integrated Postsecondary Education Data System Data Feedback Report," National Center for Education Statistics. https://nces.ed.gov/ipeds/.

11. William Kirkland, "Predictors of First to Second Year Retention at a Private Historically Black College and University" (paper, Annual Symposium on Student Retention, San Diego, November 4–6, 2013).

12. Toya Barnes-Teamer (Vice President for Student Success), in discussion with the author, October 2014.
13. Demetrius Johnson (Director of Residential Life), in discussion with the author, October 2014.
14. Carol C. Landry, "Retention of Women and People of Color: Unique Challenges and Institutional Response," *Journal of College Student Retention* 4, no. 1 (2002): 1–14.
15. James Scannell, "The Role of Financial Aid and Retention," *University Business Magazine,* May 2011, https://www.universitybusiness.com/article/role-financial-aid-and-retention.
16. William Kirkland, "Predictors of First to Second Year Retention at a Private Historically Black College and University" (paper, Annual Symposium on Student Retention, San Diego, November 4–6, 2013).
17. Eduwardo Porter, "A Simple Equation: More Education = More Income," *New York Times,* September 10, 2014, https://www.nytimes.com/2014/09/11/business/economy/a-simple-equation-more-education-more-income.html.

Chapter 9

1. Authors' calculations using data from US Department of Education, National Center for Education Statistics, 2011–12 National Postsecondary Student Aid Study (NPSAS:12), https://nces.ed.gov/surveys/npsas/index.asp.
2. *Quarterly Report on Household Debt and Credit* (New York: Federal Reserve Bank of New York, 2014).
3. Sara Goldrick-Rab. *Paying the Price: College Costs, Financial Aid, and the Betrayal of the American Dream* (Chicago: University of Chicago Press, 2016).
4. Fenaba R. Addo, Jason N. Houle, and Daniel Simon, "Young, Black, and (Still) in the Red: Parental Wealth, Race, and Student Loan Debt," *Race and Social Problems* 8, no. 1 (2016): 64–76.
5. Sara Goldrick-Rab, Laura Schudde, and Jacob Stampen, "Creating Cultures of Affordability: Can Institutional Incentives Improve the Effectiveness of Financial Aid?" in *Reinventing Financial Aid: Charting a New Course to College Affordability*, ed. Andrew Kelly and Sara Goldrick-Rab (Cambridge, MA: Harvard Education Press, 2014).
6. National Center for Education Statistics, *Digest of Education Statistics* (Washington, DC: Department of Education, 2013).
7. James C. Hearn and Janet M. Holdsworth, "Federal Student Aid: The Shift from Grants to Loans," in *Public Funding of Higher Education: Changing Contexts and New Rationales,* ed. Edward P. St. John and Michael D. Parsons (Baltimore: Johns Hopkins University Press, 2004); Gwendolyn L. Lewis, "Trends in Student Aid: 1963–64 to 1988–89," *Research in Higher Education* 50, no. 6 (1989): 547–61.
8. Arthur M. Hauptman, "Reforming the Ways in Which States Finance Higher Education," in *The States and Public Higher Education Policy: Affordability, Access, and Accountability*, ed. Donald E. Heller (Baltimore: Johns Hopkins University Press, 2001); Julie Renee Posselt, "The Rise and Fall of Need-Based Grants: A Critical Review of Presidential Discourses on Higher Education, 1964–1984," in *Higher*

Education: Handbook of Theory and Practice, vol. 24, ed. John C. Smart (Dordrecht, the Netherlands: Springer, 2009).

9. Goldrick-Rab et al., "Creating Cultures of Affordability."

10. Robert B. Archibald, *Redesigning the Financial Aid System: Why Colleges and Universities Should Switch Roles with the Federal Government* (Baltimore: Johns Hopkins University Press, 2002); F. Galloway and Derek Price, "Student Loans," in *Governing America: Major Decisions of Federal, State and Local Governments from 1789 to the Present,* ed. Paul J. Quirk and William Cunion (New York: Facts on File, 2011).

11. Middle Income Student Assistance Act, 20 U.S.C. (1978), Public Law 95-566.

12. Michael Mumper, *Removing College Price Barriers: What Government Has Done and Why It Hasn't Worked* (Albany: State University of New York Press, 1996).

13. Education Amendments of 1980, 20 U.S.C. (1980), Public Law 96-374.

14. Education Amendments of 1986, 20 U.S.C. (1986), Public Law 99-498.

15. Education Amendments of 1992, 20 U.S.C. (1992), Public Law 102-325.

16. Sandy Baum and Jennifer Ma, *Trends in College Pricing* (Washington, DC: The College Board, 2013).

17. Christina Chang Wei and Paul Skomsvold, *Borrowing at the Maximum: Undergraduate Stafford Loan Borrowers in 2007–08* (Washington, DC: National Center for Education Statistics, 2012).

18. Authors' calculations using NPSAS:12 data.

19. Sara Goldrick-Rab and Nancy Kendall, *Redefining College Affordability: Securing America's Future with a Free Two Year College Option* (Madison, WI: The Education Optimists, 2014).

20. Sara Goldrick-Rab, "The Challenge of College Affordability: The Student Lens" (testimony, US Senate Committee on Health, Education, Labor and Pensions, Washington, DC, 2013).

21. Authors' calculations using NPSAS:12 data.

22. Wei and Skomsvold, *Borrowing at the Maximum.*

23. Erin Dillon and Kevin Carey, *Drowning in Debt: The Emerging Student Loan Crisis* (Washington, DC: Education Sector, 2009).

24. Project on Student Debt, *Private Loans: Facts and Trends* (Oakland, CA: Institute for College Access and Success, 2016), http://ticas.org/sites/default/files/pub_files/private_loan_facts_trends.pdf.

25. Federal Student Aid, *FY 2011 2-Year National Student Loan Default Rates,* US Department of Education, 2014, https://ifap.ed.gov/eannouncements/attachments/2013OfficialFY112YRCDRBriefing.pdf.

26. Federal Student Aid, *Federal Student Loan Portfolio,* US Department of Education, 2014, https://studentaid.ed.gov/sa/about/data-center/student/portfolio.

27. Awilda Rodriguez, *Access to What and for Whom? A Closer Look at Federal Parent PLUS Loans* (Washington, DC: American Enterprise Institute, 2014).

28. Ibid.

29. Alicia D. Dowd, "Dynamic Interactions and Intersubjectivity: Challenges to Causal Modeling in Studies of College Student Debt," *Review of Educational Research* 78, no. 2 (2008): 232–59.

30. Stephanie Riegg Cellini and Claudia Goldin, "Does Federal Student Aid Raise Tuition? New Evidence on For-Profit Colleges" (Working Paper No. 18343, National Bureau of Economic Research, Cambridge, MA, 2012).
31. Susan Dynarski and Judith Scott-Clayton, *College Grants on a Postcard* (Washington, DC: Brookings Institution, 2007); Don Hossler, Mary Ziskin, Jacob Gross, Sooyeon Kim, and Osman Cekic, "Student Aid and Its Role in Encouraging Persistence," in *Higher Education: Handbook of Theory and Practice,* vol. 24, ed. John C. Smart (Dordrecht, the Netherlands: Springer, 2009).
32. Rong Chen and Stephen L. DesJardins, "Investigating the Impact of Financial Aid on Student Dropout Risks: Racial and Ethnic Differences," *Journal of Higher Education* 81, no. 2 (2010): 179–208; Rachel E. Dwyer, Randy Hodson, and Laura McCloud, "Gender, Debt, and Dropping Out of College," *Gender and Society* 27, no. 1 (2013): 30–55; Brandon A. Jackson and John R. Reynolds, "The Price of Opportunity: Race, Student Loan Debt, and College Achievement," *Sociological Inquiry* 83, no. 3 (2013): 335–68.
33. Kevin Carey, "The Federal Parent Rip-Off Loan," *Chronicle of Higher Education,* June 3, 2013.
34. Susan Dynarski, "PLUS Loans Are Not Student Aid," *The Cranky Analyst,* April 5, 2014, http://susandynarski.blogspot.com/2014/04/plus-loans-are-not-student-aid.html; Rachel Fishman, *Parent PLUS Loans: A No-Strings-Attached Revenue Source* (Washington, DC: New America Foundation, 2013).
35. Libby A. Nelson, "Cracking Down on PLUS Loans," *Inside Higher Ed,* October 12, 2012.
36. Michael Stratford, "Duncan Apologizes on PLUS Loans," *Inside Higher Ed,* September 27, 2013. Education secretary Arne Duncan later apologized for poor management of the PLUS loan changes and promised to expedite the appeal process for parents who were denied loans; nearly all families who appealed were granted loans in 2013. This apology was directed only to HBCUs.
37. See chapter 8 in this volume, Willie Kirkland, "The Impact of Financial Aid Limits: A View from a Leading HBCU."
38. Rodriguez, *Access to What and for Whom?*
39. Rachel E. Dwyer, Laura McCloud, and Randy Hodson, "Debt and Graduation from American Universities," *Social Forces 90,* no. 4 (2012): 1133–55; Rachel E. Dwyer, Randy Hodson, and Laura McCloud, "Gender, Debt, and Dropping Out of College," *Gender and Society* 27, no. 1 (2013): 30–55; Jason N. Houle and Cody Warner, "Into the Red and Back to the Nest? Student Debt, College Completion, and Returning to the Parental Home among Young Adults," *Sociology of Education* 90, no. 1 (2017): 89–108.
40. Caroline Ratcliffe and Signe-Mary McKernan, *Forever in Your Debt: Who Has Student Loan Debt, and Who's Worried* (Washington, DC: Urban Institute, 2013); Jason N. Houle, "Disparities in Debt: Parents' Socioeconomic Resources and Young Adult Student Loan Debt," *Sociology of Education* 87, no. 1 (2014): 53–69; Addo et al., "Young, Black, and (Still) in the Red."
41. Private loan receipt data were not available for 1995–96.

42. Debbie Cochrane and Laura Szabo-Kubitz, *At What Cost? How Community Colleges That Do Not Offer Federal Loans Put Students at Risk* (Oakland, CA: Institute for College Access and Success, 2014).

43. Lawrence Gladieux and Laura Perna, *Borrowers Who Drop Out: A Neglected Aspect of the College Student Loan Trend* (San Jose, CA: National Center for Public Policy and Higher Education, 2005).

44. Caroline Ratcliffe and Signe-Mary McKernan, *Forever in Your Debt: Who Has Student Loan Debt, and Who's Worried* (Washington, DC: Urban Institute, 2013); Jacob P. K. Gross, Osman Cekic, Don Hossler, and Nick Hillman, "What Matters in Student Loan Default: A Review of the Research Literature," *Journal of Student Financial Aid 39*, no. 1 (2009): 19–29; Derek V. Price, *Borrowing Inequality: Race, Class and Student Loans* (Boulder, CO: Lynne Rienner, 2004); Addo et al., "Young, Black, and (Still) in the Red."

45. Christian E. Weller, *Access Denied: Low-Income and Minority Families Face More Borrowing Constraints and Higher Borrowing Costs* (Washington, DC: Center for American Progress, 2007).

46. Melvin L. Oliver and Thomas M. Shapiro, *Black Wealth, White Wealth: A New Perspective on Racial Inequality* (New York: Routledge, 1995).

47. Dalton Conley, "Capital for College: Parental Assets and Postsecondary Schooling," *Sociology of Education 74*, no. 1 (2001): 59–72.

48. Rakesh Kochhar, Richard Fry, and Paul Taylor, *Wealth Gaps Rise to Record Highs Between Whites, Blacks, and Hispanics* (Washington, DC: Pew Research Center for Social and Demographic Trends, 2013).

49. Thomas M. Shapiro, Tatjana Maschede, and Sam Osoro, "The Widening Racial Wealth Gap: Why Wealth Is Not Color Blind," in *The Assets Perspective: The Rise of Asset Building and Its Impact on Social Policy*, ed. Reid Cramer and Trina Shanks (New York: Palgrave McMillian, 2014), 99.

50. Fabian T. Pfeffer, Sheldon Danzinger, and Robert F. Schoeni, "Wealth Disparities Before and After the Great Recession," *Annals of the American Academy of Political and Social Science 650*, no. 1 (2013): 98–123.

51. Signe-Mary McKernan, Caroline Ratcliffe, C. Eugene Steuerle, and Sisi Zhang, *Less Than Equal: Racial Disparities in Wealth Accumulation* (Washington, DC: Urban Institute, 2013).

52. Ibid.; Shapiro et al., "The Widening Racial Wealth Gap."

53. Min Zhan and Deirdre Lanesskog, "The Impact of Family Assets and Debt on College Graduation," *Children and Youth Services Review 43* (2013): 67–74.

54. Zhan and Lanesskog, "The Impact of Family Assets and Debt on College Graduation," 72.

55. Thomas Shapiro, Tathana Maschede, and Sam Osoro, *The Roots of the Widening Racial Wealth Gap: Explaining the Black-White Economic Divide* (Waltham, MA: Institute on Assets and Social Policy, 2013).

56. Edward N. Wolff, "The Asset Price Meltdown and the Wealth of the Middle Class" (Working Paper No. 18559, National Bureau of Economic Research, Cambridge, MA, 2012), 7.

57. McKernan et al., *Less Than Equal.*

58. Pfeffer et al., "Wealth Disparities Before and After the Great Recession."

59. Melvin L. Oliver and Thomas M. Shapiro, "Wealth of a Nation: A Reassessment of Asset Inequality in America Shows at Least One Third of Households Are Asset Poor," *American Journal of Economics and Sociology* 49, no. 2 (1990).

60. Karen Dynan, *The Income Rollercoaster: Rising Income Inequality and Its Implications* (Washington, DC: Brookings Institution, 2010); H. Luke Shaefer and Kathryn Edin, "The Rise of Extreme Poverty in the United States," *Pathways*, Summer 2014, https://inequality.stanford.edu/sites/default/files/media/_media/pdf/pathways/summer_2014/Pathways_Summer_2014_ShaeferEdin.pdf; Jonathan Morduch and Rachel Schneider, *The Financial Diaries: How American Families Cope in a World of Uncertainty* (Princeton, NJ: Princeton University Press, 2017).

61. Conley, "Capital for College"; Dalton Conley, *Being Black, Living in the Red* (Berkeley: University of California Press, 1999); Min Zhan and Michael Sherraden, "Assets and Liabilities, Race/Ethnicity, and Children's College Education," *Children and Youth Services Review* 33, no. 11 (2011): 2168–75.

62. Michael F. Lovenheim, "The Effect of Liquid Housing Wealth on College Enrollment," *Journal of Labor Economics* 29, no. 4 (2011): 741–71.

63. See, for example, Liz Weston, "10 Ways to Boost Financial Aid," *MSN Money*, December 11, 2012.

64. While Dynarski and Scott-Clayton (2007) find that few changes in Pell eligibility would occur under FAFSA simplification, this is primarily because students with negative EFCs are unable to receive larger grants. Susan Dynarski and Judith Scott-Clayton, "College Grants on a Postcard: A Proposal for Simple and Predictable Federal Student Aid," Brookings Institution Hamilton Project Discussion Paper 2007-1, https://www.brookings.edu/wp-content/uploads/2016/06/200702dynarski-scott-clayton.pdf.

65. Conley, "Being Black, Living in the Red."

66. Rakesh Kochnar, Richard Fry, and Paul Taylor, *Twenty-to-One: Wealth Gaps Rise to Record Highs Between Blacks, Whites, and Hispanics* (Washington, DC: Pew Social and Demographic Trends, 2011).

67. Courtney McSwain, *Window of Opportunity: Targeting Federal Grant Aid to Students with the Lowest Incomes* (Washington, DC: Institute for Higher Education Policy, 2008).

68. National Opinion Research Center and University of Chicago, *National Longitudinal Survey of Youth 1997 Cohort, 1997–2013 (Rounds 1–16)*, US Department of Labor, Bureau of Labor Statistics (Columbus: Ohio State University, 2015).

69. Addo et al., "Young, Black, and (Still) in the Red."

70. Oliver and Shapiro, *Black Wealth, White Wealth.*

71. Jackson and Reynolds, "The Price of Opportunity."

72. This rate of growth was higher for PLUS loans than for other types of loans primarily since federal loan limits make it difficult to increase take-up of those loans.

73. Jackson and Reynolds, "The Price of Opportunity."

74. Ibid.

75. Rodriguez, *Access to What and for Whom?*

76. Pamela Bennett, "Black Immigrants' Use of an African-American Strategy for Mobility: Implications for Segmented Assimilation Theory" (Working Paper, Queens College, NY, 2014).

77. Theodore Cross and Robert B Slater, "The Commanding Wealth Advantage of College-Bound White Students," *Journal of Blacks in Higher Education* 15 (1997): 85.

78. Noah Drezner and Anubha Gupta, "Busting the Myth: Understanding Endowment Management at Public Historically Black Colleges and Universities," *Journal of Negro Education* 81, no. 2 (2012): 107–20.

79. Marybeth Gasman, *The Changing Face of Historically Black Colleges and Universities* (Philadelphia: University of Pennsylvania Graduate School of Education Center for MSIs, 2013).

80. Rachel Fishman, *The Parent Trap: Parent PLUS Loans and Intergenerational Borrowing* (Washington, DC: New America Foundation, 2014); Rachel Fishman, "PLUS Loans Are Not Grants," *New America* (blog), April 3, 2014, http://www.edcentral.org/plus-loans-grants/.

81. This measure likely understates the difference in financial need between HBCU and non-HBCU students, because not all high-income students file the FAFSA. But given that very few HBCU students who filed the FAFSA come from households making more than $110,000 per year, it is unlikely that many students at HBCUs are not filing the FAFSA because they have high incomes. Data available on request.

82. Education expenditures per students have been higher at HBCUs than at other institutions dating back to at least the early 1970s. Ronald G. Fryer and Michael Greenstone, "The Changing Consequences of Attending Historically Black Colleges and Universities," *American Economic Journal: Applied Economics* 2, no. 1 (2010): 114–48.

83. Data on PLUS Loan receipt are from Federal Student Aid (FSA) records instead of the Department of Education's Integrated Postsecondary Education Data System (IPEDS). FSA data aggregate some colleges to the system level for reporting purposes (e.g., Rutgers and Pennsylvania State systems) but no others (e.g., University of Wisconsin and University of California systems). To get accurate comparisons of loan volume by campus, we limit our analyses to colleges not aggregated to the system level; four-year HBCUs are not aggregated to the system level. For more details about limitations of FSA data, see Ozan Jaquette and Edna Parra, "Using IPEDS for Panel Analyses: Core Concepts, Data Challenges, and Empirical Applications," in *Higher Education: Handbook of Theory and Research,* vol. 29, ed. Michael B. Paulsen (Dordrecht, Netherlands: Springer, 2014).

84. This may be a lower fraction than in previous years. Between 1977 and 2001, 61 percent to 73 percent of public HBCUs' revenue came from public funds (today it is just under 66 percent). See Fryer and Greenstone, "The Changing Consequences of Attending Historically Black Colleges and Universities."

85. William Casey Boland and Marybeth Gasman, *America's Public HBCUs: A Four State Comparison of Institutional Capacity and State Funding Priorities* (Philadelphia: University of Pennsylvania Graduate School of Education Center for MSIs, 2014).

86. Pearl Stewart, "Three Mississippi HBCUs Finding Diversity Fuels Their Mission," *Diverse Education*, October 18, 2012, http://diverseeducation.com/article/48872/.

87. Conley, *Being Black, Living in the Red*; Oliver and Shapiro, *Black Wealth, White Wealth*.

88. Rodriguez, *Access to What and for Whom?*

89. Stacy Berg Dale and Alan B. Krueger, "Estimating the Payoff to Attending a More Selective College: An Application of Selection on Observables and Unobservables," *Quarterly Journal of Economics* 117, no. 4, (2002): 1491–527; Stacy Berg Dale and Alan B. Krueger, "Estimating the Return to College Selectivity over the Career Using Administrative Earnings Data" (Working Paper No. 17159, National Bureau of Economic Research, Cambridge, MA, 2011). See, for example, Sigal Alon and Marta Tienda, "Assessing the 'Mismatch' Hypothesis: Differences in College Graduation Rates by Institutional Selectivity," *Sociology of Education* 78, no. 4 (2005): 294–315; William G. Bowen and Derrick C. Bok, *The Shape of the River: Long-Term Consequences of Considering Race in College and University Admissions* (Princeton, NJ: Princeton University Press, 1998); Tatiana Melguizo, "Quality Matters: Assessing the Impact of Attending More Selective Institutions on College Completion Rates of Minorities," *Research in Higher Education* 49, no. 3 (2008): 214–36; Mario L. Small and Christopher Winship, "Black Students' Graduation from Elite Colleges: Institutional Characteristics and Between-Institution Differences," *Social Science Research* 36, no. 3 (2007): 1257–75.

90. Stephanie R. Cellini and Latika Chaudhary, "The Labor Market Returns to a For-Profit College Education" (Working Paper No.18343 National Bureau of Economic Research, Cambridge, MA, 2012); Kevin Lang and Russell Weinstein, "The Wage Effects of Not-for-Profit and For-Profit Certifications: Better Data, Somewhat Different Results," *Labour Economics* 24 (2013): 230–43; David J. Deming, Claudia Goldin, and Lawrence F. Katz, "The For-Profit Postsecondary School Sector: Nimble Critters or Agile Predators?" (Working Paper No. 17710, National Bureau of Economic Research, Cambridge, MA, 2011).

91. In "The Changing Consequences of Attending Historically Black Colleges and Universities," Fryer and Greenstone note similar difficulties in identifying appropriate counterfactuals and making sense of shits in the wage returns associated with attending HBCUs. Their longitudinal analysis suggests that while in the 1970s students who attended HBCUs appear to gain from higher probabilities of graduation and higher wages, by the 1990s that advantage appears to have disappeared, and may have even become a disadvantage. They report great difficulty assessing the precise channels through which the shift occurred but point to the growing academic disadvantages among students attending HBCUS and declining resources. Moreover, Price, Spriggs, and Swinton do not reproduce evidence of a declining premium and in fact find continued advantage in long-term labor market outcomes. Gregory N. Price, William Spriggs, and Omari H. Swinton, "The Relative Returns to Graduating from a Historically Black College/University: Propensity Score Matching Estimates from the National Survey of Black Americans," *Review of Black Political Economy* 38.2 (2011): 103-30.

92. Addo et al., "Young, Black, and (Still) in the Red."

93. This result is not shown but is available from the authors on request.

94. Danielle-Joy Davis, Lisa C. Green-Derry, and Brandon Jones, "The Impact of Federal Financial Aid Policy upon Higher Education Access," *Journal of Educational Administration and History* 45, no. 1 (2013): 49–57.

95. Glenda F. Carter, "Financial Aid and Tuition: Factors Contributing to the Decline of Black Student Enrollment in Higher Education," in *Recruitment and Retention of Black Students in Higher Education*, ed. Johnson N. Niba and Regina Norman (Lanham, MD: University Press of America/National Association for Equal Opportunity in Higher Education, 1991).

96. Nick Anderson, "Tighter Federal Lending Standards Yield Turmoil for Historically Black Colleges," *Washington Post*, June 22, 2013; Justin Doubleday, "With Parents Denied Loans, Students Scramble at HBCUs," *Chronicle of Higher Education*, October 7, 2013.

97. Bennett, *Black Immigrants' Use of an African-American Strategy for Mobility*.

98. Fishman, *The Parent Trap*; Fishman, "PLUS Loans Are Not Grants"; Rodriguez, *Access to What and for Whom?*

99. Fishman, *The Parent Trap*; Fishman, "PLUS Loans Are Not Grants."

Conclusion

1. Nolan McCarty, Keith T. Poole, and Howard Rosenthal, *Polarized America: The Dance of Ideology and Unequal Riches*, 2nd ed. (Cambridge, MA: Massachusetts Institute of Technology Press, 2016).

2. Suzanne Mettler, *Degrees of Inequality: How the Politics of Higher Education Sabotaged the American Dream* (New York: Basic Books, 2014).

About the Editors

Gary Orfield is a Distinguished Research Professor of Education, Law, Political Science & Urban Planning at the University of California, Los Angeles, where he is also codirector of the Civil Rights Project, which he co-founded at Harvard University in 1996. He is a political scientist whose work includes more than a dozen authored or edited books, one of which was cited by the Supreme Court in upholding affirmative action. Orfield's work focuses on equal opportunity and civil rights and has been included in testimony in more than twenty major class action civil rights lawsuits on school segregation, housing discrimination, and other civil rights violations. He has taught at six universities, including Harvard University and the University of Chicago, and is a member of the National Academy of Education.

Nicholas Hillman is an associate professor in the Department of Educational Leadership and Policy Analysis at the University of Wisconsin–Madison, where he is also a faculty affiliate in Wisconsin Center for the Advancement of Postsecondary Education and the La Follette School of Public Affairs. His research focuses on postsecondary finance and financial aid policy, primarily as they relate to college access and equity, and his work includes research on student loan debt and default, performance-based funding, and college affordability. Hillman teaches courses in politics of higher education, higher education finance, educational policy, and research methods.

About the Contributors

Adriana Ruiz Alvarado is an assistant professor in the School of Education at the University of Redlands. Her research focuses on improving conditions and increasing the success of historically underrepresented students in college, particularly with regard to persistence to the baccalaureate degree and experiences with the campus climate for diversity.

Dominique J. Baker is an assistant professor of education policy and an associate with the John Goodwin Tower Center for Political Studies at Southern Methodist University. She conducts research on policies that affect the access and success of students within higher education, with an emphasis on student financial aid.

Daniel Corral is a PhD student in the Department of Educational Leadership and Policy Analysis at the University of Wisconsin–Madison.

Valerie Crespín-Trujillo is a doctoral student in the Department of Educational Leadership and Policy Analysis at the University of Wisconsin–Madison. As a practitioner and a scholar, she has experience advising federal, state, and institutional policy makers on issues of higher education finance, college readiness, and access to postsecondary education for traditionally underrepresented students.

Kevin Eagan is an assistant professor of education at the University of California, Los Angeles, where he is also the managing director of the Higher Education Research Institute, which administers six national surveys targeted to college students, faculty, and staff. His research interests include issues related to undergraduate STEM education, contingent faculty, structures of opportunity, and advanced quantitative methods.

Stella M. Flores is an associate professor of higher education and director of access and equity at the Steinhardt Institute for Higher Education Policy at New York University. Her research examines the effects of public policies on college access and completion for underserved and immigrant populations using a K–20 perspective.

Marybeth Gasman is the Judy & Howard Berkowitz Professor of Education in the Graduate School of Education at the University of Pennsylvania. She also serves as the director of the Penn Center for Minority Serving Institutions.

Sara Goldrick-Rab is a professor of higher education policy and sociology at Temple University and founder of the Wisconsin HOPE Lab. She is best known for her innovative research on food and housing insecurity in higher education and for her work on making public higher education free.

Jason Houle is an assistant professor of sociology at Dartmouth College. His research interests include social stratification and mobility, the sociology of mental health, and medical sociology. His current work examines the causes and consequences of rising debt in the United States.

Sylvia Hurtado is a professor in the Graduate School of Education and Information Studies the University of California, Los Angeles, where she also served as the director of the Higher Education Research Institute at. Her research focuses on campus climate, equity in higher education, STEM postsecondary education, and student outcomes.

Willie Kirkland is the director of institutional research and an adjunct professor of political science at Dillard University.

Thai-Huy Nguyen is an assistant professor of education at Seattle University.

Anne-Marie Núñez is an associate professor in the Higher Education and Student Affairs program at The Ohio State University. She employs sociological approaches to explore how diverse higher education institution types, linkages between K–12 and postsecondary education systems, and scientific disciplinary cultures structure equitable postsecondary education opportunities for historically underserved groups in education.

Toby J. Park is an assistant professor of economics of education and education policy and an associate director of the Center for Postsecondary Success at Florida State University. His research investigates student access and success in postsecondary education, with a particular focus on minority-serving institutions, community colleges, and developmental education.

Awilda Rodríguez is an assistant professor in the Center for the Study of Higher and Postsecondary Education. Her research is at the intersection of higher education policy, college access and choice, and the representation of Black, Latino, low-income, and first-generation students in postsecondary education.

Andrés Castro Samayoa is an assistant professor of education in the Lynch School of Education at Boston College.

Index

accountability
  balancing with civil rights, 11–14, 43–44,
    175–180
  policies and programs for. *see* policies and
    programs
  recommended strategies for, 70–72, 73–
    75, 86–88, 107–110, 124–126, 128,
    137–139, 149–150, 173–174, 175–179
  regulations for. *see* regulations
  research regarding, importance of, 13–14,
    44, 111–112
  as response to limited resources, 1–4, 7,
    26, 27, 45–47, 175
  strategies contributing to inequality,
    2–6, 12–13, 21, 73–74, 90–91, 109,
    111–112, 117, 122–124, 137–139,
    144–145, 151–154, 157–158, 169–
    173, 179–180
accountability metrics
  college costs as, 41–42
  in College Scorecard, 30–31, 40–43
  data needed for, 17, 37, 43–44, 118–121,
    124–125, 176
  data used for, limitations of, 29, 34–35,
    36–38
  efficiency scores, 73–74, 76–77, 78,
    82–83
  employment as, 40–41
  input-adjusted performance indices,
    75–77, 86, 178, 180
  loan default rate as, 42–43
  in performance funding, 48–49,
    50–51
administrations. *see* presidential administra-
    tions
affirmative action, 6–7, 11
African American students. *see* Histori-
    cally Black Colleges and Universities
    (HBCUs); minority-serving institutions
    (MSIs); racial/ethnic minority students

Alaska Native students, 66–69
American Dream, 2–6
American Graduation Initiative, 74
American Indian students. see Alaska Native
    students; Native American students
American Recovery and Reinvestment Act,
    24
Asian students, 1, 64, 66–67, 82–83, 135,
    136. *see also* racial/ethnic minority
    students
at-risk students, 49–52, 58. *see also* low
    income students; racial/ethnic minority
    students

Bakke; *Regents of the University of Califor-
    nia v.* (1978), 7
Black students. *see* African American stu-
    dents
Bush (George W.) administration
  Spelling Commission, 31, 37
  tax subsidies, 8–9

California Proposition 13, 7
Carter administration, 8
civil rights. *see also* minority-serving institu-
    tions (MSIs); racial/ethnic minority
    students
  balancing with accountability, 11–14,
    43–44, 175–180
  decreasing support for, 11, 21
  policies supporting, 6–7, 111
  stratification of society and, 3–5, 10–13,
    89–91
Civil Rights Act of 1964, 6–7, 111
Clinton administration
  DLC affecting, 8
  tax benefits, 24
  tax subsidies, 9
college completion
  importance of, 89–90